How We
Do It

Previous books by the author

*Redbook's 500 Sex Tips: How to Make Sex
More Exciting, Satisfying & Fun*

How the Science of Sex Can
Make You a Better Lover

How We Do It

Judy Dutton

Broadway Books, New York

Published in the United States by Broadway Books, an imprint of
the Crown Publishing Group, a division of Random House, Inc., New York.
www.crownpublishing.com

BROADWAY BOOKS and the Broadway Books colophon are trademarks of
Random House, Inc.

Library of Congress Cataloging-in-Publication Data

Dutton, Judy.
How we do it : how the science of sex can make you a better lover /
Judy Dutton.—1st ed.
p. cm.
Includes bibliographical references.
ISBN 978-0-7679-3028-4
1. Sex.   I. Title.

HQ21.D875 2009
613.9'6—dc22   2008053033

PRINTED IN THE UNITED STATES OF AMERICA

Book design by Ralph Fowler / rlfdesign
Illustrations by Margarita Reyfman

10 9 8 7 6 5 4 3 2 1

First Edition

For Jason

CONTENTS

ACKNOWLEDGMENTS

I have learned so much while writing this book, and am deeply grateful to the many researchers who devoted their time, intelligence, and patience to helping me understand their fascinating work. I owe a special thanks to Barry Komisaruk, a saint in scientist's clothing who spent countless hours explaining the intricacies of sexual arousal. Gordon Gallup also greeted my seemingly infinite barrage of questions with aplomb and plenty of engaging stories. I am also thankful for the insights contributed by Daniel Amen, Chua Chee Ann, Arthur Aron, Dan Ariely, Michael Bader, Rosemary Basson, Peter Bearman, Eric Bressler, Stuart Brody, Norman Brown, Meredith Chivers, Andrew Clark, Michael Cunningham, John DeLamater, Bella DePaulo, Denise Donnelly, Edward Eichel, Harry Fisch, Helen Fisher, Terri Fisher, Steven Gangestad, James Giannini, David Givens, Martie Haselton, Elaine Hatfield, Alan Hirsch, Emmanuele Jannini, Erick Janssen, David Jay, Brent Jordan, Eric Klinger, Daniel Kruger, James Laird, Mats Larsson, Harold Leitenberg, Tommer Leyvand, Marlene Maheu, Rachel Maines, Ken Maravilla, Stuart Meloy, Barry McCarthy, Samantha McGlone, Beatriz Mileham, Geoffrey Miller, Monica Moore, Daniel Nettles, Philip Ney, Gina Ogden, Andrew Oswald, Paige Padgett, Lou Paget, Erdman Palmore, Robert Pellegrini, Timothy Perper, David Perrett, Robert Provine, David Schmitt, Ian Shrier, Todd Shackelford,

Sarah Sitton, Tom Smith, Timothy Spector, Annie Sprinkle, Richard Sprott, Randy Thornhill, Martin Tovée, David Vitalli, David Weeks, Beverly Whipple, Allen Wilcox, and Larry Young.

Gathering the research in this book would have driven me nuts if it hadn't been for the generous help of many publishers whose articles are highlighted in this book. I am especially indebted to Renate Bayaz at Springer Publishing in Germany for cheerfully sending me what must amount to over a hundred studies. My access to ScienceDirect.com, granted by Anna Hogrebe at Elsevier Publishing in the Netherlands, was also invaluable.

A heartfelt thank-you goes to Hallie Falquet and other staffers at Broadway Books for their smarts, sense of humor, and unerring instincts steering this project in the right direction from beginning to end—you have made my year.

Last but not least, I feel amazingly lucky to have Doug Stewart at Sterling Lord Literistic as my agent; his brilliant ideas, support, and enthusiasm have turned the once daunting world of book publishing into a delight (a big thanks goes to Seth Fishman, too).

I am also forever indebted to my friends (and friends of friends) who were brave enough to share their personal stories from the dating trenches and in-bed encounters. I can't name names because some of you would kill me if I did, but you know who you are.

The Surprising Truth About Science and Sex

Tim and Sally are a baffling couple. Tim loves sailing. Sally can't swim. Sally loves musicals. Tim would rather gnaw his own hand off than sit through *Hairspray*. Sally swore she'd never date a guy who watches sports. Every weekend, Tim plants himself in front of ESPN in their home in Hoboken, New Jersey, with a six-pack of Pabst Blue Ribbon. Sally never drinks beer. Ever.

"We always joke that we would never have met on a dating Web site like Match.com because we're such polar opposites," says Tim. So what prompted Tim to propose to Sally last year? And why did Sally accept?

For one, the sex is fantastic—and they swear they both knew it would be from the moment they met. Tim and Sally first worked at the same publishing company. Tim was in ad sales; Sally in public relations. The minute they first bumped into each other at the coffee machine, Tim started teasing Sally about using skim milk rather than creamer in her coffee. "It definitely wasn't love at first sight," Sally says. "At first, I didn't even like Tim that much." And yet, every single molecule in

Sally's body clearly disagreed with her mind. Whenever Tim came within ten feet of her, her breathing would get shallow, her mouth dry, her hands sweaty. Not that the sensation was unpleasant. On the contrary, it felt a lot like those moments in high school right before she'd step on stage to perform a role in a play—nerve-wracking but exhilarating, as if something amazing were about to happen. Could that something amazing be Tim? She decided to find out.

Sally began "bumping into" Tim regularly at the coffee machine, timing her trips for when she knew Tim would be there. Conversations over coffee morphed into lunch outings, then dinner. "Is this a work date or a date date?" Tim asked at the end of one evening with a grin. "Because if it's the latter, don't worry, I won't sue for sexual harassment." Then Tim leaned over the plate of calamari they'd been sharing and kissed her.

He knew Sally wasn't his type. Plus, the fact that they worked together was far from ideal. Still, for some unexplainable reason, he'd been wondering what it would be like to kiss Sally ever since she'd first frowned at his creamer remark by the coffee machine. As he'd hoped, kissing Sally felt great. It felt right.

After that night, Tim and Sally started officially dating. Soon, they discovered that while they didn't see eye to eye on everything, they got along fantastically well in bed. Their health profiles also complemented each other in uncanny ways. Sally has excellent eyesight. Tim's vision is terrible. Sally has high cholesterol. Tim's cholesterol levels are low. Sally has never had a cavity. Tim's teeth are soft and prone to them. "I always thought stuff like that was weird with us," Tim says. "Did our DNA somehow know that we could balance out each other's weaknesses and create a healthy baby? I guess we'll have to find out someday if my hunch is right."

Given all that was conspiring against them—different interests, personalities, an awkward first encounter over coffee creamer—how did Sally and Tim end up together? Was it fate? Luck? Or was it because of a far less mysterious force called science? Applying the clinical precision of science to the messy arena of sexual passion might seem like a strange combination, but behind closed laboratory doors, scientists have been scrutinizing sex for centuries. You're probably familiar with Alfred Kinsey, who rocked America's perceptions of what people do in bed in the 1950s, but he is only one of hundreds of researchers who have examined sex and come to some startling conclusions. Here are just a few of the more recent discoveries from the field of sex research:

- To find your perfect partner, you should sleep with twelve people before settling down.

- If you ride a roller coaster with your date, you will appear more attractive once the ride's over.

- An MRI scan of your brain can reveal if you're in love or just in lust.

- There's a genetic test that can predict who will cheat— and a vaccine may one day exist to keep cheaters faithful.

- Some people can have nose orgasms, or knee orgasms.

"If You Could See What I've Seen . . ." A Day in the Life of a Sex Scientist

Sex makes us act in mysterious ways. Try as we might to explain it, all too often we're left scratching our heads, stirred by forces that seem beyond our control or comprehension. One minute, you're at a party digging into the cheese dip. The next, you've dragged someone home and are burrowing into each other as if the meaning of life were buried between you. How does that happen?

To a certain extent, the how's and why's of sex may seem obvious. After all, we all know that humans are programmed to reproduce. Without sex, we would cease to exist. End of story. Still, saying sex boils down to baby making is like saying we eat so we don't die of starvation. Scores of five-star restaurants are testament to the fact that eating is a far more sophisticated experience than can be explained by our daily requirement for nutrients. The same is true with sex. Procreation is important, but sex is also pleasurable—bed-shakingly, mind-blowingly pleasurable. What tips and tricks can we learn from all of the research being done on sex to kick things up a notch and make sex even better?

That's where this book can help. Every day, scientists who study sex pack their lunch, go to work, and study in detail something that most of us do while fumbling around in the dark. If their advice seems a little out there, that's because they're pioneers, going where none have gone before, probing nooks and crannies and embarrassing topics that would make most of us blush. To conduct their research, scientists have searched for volunteers who are willing to come into their laboratory, strip down, and go at it while researchers scribble notes from the sidelines. To get a glimpse beyond what the naked eye can see, they've inserted "penis cameras" into women's nether regions. Under microscopes, they've identified new kinds of sperm called "killers" and "blockers" that contribute to reproduction in surprising ways. On tumbling mats, they've forged new sex positions like the Coital Alignment Technique, which, while it might not sound sexy, has a great track record yielding orgasms. With a few well-placed electrodes, scientists invented an orgasmatron that triggers peaks with the push of a button. Really.

In her delightful and informative book *Bonk: The Curious Coupling of Science and Sex*, writer Mary Roach gives her readers a peek at life behind the doors of a sex laboratory and the personalities under the lab coats. This book reveals not only the juicy details of their discoveries, but the practical know-how that will enable you to put this information to good use in your own bedroom. Each chapter in *How We Do It* highlights a stage of the seduction process from beginning to end. In the early chapters, you'll get a crash course on what creates chemistry. After that, we'll take a tour of the naked body and all its attractions, then lift the lid on the brain and learn how to read someone's secret thoughts. From there, we'll romp through the wild kingdom of kinky sex, then finish up with a bang by revealing everything you ever wanted to know about orgasms.

Our guides on this journey are John and Jane. While they are fictional characters, their experiences will feel familiar to anyone who has ever faced the classic questions that crop up during the seduction process. As we follow John and Jane from the moment they meet, fall into bed together, hit their high notes, then bask in the afterglow, you will learn about the science going on behind the scenes, and how to harness these forces so they can be used to your benefit. You will also hear from real men and women like Tim and Sally (names and some identifying details have been changed) about what's baffled them most about sex, followed by explanations that can help shed some light on these mysteries, and provide some much-needed solutions to boot.

This book focuses primarily on what happens when sex goes right—bad stuff (for example, STDs) not included. Even so, before following any of the advice in this book, you should take steps to protect yourself by using condoms, getting tested for STDs, and discussing the monogamy question with partners (for more information, turn to chapter 4). The term "safe sex" is a bit of a contradiction since sex, by definition, is never entirely safe. Still, there are things you can do to lower your risk of some nasty surprises that would undoubtedly put a damper on the fun. Take a few precautions, and that leaves less room for worrying and more room for good old sexual pleasure.

Sex scientists have seen things. Weird things. Wonderful things. And now is your chance to cash in on their hard work. By the end of your journey, you're going to be armed with more than a few new ideas to try in bed.

How We Do It

CHAPTER 1

Why We Have Sex
(Do You Really Need to Ask?)

It was Friday night. John was out at a bar, drinking a beer, scoping out prospects. His goal that night was simple: to find someone cute and get her phone number. Then, after a few dates, more conversation, and maybe a make-out session or two, if all went well she'd deem him worthy of the grand prize of the getting-to-know-you game: sex, of course. If John were really lucky, he'd convince some woman to head to bed with him tonight. After all, if they got along, they'd end up having sex sooner or later anyway, and sex felt great. What was the point of waiting?

Standing no more than three feet from John, Jane was ordering a Stoli and soda. Jane was on a girls' night out with a few of her friends who'd congregated in the back of the bar, but Jane knew that bonding with her pals wasn't the only thing on her agenda. Jane, who was in her late twenties, was ready to meet Mr. Right. Her criteria were simple: He had to be smart, make her laugh, and—last but not least—rock her world in bed. She'd had plenty of relationships that seemed perfect on paper but were lacking on that last point, and she'd made up her mind to hold out for the whole package. Wasn't that what pretty much every single man and woman in the bar was looking for, more or less?

While neither John nor Jane were aware of it yet, tonight was the night they would both find exactly what they were hoping to find, in each other.

F OR JOHN, JANE, and millions of other men and women around the world, the pursuit of sex is a powerful urge. Every day, the World Health Organization estimates that more than one hundred million couples strip down and get busy in high-rise apartments, hotel rooms, mud huts, igloos, and anywhere else the mood might strike. The reasons for this may seem obvious: We have sex because we're in love, or because we're in lust, or because we want babies. Still, is that everything?

To get a full look at what inspires people to have sex, Cindy Meston and David Buss, two professors at the University of Texas in Austin, asked hundreds of men and women to spill all their reasons for going at it. After tabulating the results and eliminating any repeats, they announced their final tally in an article published in the *Archives of Sexual Behavior*. Their list had 237 reasons.

No, that number wasn't a typo. Here's a sampling to give you an idea:

I wanted to burn calories.

I wanted to feel closer to God.

I wanted to get a promotion.

I wanted to make the person feel better about herself/himself.

Someone dared me.

I wanted to keep my partner from straying.

I wanted to get back at my partner for having cheated on me.

The person was famous and I wanted to be able to say I had sex with him/her.

I was bored.

Some of these 237 reasons may seem sleazier than an episode of *Jerry Springer*, and they might actually add up to one very good reason to *not* have sex, at least until you know someone better. Still, what this study proves is that what motivates humans to hop in bed isn't as simple as some of us might think, and the benefits don't end with orgasms and babies. Not by far. If you've ever doubted just how much effort and ingenuity people are willing to put into scoring sex, look no further than Andy, a psychologist in Lincoln, Nebraska. Today, he's a happily married man in his thirties. Flash back to ten years ago, though, and he swears he would have done anything—and he means anything—to get laid.

"My sex life could have been Sting's inspiration when he wrote his song 'King of Pain.' I went to painful lengths to get sex," Andy admits. Part of the problem was that he'd grown up in a small town that didn't offer a guy tons of sexual opportunities. "After an adolescence nearly devoid of sexual contact, times were desperate," he recalls. Turning twenty-one and having access to tipsy girls in bars helped, but even that wasn't enough. As a result, whenever a woman showed Andy even a glimmer of interest, he would bend over backward to close the deal. He would drive for hours to meet up with a woman he felt a connection with, or book plane tickets and fly to another continent if sex was hovering on the horizon. No distance was too far, no fib too big, if it upped the odds that sex would ensue. "One regular lie involved telling women in a bar that I was a fighter pilot going off to war. I've even paid homage to George Costanza and pretended to be an architect," Andy admits. "I know this makes me sound like a jerk, but lying is like signing up for an adjustable rate mortgage. You know you might have to deal with the consequences someday, but that seems way down the road."

Occasionally, Andy's efforts would come back to haunt him. Once while on vacation, he met a wealthy divorcée who looked him up and down and remarked, *It's about time I met a guy who knows how to dress.* "I had on my best clothes that day, but after that, it was BBQ attire and basketball shorts," he recalls. "She wanted to see me again, and Old Navy was not going to cut it. So I went on a shopping spree and dropped nearly a thousand bucks I didn't have on my credit cards. It took me a few years to polish off that debt, but it was worth it. It was all worth it."

At this point in his life, Andy is grateful that having sex no longer requires that much work. Still, between his job, two kids, and his wife's residency at a local hospital, he's not exactly getting laid left and right, either. While he and his wife might not have sex as often as they used to, they've learned how to cut corners to squeeze some in. "In one sense, finding time for sex is easy, since commercials during *Law & Order* are about three minutes, and that's all we need now," he jokes. "Wooing consists of 'I took a shower today, interested?' We're blunt at this stage."

How Much Is Sex Worth? The $50,000 Question

Let's return, for a moment, to one of our favorite reasons for having sex: because it feels good. How good? Very good? Very, *very* good? Is there any way to measure—in watts, volts, or Nielson ratings—just how enjoyable sex is? To get a ballpark idea of where sex stands on our list of priorities, a team of researchers led by Daniel Kahneman at Princeton University asked more than a thousand women to rank nineteen daily activities from most to least enjoyable. Sex topped the list, beating out eating, socializing, spending time with their kids, and, yes, even shopping. But beyond saying sex trumps a Saks sale or cheering on Junior during soccer practice, is there any way to gauge how amazing sex feels in its own right?

In 2004, two economists—David Blanchflower from Dartmouth College and Andrew Oswald at Warwick University—announced they had come up with an equation to measure just how much sex was worth in terms we can all understand: cold hard cash. Most people, of course, rarely pay for sex, but these economists had found a way to peg what we *would* pay if we had to. They analyzed data from 16,000 Americans who had participated in social surveys since the early 1990s, comparing how often respondents claimed they had sex with their reported happiness levels. Then, the economists compared the happiness levels brought on by sex to levels of other activities we do usually pay for, such as Superbowl tickets or a trip to Tahiti. Blanchflower and Oswald were able to extrapolate an estimate of how much sex is worth—and it doesn't come cheap. Having sex once a week compared to once a month increased happiness by the same amount as earning an extra $50,000 per year. So if you're getting laid regularly, you can think of yourself as $50,000 richer than you thought you were five minutes ago.

Hot Monogamy

Blanchflower and Oswald didn't just calculate how much sex was worth, they also looked at the quality of sex. Many of us might assume we'd be in heaven if we had a roster of hot prospects at our beck and call, but their study proved that the most "happiness-maximizing" number of sex partners was just one, most likely since this arrangement is more stable than juggling numerous partners, says Oswald. Monogamists, rejoice. The study also found that while single people are often rumored to have the most action-packed sex lives, married couples actually get it on far more often, which may explain why marriage—the sex, the intimacy, the extra hand with the dishes, the whole package—was calculated to deliver a whopping $100,000 worth of additional happiness per year, twice what you'd get from having regular sex alone. On the other hand, getting a divorce imposes an emotional toll of $66,000 a year.

According to the economists' calculations, having money does increase happiness levels to a certain extent. And yet, "research suggests that people overrate the well-being gains from purchasing things," says Oswald. Does this mean people should invest more time in their relationships rather than slaving away on making more money? "Very probably they should," says Oswald.

Another myth this study debunked was that rich people find partners more readily than those of us with slimmer bank accounts. On the contrary, people with higher-than-average incomes were found to have no more sex with no more partners than those with below-average incomes. The old adage is true, then, that money can't buy love. "That was surprising to us as economists, because by and large, we think money can buy anything," Oswald says. "I suppose you could say the data show that sex and the enjoyment of sex are spread around in a surprisingly egalitarian way."

How Semen Makes You Happy

At first, Dr. Philip Ney was mystified as to what was wrong with Mrs. Jones. In 1984, the twenty-three-year-old mother had been referred to the New Zealand doctor for consultation because she'd become depressed and occasionally violent toward her three-year-old daughter. After hearing more about Mrs. Jones's sexual history, Dr. Ney formed a novel hypothesis: Mrs. Jones wasn't getting enough sex—or, more specifically, enough of the health-sustaining hormones normally found in seminal plasma.

Ney was informed that Mrs. Jones normally had sex with her husband four or five times a week. They had largely stopped having sex following the birth of their child. Her mood had spiraled downward. Ney also knew that seminal fluid contained, in addition to sperm, at least thirteen different kinds of prostoglandins, hormones known to affect neurotransmitter levels in the body that control people's moods. In Ney's study, published in 1986 in *Medical Hypotheses*, he also noted that "the vagina appears to have an active transport mechanism which readily absorbs the hormones found in seminal plasma." As a result, "when hormones found in seminal fluid are absorbed in significant amounts, there is likely to be an effect on the thinking, mood, and behavior of women." Based on these findings, during their next visit, Ney recommended to Mr. and Mrs. Jones that more sex might help improve Mrs. Jones's outlook. "The husband said, 'That's fine with me,'" Ney recalls. Once the couple resumed having sex, Mrs. Jones's depression quickly dissipated.

In 2002, Gordon Gallup, a professor at the New York State University in Albany, took Ney's hypothesis one step further by publishing a paper in the *Archives of Sexual Behavior* titled "Does Semen Have Antidepressant Properties?" Gallup polled nearly three hundred women about how regularly they used condoms, then assessed their mental health using the Beck Depression Inventory (BDI), where scores under 10 indicate someone is not depressed, scores 10-18 indicate mild depression, and scores above that indicate more severe depression. Women who never used condoms, Gallup found, scored the least depressed at 8 on average. Those who occasionally used condoms scored 10.5, while those who always used condoms scored most depressed at 11.3.

Was semen really the secret ingredient keeping condomless women happy? Gallup explored other possibilities, such as the use of oral contraceptives (since the Pill can also affect mood) and the nature of the women's relationships, in case women who weren't using condoms were happier because they had committed boyfriends who kept them in higher spirits. None of these variables were found to explain Gallup's results. Women in loving, long-term relationships who used condoms were more depressed than women who were single and not using condoms. Gallup even found evidence of "semen withdrawal," where women who lose their semen supplier will do just about anything—or more accurately, anyone—to find a new fix. After a breakup, women who don't use condoms are especially prone to rebound relationships, and will hop into bed with a new guy three times faster than their Trojan-packing peers.

Gallup is by no means recommending that women chuck condoms for the sake of their happiness levels. "Clearly, an unwanted pregnancy or a sexually transmitted disease would more than offset any advantageous psychological effects of semen," he points out. Those who can safely abstain from this method of contraception, though, may reap some positive benefits, and vaginal intercourse is not their only recourse. Given the chemicals in semen can also be absorbed through the digestive tract and rectum, oral sex and anal sex might also help ward off depression. "I recently received an e-mail from a gay male saying he notices a marked improvement in his sense of well-being the day after oral sex," Gallup says. When asked whether he's received any negative response to his study, he adds, "I've also received a lot of hate mail from lesbians."

Facial, Anyone?

In China, a group of women called the White Tigresses harvest semen from willing subjects via oral sex and use it as a facial cream and hair conditioner. According to the book *The Sexual Teachings of the White Tigress* by Hsi Lai, "The ancients . . . know that semen was without question the very best of skin rejuvenators. After [semen] is spread over the face, especially the nose, forehead, and oily areas, it dries and then closes the pores. This drying effect is like an astringent reaction that will tighten and shrink wrinkles, feed skin cells, and leave the skin feeling light, clean, and smooth."

How Do You Spell Relief? S-E-X

For many of us, public speaking is about as stressful as it gets. To study people's reactions to this anxiety-inducing ordeal, Stuart Brody at the University of Paisley in Scotland recruited forty-six men and women to give a speech to a panel of judges—who had been surreptitiously instructed to look bored. After the speakers stammered through their oratory, Brody took their blood pressure. Many people's readings had shot through the roof. One group, however, had lower blood pressure readings and stress levels than others. The reason? According to diaries subjects had kept of their activities for two weeks leading up to their speech, they'd had penile-vaginal intercourse at some point during this time period. Sex can help keep us calm, which is why people hoping to sail through an upcoming public speaking engagement or work presentation should consider scheduling some sex before the big event.

Might sex mellow us out *too* much, draining our drive to tackle tough challenges? This has long been the belief among certain athletes, who often avoid sex the night before they compete. Muhammad Ali claimed he'd abstain from sex for weeks before a fight. To keep wives and girlfriends at bay before home games, football players for the Pittsburgh Steelers and the Indianapolis Colts were once required to check into hotels, even before home games. American swimmer Josh Davis, who won three gold medals at the 1996 Olympics, claimed he didn't qualify for the 2004 Olympics because he'd had sex with his wife the day of the trials. As Marty Liquori, one of the world's top-ranked 5,000-meter runners, once said, "Sex makes you happy, and happy people don't run a 3:47 mile."

Olympic triathlete Samantha McGlone had heard that sex could hex her performance, but was skeptical whether the rumor held water. As an undergraduate at McGill University, she decided to see if these superstitions had any basis in science. In 2000, she and her professor Ian Shrier reviewed the medical literature and published their findings in the *Clinical Journal of Sports Medicine* under the title "Does Sex the Night Before Competition Decrease Performance?" Of the studies reviewed, none could establish a link between sexual activity and athletes' physiological performance. In one experiment, in which men submitted themselves to a battery of tests measuring grip strength, reaction time, aerobic power, and VO2 max (a measure of cardiorespiratory endurance), no differences were noted between men who'd had sex and those who hadn't.

Today, McGlone says that few triathletes believe the old abstain-from-sex superstition. "The younger generation is coming to realize it's a bit of a myth," she says. Occasionally, her fellow triathletes will joke about how sex can help them mentally prepare for a race. "I remember being in a race with a friend of mine who, the night before the race, said, 'I guess it's time to go take care of business,'" McGlone recalls. "He didn't have a girlfriend, but I guess you could say he took care of himself."

An Orgasm a Day . . . ?

From 1979 to 1983, over 2,500 Scottish men in their forties and fifties visited their local clinic to get what was, for the most part, a fairly routine checkup. There was, however, one catch. In addition to recording height, weight, blood pressure, cholesterol levels, and other aspects of the patients' health such as diet and exercise habits, doctors also asked them a far more personal question: How often did they have sex? After no doubt blushing a bit, men gave their answers, then were sent on their way.

Ten years later, in an article titled "Sex and Death: Are They Related?" in the *British Medical Journal*, epidemiologist George Davey Smith announced that in a decade's time, men who had reported having sex less than once per month were twice as likely to be dead as those who had had sex more than once per week. An active sex life, Davey Smith concluded, keeps men from keeling over. In another study by Erdman Palmore at Duke University following 252 North Carolina residents over twenty-five years, men who had sex more than once per week lived an average of two years longer than men who had sex less often. Regular sex was found to have a more significant impact on men's life spans than obesity, intelligence, education levels, or contact with family and friends.

And what about women? For them, the *quality* of sex was what mattered. In Palmore's study, women who had reported enjoying sex "very much" lived seven to eight years longer than women who said they could take it or leave it. Enjoyable sex trumped a whole array of factors often assumed to be crucial to a woman's health, including tobacco use, obesity, intelligence, education, income, contact with family and friends, and even genetic factors such as the father's age at death. "Everyone thinks that if you want to live a long time, have parents who live a long time. Not in our sample," says Palmore. Why did quality matter for women, and quantity for men? Palmore isn't sure, although he points out it does seem to be anecdotally true.

What is it about sex that keeps us alive and kicking? According to Palmore, sex packs a one-two punch of physical and psychological benefits. "It gets your heart pumping, plus it makes you feel good about life," he says simply. On average, sex burns 5.25 calories per minute if you weigh 160 to 170 pounds—about the same rate as walking, weeding, or playing table tennis. In Davey Smith's study, men who had reported having sex two or more times per week were half as likely to suffer a heart attack or stroke than those who had sex less frequently. Most likely, this is because orgasm triggers our adrenal glands to release the hormone dehydroepiandrosterone (or DHEA for short), which not only serves as the building blocks for male and female sex hormones such as estrogen and testosterone, but also improves arterial dilation and inhibits the formation of blood clots.

As for those rumors you've heard that sex *causes* heart attacks, two cardiologists named Geoffrey Tofler and James Muller decided to get to the bottom of this by conducting bedside interviews with nearly 1,700 heart attack survivors, asking them what they were doing right before the attack. Sex was rarely the culprit. According to their calculations, people risk only a two in a million chance of having a heart attack during sex, and even those with a heart attack in their past face only a one in 50,000 chance. For those unfortunate few who do suffer a so-called "death in the saddle," medical examiner A. W. Green found that fourteen out of the twenty cases he observed occurred when men were having affairs, engaging in sex "with a non-spouse in unfamiliar surroundings after a big meal with alcohol." Isn't there an expression about making your own bed? Hmmm.

Sex not only keeps your circulatory system running

smoothly, but may help prevent cancer, as well. Timothy Murrell, a doctor and lecturer at the University of Adelaide, Australia, first developed this hunch after witnessing a patient who had suffered from breast pain improve dramatically upon her next visit. Baffled, Murrell asked his patient what had caused this miraculous turn of events. "I've remarried," the woman explained. "And my second husband is much better at loving my breasts."

That got Murrell thinking: Might frequent breast-fondling help flush toxins from the area? To test his theory, Murrell recruited 5,000 of his female patients to stimulate their breasts regularly (on their own or with the help of a partner) for two to three minutes at least twice a week. Three years after embarking on this experiment, Murrell announced his findings at a conference on breast cancer care. "We would expect to be seeing two or three breast cancers a year based on a population of this size," he said. "All I can say is that we have not seen one since we began." Men, too, may be able to flush carcinogens by fondling their anatomy. In one survey of 2,000 men, Graham Giles, a cancer specialist in Victoria, Australia, found that those who ejaculated four or more times per week had one-third the risk of developing prostate cancer than men who did so less often.

Even the common cold seems to cower under the powers of passionate lovemaking. Carl Charnetski at Wilkes University in Pennsylvania asked 112 college students how often they had sex, and then tested their saliva for levels of immunoglobulin A, an antibody that battles microbes and serves as the muscle behind your immune system. College kids who frolicked with one another during their study breaks one to two times per week had 30 percent higher levels of immunoglobulin A than those who got it on less than once a week. Students who were sexually active more than twice a week had the same levels of immunoglobulin A as those who were celibate. So, like many things, moderation is key.

Is Sex Good for Your Looks?

Sex not only helps you live longer, but look younger, too. David Weeks, a neuropsychologist and author of *Secrets of the Superyoung*, questioned ninety-five men and women aged 30 to 101 about their love lives, then showed their photos to a panel of judges who were asked to guess how old they were. On average, men and women who had sex regularly were judged four to seven years younger than their actual age. The reason may be because sex increases the body's production of human growth hormone, a chemical that helps improve muscle tone and keeps things from sagging or wrinkling quite so quickly.

"Hold the Sex, Thanks"

In many ways, David Jay is your typical twenty-six-year-old guy. An MBA student in San Francisco, he spends his free time going swing dancing with friends, making homemade pizza, and watching TV shows like *The Wire*, *Dexter*, and *Dr. Who*. Ask him his sexual orientation, however, and his answer is rather atypical. Jay is not heterosexual, homosexual, bisexual, transsexual, pansexual, or anywhere in between. Jay is asexual, which means he isn't sexually attracted to anyone at all. He's never had sex and doesn't plan to, and his reasons aren't religious. He hasn't been badly burned in the dating market, and he says it's not because he just hasn't met the right person yet. "It's not a choice," Jay explains. "This is the way I was born." During his freshman year in high school, he hit upon the term "asexual" to describe his sexual orientation, and tried Googling it to see if there were others like him out there. At first, the only Web sites he found were about amoebas, although with further digging, he came across a few references to asexuality in humans, too.

In 2001, Jay created an online forum for people who shared his outlook called the Asexual Visibility and Education Network (AVEN) at Asexuality.org. Today, AVEN has 26,000 members worldwide. To publicize their cause, they've coined catchphrases like "A-pride" and printed T-shirts with slogans like "Asexuality: It's not just for amoebas anymore." Scientists have also taken an interest in asexuality, and say it may be as common as homosexuality. In one 2004 study in the *Journal of Sex Research* polling a nationally representative sample of over 18,000 men and women, one in every hundred people said they'd never felt an iota of attraction to either males or females. Asexuality is also prevalent in animals such as sheep, according to scientists at the U.S. Sheep Experiment Station in Dubois, Idaho, who have paired up rams and ewes in pens and kept tabs on their mating patterns. Only 55.6 percent of sheep turned out to be straight. As for the rest, 9.5 percent were homosexual, 22 percent bisexual, and a full 12.5 percent expressed no interest in having sex at all.

Asexuals may be at the extreme end of the continuum, but their lack of enthusiasm for sex isn't as uncommon as you might think. Some of us are too tired for sex. Others are too busy. Former Labor Secretary Robert Reich has even coined an acronym to replace yuppies (young urban professionals) and DINKs (dual income, no kids): DINS, which stands for Dual Income, No Sex. Experts estimate that 15 to 20 percent of couples are in what's defined as a "sexless marriage," which means they have sex fewer than ten times per year.

Is modern-day life too hectic for sex? Researchers who have closely scrutinized our packed itineraries have found that, on the contrary, we have more free time today than ever. Since 1965, Americans have gained leisure time—four to eight hours per week, which adds up to an extra five to ten weeks of vacation per year. This is due not only to declining office hours, but technological advances like the washing machine (try scrubbing your clothes on a washboard and you'll understand).

One nationwide study of over 1,700 married Americans—including those who worked part time, full time, and overtime, or not at all—found *no* relation between the number of hours we work and how often we have sex. According to the study's authors, Janet Hyde and John DeLamater at the University of Wisconsin, how much we work isn't the issue. It's whether we enjoy the work we do. People who like their jobs are happier, cope better with stress, and are less likely to shut down sexually than those who work fewer hours in a job they dislike. Another study in the *Journal of Marriage and the Family* shows that having kids up to age four may moderately decrease couples' levels of sexual activity, but having kids ages five to eighteen has a positive impact on the frequency of sex.

Another common reason couples cite for their lackluster libidos is boredom. In fact, the proverbial "seven-year itch" may no longer be considered the point at which couples' passion levels start to slide. According to anthropologist Helen Fisher, author of *Why We Love*, the intense high we experience during the honeymoon phase typically dies down one to three years into a relationship, so even in the best circumstances, a "three-year itch" may be more accurate.

But all is not lost. Scientists have also found ways couples can alleviate their doldrums, and ironically, shaking up what we do *in* bed isn't the answer. The trick is to take on challenges in other areas of life, from running a 5K race to learning a foreign language. Novel activities that test our abilities stimulate the brain's reward system—the same circuits that get activated during those exhilarating early days when couples first fall in love, says Fisher. By adding a few new accomplishments to their roster of achievements, couples can goose their brain chemistry into thinking their partners are as fascinating ten years into a relationship as they seemed the day they first met.

In one telling study, Arthur Aron at the University of New York in Stony Brook set up an experiment in his laboratory where some couples were asked to complete mundane tasks such as walking back and forth in a room. Other couples were assigned trickier missions, such as having their wrists and ankles bound as they crawled around nudging a ball in front of them. Afterward, Aron asked the couples questions such as "How bored are you with your relationship?" Couples who'd crawled around with balls reported they were happier with their partners than those who had merely paced around the room.

And the Most Sexually Active Americans Are . . .

According to *American Demographics*, the most sexually active Americans include jazz fans, gun owners, and people who lack confidence in the president.

While binding your hands and feet and nudging a ball around might be a little strange to try on your next date night, clearly it pays to tackle a new activity rather than always re-

How to Find Time for Sex

Log off. Making room for sex may simply be a matter of canning distractions, including your Internet habit. In one survey of 1,000 Americans, 20 percent of respondents admitted they spent less time having sex because they're online. If you need another reason to log off, one study by Kings College showed that constantly checking e-mail and phone messages can be so distracting it temporarily lowers your IQ by ten points—more than double the brain drain of smoking marijuana.

Ban TV from the bedroom. One study of more than five hundred couples by Italian researcher Serenella Salomoni found that those who didn't have a TV in their bedroom had sex an average of eight times a month, while those with TVs got it on half as often. If you channel surf come bedtime, try turning it off and see what happens. Or, if you can't resist the comforting drone of a TV as you drift off to sleep, steer clear of reality shows, which were found to be among the biggest libido killers.

Shake up date night. New experiences can trigger the same chemical rush that's produced when couples first fall for each other. Instead of sticking with your usual dinner date, try a cooking class or tango lessons, then ride that wave of excitement into bed.

Adhere to the 2-6-2 rule. Expecting that sex will always be earth-moving is unrealistic, and will only set you up for disappointment. In couples therapy, British sexologist Paula Hall often teaches the 2-6-2 rule, which means that out of every ten times you have sex, twice it'll be wonderful, six times it'll be nice but nothing special, and twice it'll be such a snooze-fest, you'll wonder why you ever bothered. Still, unless you keep trying, you'll never get around to those two-out-of-ten amazing encounters, so it's worth rolling the dice.

Speak up. Few problems in life ever get solved by sweeping them under the carpet, so if you're worried about how your sex life has waned, don't be afraid to bring it up with your partner. Avoid accusatory statements such as "Why aren't you into sex anymore?" and treat it like a joint problem by saying, "I've noticed we haven't been having sex very often and it concerns me. Can we talk about it?" If an argument erupts as a result, that's not necessarily a bad thing. According to one study, couples who fight about sex have it more often than those who don't. The reason? Those who fight for their relationship show they care, which sets the stage for intimacy later (or maybe even some hot make-up sex).

Nix the annoying habits. So you know that leaving your dirty socks on the floor or hogging the bathroom bugs your partner. While it's tempting to think these pet peeves aren't all that important, one study titled "Social Allergies in Romantic Relationships" argues to the contrary. By charting the "deromantization" of 137 couples, Michael Cunningham at the University of St. Louis found that couples can become even *more* sensitive to their significant others' quirks over time. Men, for example, claimed they couldn't stand when women complained that they were too hot or too cold, constantly fussed with their appearance, or dragged them out shopping. Women had all but had it with men's belching, farting, nose-picking, and profanity. If you know something you do annoys your partner, make an effort to change your ways to keep the romance rolling . . . or else.

turning to your old favorites. In another experiment, Aron administered a questionnaire to couples to measure their satisfaction levels with their relationship. Then, Aron asked one group of couples to spend ninety minutes a week together engaged in familiar pastimes, such as dining out or going to a movie. The other group of couples spent ninety minutes a week on pursuits that didn't typically make it into their usual routines, such as hiking, dancing, or going to art galleries. After ten weeks, couples filled out the same questionnaire again to gauge their marital happiness levels. Duos who had gone on unfamiliar dates improved their scores significantly over those who had stuck with the same old stuff.

Sex might not be the answer to all of the world's problems, but overall, it deserves a lot more credit than it usually gets. Of course, as they say, getting those sparks flying isn't always easy. That's why, in our next chapter, we'll explore the elements that get sexual chemistry brewing.

The Laws, Bylaws, and Loopholes of Attraction

As soon as John spotted Jane ordering a drink a mere few feet from where he was seated at the bar, he knew that she had . . . something. John wasn't sure what. Jane wasn't a bombshell, but had an understated beauty, perhaps. Brunette, sweet smile, slim but not rail thin. As Jane breezed by John to join her girlfriends in the back of the bar, John caught a whiff of an intoxicating aroma—was it her perfume? Her shampoo? He wasn't sure. All he knew was that the way Jane smelled, looked, talked, and walked was oddly mesmerizing. Was he crazy? John decided to get a second opinion from his friend Bob, who was seated next to him.

"What do you think of that brunette back there?" John asked Bob under his breath.

Bob looked, then shrugged. "She's okay. But what about that blonde in the miniskirt to her right? That's who I'd go for." Bob continued to tease John on his questionable taste in women, but John stood firm that Jane was the best of the bunch. He couldn't put his finger on why. He didn't know anything about her, in fact. Still, before the night was over, John vowed that he would get to know her by mustering up the courage to buy her a drink.

Meanwhile, as Jane chatted with her girlfriends, she could sense John was checking her out. At first, she wasn't all that interested, but after pointing him out to her posse and hearing them sigh collectively and say, "Ooh, he's cute!" she took a second look and decided her friends were right. Jane often marveled at how her pals' opinions could change her own assessment of men. Was she really that impressionable? It had also occurred to Jane that she was feeling especially frisky that night, which tended to happen during certain times of the month for no apparent reason. Were hormones to blame? Jane wasn't sure what was going on. All she knew was that John was looking better and better by the minute. Only did she?

"Bathroom break," Jane announced. She and her friends moved en masse toward the restroom, where Jane touched up her makeup, fussed with her hair, and bemoaned the fact that she hadn't worn that slinky top she'd bought last week. As she looked in the mirror, she wondered: Was she hot enough? Would John say hi? There was only one way to find out. She stepped out of the bathroom to see what would happen.

TAKE A LOOK AT HOW Americans spend their time and money, and it quickly becomes clear that looking attractive is one of our top priorities. Every year, Americans spend $18 billion on makeup, $38 million on hair care, and $15 billion on perfume and cologne. We shell out another $82 billion on clothes, $12 billion on gym memberships, and $8 billion on self-help books and programs. On average, women spend 63 minutes applying makeup and trying on outfits before they head out the door. Meanwhile, men spend 28 minutes in front of the mirror tweezing stray hairs and messing with hair gel. Who, exactly, is all this effort and expenditure for? For many of us, it's to attract a mate.

For some singletons, the desire to meet Mr. or Mrs. Right is so strong that their pre-date preparations can take all day. Ellen, a Web site designer in New York City, has been known to start getting ready at dawn for a date in the evening. "Typically, I might have a teeth-whitening appointment at ten, a manicure at twelve, a blowout at the hairdresser at five, and in between all that, I shop for a new outfit," Ellen explains. She knows it sounds ridiculous, but swears her efforts aren't driven by vanity or the need to wear whatever's in the latest issue of *Vogue*. "It's because I really, really want to find a great guy and settle down," she says. "And in this city, the competition is fierce!"

And yet, even after a whole day of preparation, Ellen often finds herself sitting across from her date over dinner realizing that there's one crucial thing missing: chemistry. "The guy can be cute, polite, and a total catch by objective standards, but if sparks aren't flying, that date is most likely our last," Ellen admits. "Talk about a waste. Sometimes it makes me wonder: Are all my shopping sprees and hair appointments a moot point?"

Sexual attraction is a funny thing. While cosmetics and fashion companies might like us to think that expensive aftershave or the right shirt will make a difference, the internal compass that steers us into certain people's arms but not others' operates on a more subliminal level. John and Jane, for example, couldn't even pinpoint why they were drawn to each other, all they knew was that they were. So what was their secret? The answer may boil down to science. Researchers have discovered that some pretty strange things—like the vowels in our names, the time of month, or the length of our fourth fingers—can nudge us closer or farther away from romantic prospects for their own mysterious reasons. Understand how these subtle factors work their magic, and you can start bending the laws of attraction in your favor.

Would a Rose by Any Other Name Sound as Sweet?

One afternoon, as students at Tulane University ambled to and from class, a sign posted in the student center caught their attention:

ST JOSEPH'S MARCHING SOCIETY BEAUTY QUEEN
They are all so pretty we can't decide.
Please help us by voting for your choice.

Throughout the day, numerous students stopped to cast their vote, entering a small booth to assess photos of the six finalists. All six—Kathy, Jennifer, Christine, Ethel, Harriet, and Gertrude—were similarly stunning. But who won?

What the students didn't know was that the St. Joseph's beauty pageant had been rigged. All six photos had been previously rated as equally attractive. But their names—which weren't their real names, but had been assigned at random— had been previously rated as very attractive, or very unattractive. The mastermind behind this experiment, professor Gary Garwood, had set out to prove that beauty doesn't merely boil down to appearance. The results of his study, aptly titled "Beauty Is Only 'Name' Deep," proved he was right. Even though the six contestants were equally attractive, those with the appealing monikers (Kathy, Jennifer, and Christine) won the most votes (47, 52, and 59 votes respectively), while the dowdier eponyms (Ethel, Harriet, and Gertrude) garnered fewer votes

(11, 14, and 14). Attractive names make their owners appear more attractive, which may also explain why celebrities often do name upgrades to increase their appeal. Would Marilyn Monroe be half the bombshell named Norma Jean Mortenson, or Snoop Dogg half the bad boy as Calvin Broadus, or Jennifer Aniston as all-American as Jennifer Anastassakis?

To pinpoint what makes certain names more appealing than others, Amy Perfors, a linguist at the Massachusetts Institute of Technology, posted photos of her friends on Hotornot.com, a Web site where the public views and rates the attractiveness of submissions. Each photo was posted several times, with different names, to see how changing names affected their score. The secret, Perfors found, was all in the vowels. Linguists classify vowels by where in the mouth they're articulated: "Front" vowels are formed in the front of the mouth to create sounds like the *i* in *bit*, the *e* in *bet*, or the *a* in *bait*. "Back" vowels are formed in the back of the mouth to create sounds like the *o* in *hot* or the *u* in *hut*.

In Perfors' study, men with names containing front-vowel sounds (like Ben, Dave, Rick, or Steve) were rated as more attractive than those with back-vowel sounds (like John, Luke, or Paul). For women, it was the exact opposite. Names with back-vowel sounds (like Julie, Laura, or Robin) were rated as more ravishing than those with front vowels (like Anne, Kate, or Mindy). Front vowels are perceived as sounding small, back vowels large. Women prefer men with small-sounding names because it suggests the guy is less threatening and more sensitive, while men dig women with big-sounding names since it suggests a woman's aggressive and outgoing. Names add a refreshing twist to traditional gender stereotypes that can increase someone's appeal. It's like finding out a gorilla of a guy plays the flute, or a mousy gal is a champion arm wrestler. Given that the majority of the study's respondents were heterosexual, Perfors' findings probably apply best to straight people, although, as Perfors points out, "There's no reason that gay men couldn't also like men that aren't supermasculine, and lesbians couldn't like women who aren't super feminine," just like straight folks.

Whose Names Are Hot—or Not?

HOT NAMES (MEN)	HOT NAMES (WOMEN)
Matt Damon	Julia Roberts
Ben Affleck	Carmen Electra
Jake Gyllenhall	Lauren Bacall
Steve Martin	Robin Wright Penn
Denzel Washington	Susan Sarandon
Richard Gere	Holly Hunter
Eminem	Drew Barrymore
David Duchovny	

NOT HOT NAMES (MEN)	NOT HOT NAMES (WOMEN)
Jonathan Rhys-Meyers	Jennifer Aniston
Luke Wilson	Melanie Griffith
Tom Selleck	Natalie Portman
Paul Newman	Gillian Anderson
Charles Bronson	Amy Sedaris
George Clooney	Anne Heche
Jon Stewart	Lindsay Lohan

So if your name is a dud, should you change it—or adopt a nickname with nicer overtones? Before you head to city hall and file a name-changing petition, there is an easier option:

Find people whose names are similar to your own. In a study titled "How Do I Love Thee? Let Me Count the J's," John Jones at the United States Military Academy scanned hundreds of marriage records spanning back to the 1800s and found that a considerable number of women's maiden names began with the same letter as their husband's last name. To test this tendency further, Jones conducted an experiment asking men to write an essay focusing on their flaws, then rate the attractiveness of women's personal ads where the full first name and first three letters of their last name were listed. By and large, the men preferred ads where the names closely matched their own, most likely because we tend to find familiarity comforting in situations where we might feel insecure. Given dating can definitely induce some jitters, it would make sense we'd be drawn to names that mimic our own.

This'll Come in Handy . . .

Gordon Gallup was at Pizza Hut with his wife and kids when, among the video games in one corner of the restaurant, he spotted a device that would play a critical role in his research more than a decade later: a grip-strength machine. "I inserted a quarter, grabbed the handle, and squeezed as hard as I could," Gallup recalls. According to the machine, Gallup's grip strength was off the charts. "My five-year-old son was very impressed," he says.

In 2008, Gallup and his son—who by then was an undergrad at the University of New York in Albany, where Gallup was a professor—revisited grip strength in a laboratory setting. Eighty-two male students had their grip strength measured with a stapler-sized device called a handgrip dynamometer, then submitted themselves to a battery of tests and questions about their love lives. After analyzing the results, Gallup found that men with firm grips also had more manly physiques (broad shoulders, narrow waists), more outgoing personalities, and had slept with more women than more limp-lilied hand shakers. Most likely caused by higher testosterone levels, firm grips are largely genetic, a hand-me-down from our primitive past when swinging from trees was our main mode of transportation. By shaking a man's hand hello, women can get an instant gauge of whether a guy is a catch. Shake a woman's hand, and men can glean very different information—namely, where she's at in her menstrual cycle. Women's grips get stronger when they're ovulating and most fertile.

Hands contain other clues to compatibility, specifically in the length of our second and fourth fingers. Researchers call this the 2D:4D ratio, which is critically affected by hormone levels in the womb during fetal development. As a result, these two fingers act like a secret hand signal, giving away top-secret information about who we are. In most men, the fourth finger is a couple millimeters longer than the index. If it's a lot longer (approximately 5 mm is notable, 15 mm the max), studies suggest these men may be more aggressive, ambitious, and have higher sperm counts. In women, the index and fourth fingers are typically the same length, although often the index finger is longer. If it's a lot longer (approximately 8 mm is notable, 20 mm the max), this can signal a more feminine demeanor and higher fertility levels.

Kiss Me, I'm . . . Ovulating?

At a swarthy 6'2" with a crew cut, Brent Jordan cheerfully admits, "I look like a big doofy jock. In fact, it took me a while to figure out that I had a brain." In his twenties, Jordan worked as a lifeguard, as a cage fighter, and on an offshore oil rig. In his early thirties, he decided to apply himself to a different pursuit: academics. Enrolling as an undergrad at the University of New Mexico, Jordan paid his way through college by managing a strip club called TD North, where, in addition to bouncing unruly clients, he served as a foreman of sorts to the dancers, collecting nightly reports on their tip earnings and, on occasion, handing out tampons (the ladies' room lacked a dispenser).

One night, Jordan noticed something peculiar: The dancers asking for tampons weren't earning as much as the other girls. Were their cramps making them cranky toward customers? Jordan doubted it, but was stumped as to what else could be causing this monthly dip in tips. He raised this question with his evolutionary psychology professor, Geoffrey Miller, and together they started scrutinizing the tipping/tampon mystery in depth by tracking the menstrual periods and earnings of eighteen strippers. Two months, 296 work shifts, and 5,300 lap dances later, Miller and Jordan published their findings, "Ovulatory Cycle Effects on Tip Earnings by Lap Dancers," in the journal *Evolution and Human Behavior*. Miller and Jordan found that on average, strippers made $70 an hour when they were ovulating (which, in this study, was estimated to occur nine to fifteen days after the start of their last period), $35 while menstruating, and $50 in between. Assuming men's tips were a reflection of how drawn they were to certain dancers, that meant that strippers—and all women, for that matter—were hotter at certain times of the month. The reason, Miller and Jordan theorized, was that men were subconsciously picking up on a phenomenon known as human estrus.

Estrus is a period when a female is ovulating—and, as a result, is fertile and ready for sex. In many mammals, estrus is announced loud and clear. Baboons' behinds, for example, turn red. Cats caterwaul. Dogs emit an odor that attracts all the strays in the neighborhood. Until recently, humans weren't thought to have a "come one, come all" clarion call that they're ready to copulate, but Miller and Jordan's study proves otherwise. Exactly *how* women advertise they're in estrus is still unknown, although Miller and Jordan posit it might have to do with subtle fluctuations in the way women look, walk, talk, smell, flirt, or dance. Other studies confirm these findings. In one experiment, men were asked to sniff T-shirts previously worn by women at various points in their menstrual cycle; time and again men picked the shirts of ovulating gals as their favorites. In another study of women in nightclubs, researchers determined that as ovulation approached, their outfits got skimpier in an effort to attract more attention. And if they do head home with a cute stranger, studies show that ovulating women are 25 percent more likely to initiate sex and have twice as many orgasms as women who are at other points in their cycle.

Women in estrus are primed for reproduction, and men appear programmed to respond. At strip clubs, they'll increase their tips. At home, studies show that men become more amorous when their wives or girlfriends are ovulating. Women on birth control, however, may be at a disadvantage. In Miller and Jordan's study, strippers taking oral contraceptives made less money month-round, most likely because they render a woman infertile and cancel out her abilities to use estrus to her advantage.

Like It or Not, Looks Matter—a Lot

Elaine Hatfield admits she's no social butterfly. And yet there she was, in her first job at the University of Minnesota's Student Activity Bureau, arranging the Freshman Welcome Week dance. "Anyone who knows how shy and nonsocial I am finds that a big joke!" she says. A recent Ph.D. graduate in psychology from Stanford, Hatfield's true calling was scientific research in human relations. Trying to spin gold from straw, she decided to use the dance to conduct her own experiment. Hatfield announced that each ticket-purchaser would get set up on a date with another attendant. Pairs would be matched by a computer, based on their answers to a variety of personality and aptitude tests. In her book, *Mirror, Mirror*, Hatfield recounts the results.

"Four hundred couples who attended did what people always do at dances—they danced, talked, and got to know one another," Hatfield remembers. "Then during the 10:30 p.m. intermission, we swept through the building, rounding up couples from the dance floor, lavatories, fire escapes—even adjoining buildings. We asked them to tell us frankly (and in confidence) what they thought of their dates." Hatfield had assumed that couples matched for similar interests, personalities, and intelligence levels would hit it off, but her hypothesis didn't pan out. Only one criterion served as a significant predicator of whether the students wanted to see their date again: looks.

We all know looks are important. And yet Hatfield's study, which was published in 1966, was the first of its kind to suggest that physical appearance wasn't just important, but downright crucial. "Every effort to find anything else that mattered failed!" Hatfield recalls. "Men and women with exceptional IQs and social skills, for example, were *not* liked any better than those less well endowed." In today's fast-paced world, where speed-dating has become a popular way to sift through romantic prospects, Hatfield believes that people are even more prone to base their picks on appearance. When Jason Weeden at the University of Pennsylvania examined data from over 10,000 speed-daters who had met a variety of potential mates for three minutes, all the qualities the speed-daters claimed would sway their decision—similar goals, religion, education level, and interest in having kids—didn't mean squat. All that mattered was whether the person sitting across from them was hot.

Men especially are suckers for beauty. In one study conducted by Michael Cunningham at the University of St. Louis, men showed greater willingness to move furniture, donate a kidney, or even jump on a hand grenade if the damsel in distress were pretty rather than plain (the only thing men were reluctant to do was loan pretty gals money for fear they'd never get it back, says Cunningham). Even when men are happily ensconced in a relationship, their eye still wanders toward the alternatives every time one breezes by. As for men's claims that they're "just looking," that's not as harmless as it sounds. In one study, where men viewed photos of *Playboy*-type centerfolds then were asked how they felt about the woman they were currently dating, men expressed that they were less attracted, less happy, and less committed to their significant others, all because a few beauties had been paraded before their eyes.

While women are often painted as more forgiving of men's beer guts and balding heads, one study suggests that deep down, women may be more superficial than they let on. Female volunteers were asked to choose the most date-worthy guys from an array of profiles containing photos and other personal information. Looks mattered somewhat with their picks. And yet, when this same experiment was repeated with women hooked up to a lie detector, their answers changed. Fearing that any fibbing would be found out, they picked the best-looking guys largely regardless of their other attributes, which suggests that women who say "looks don't matter that much" are merely trotting out a white lie to be polite.

But wait a minute, isn't beauty only skin deep? Not according to an experiment by Arthur Miller at Miami University in Ohio, where men and women viewing photos of good-looking people rated them as more confident, complex, careful, perceptive, and friendly than average-looking folks. This bias, which is called the "halo effect," occurs because the human mind prefers simplicity. Once we spot one positive quality, we tend to assume the whole package is top-notch, inside and out (likewise, the "horns effect" makes us assume ugly people are mean, insecure, and unintelligent). As for whether these assumptions are true, that depends on which quality you're talking about. Pretty people do have better social skills, but perhaps because of all their partying, their intelligence scores may suffer. In one study comparing high school students' yearbook photos to their IQ scores, attractive men and women scored 8 and 5.5 points lower respectively than their homelier peers. Attractive people also suffer from low self-confidence levels. In one experiment, Brenda Major at New York State University in Buffalo asked students to write an essay, for which they all received high praise. While the ugly students attributed their success to their stellar writing abilities, the attractive students automatically chalked it up to the fact that the grader thought they were good-looking.

Most of us, of course, aren't blessed with bombshell looks. But the key to beating the beautiful crowd is simple: Just stay in the race. Attractive people may have the edge straight out of the gates during those first few minutes or hours of meeting someone, but less good-looking sorts, if they're nice, become more attractive over time. Kevin Kniffin at the University of Wisconsin-Madison conducted an experiment where participants on an archaeological dig rated the attractiveness of their peers at the outset of the dig as well as six weeks later. In that time, homely people who worked hard became hotter in the participants' eyes. Cute slackers got uglier.

Why Women Should Wear Red—and Men Blue

The color red really can rev up a guy's sexual appetite. According to a study by Andrew Elliot at the University of Rochester published in the *Journal of Personality and Social Psychology*, male study subjects rated photos of women wearing red as more attractive than when their clothes were a different hue. The reason for this is part scientific (red stimulates the metabolism) and part social conditioning (red is a color we associate with romance, Valentine's Day, and even the red-light district). Men who want to wow women, on the other hand, should wear blue, says Leatrice Eiseman, director of the Pantone Color Institute and author of *More Alive with Color*. People tend to subconsciously associate the color blue with a sense of calm, stability, and reliability—all qualities women typically value in a long-term mate.

Weighty Issues

Attractive SWF, nonsmoking, drug and disease-free, 44-year-old redhead, nurturing, affectionate, intelligent, 50 pounds overweight, with good sense of humor and a loving heart seeks male 40–50 years old for companionship, love, and possible marriage.

In 1994, men in Austin, Texas, browsing the personal ads in their local newspaper came across this woman's profile. Only eight men responded. One week later, local papers ran another personal ad that was identical, except for one small phrase. Rather than being fifty pounds overweight, the woman was a recovering drug addict. In spite of this liability, thirty responses rolled in from men willing to date her. None of these hopeful bachelors, however, ended up meeting either woman. Why? The ads were fake, posted by Sarah Sitton at St. Edwards University, who was curious how much a woman's weight affected her dating prospects. Given that the hefty bachelorette received one-third the interest as the recovering drug addict, it was clear that at least in American culture, slim wins.

While men's preference for slender figures may seem unfair, men actually aren't as obsessed with thinness as women think. Paul Rozin, a professor at the University of Pennsylvania, showed a panel of men and women images of nine female figures that varied from rail-thin to rotund. When women were asked to choose which body men would find most attractive, they gravitated toward the slim end of the scale. When men were asked the same question, they picked the body of average weight. In other studies on body-mass index, or BMI, which is someone's weight scaled for their height, Martin Tovée at Newcastle University found that men preferred photos of women with a BMI of twenty, which falls within the normal range. What's more, women deemed a BMI of twenty-one to twenty-two as most attractive on men, which means guys don't need to worry too much about having a little extra padding, either.

Men's tastes in a woman's figure also fluctuate based on other factors, some quite peculiar. Take, for example, an experiment conducted by Leif Nelson at New York University, who asked students entering and exiting the college cafeteria to fill out a questionnaire stating their weight preferences in a mate. While women's responses remained the same across the board, men who hadn't eaten yet preferred women 2.7 pounds heavier than those who had already eaten dinner. Nelson also found that men who weren't carrying any money in their wallets preferred women 2.3 pounds heavier than men who were packing cash. Men who are hungry or short on funds, in other words, dig bigger women. Why? Nelson theorizes that deep in the most primitive parts of their brains, men feel it's their job to put food on the table. When valuable resources like food or cash are scarce, a little extra padding on a woman is seen as a beneficial buffer against malnutrition that will keep him from feeling overwhelmed with this task. Men who are rolling in resources, on the other hand, prefer thin women because of a subconscious concern that their largess would merely make a fat woman fatter.

Still other scientists argue that women can look great at any weight, and what really matters is something different: proportion. After measuring the curves of *Playboy* centerfolds and Miss America Pageant winners through the years, Devendra Singh at the University of Texas in Austin found that a waist-to-hip ratio of .70 was consistently deemed ideal (that means a woman's waist is 70 percent the size of her hips). The reason this ratio is so revered has to do with fertility, which is highest in women with soaring estrogen levels that cause fat to situate itself around the hips and thighs verses the stomach. Both the buxom Marilyn Monroe and emaciated Kate Moss have a WHR hovering around .70, which supports the idea that sexiness is more about having an hourglass shape than the size of the hourglass.

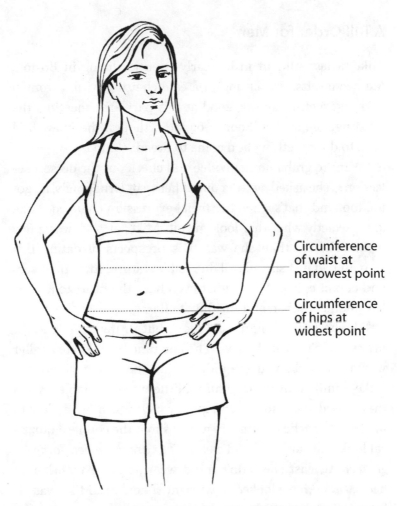

Circumference
of waist at
narrowest point

Circumference
of hips at
widest point

How women can calculate waist-to-hip ratio (WHR). Using a measuring tape, measure the circumference of your waist at its narrowest point. Then, measure the circumference of your hips at their widest point. Divide the circumference of your waist by the circumference of your hips. According to studies, a waist-to-hip ratio of .70 is deemed ideal.

A Tall Order for Men

Mike, a law student in his early twenties living in Boston, Massachusetts, was sitting in a café chatting with a woman he'd just met. Mike was good at this part—the meeting, the chatting, the sitting. Sooner or later, though, he knew he'd have to do something he'd come to dread: stand up.

"Want to grab another coffee and check out the dessert selection?" she asked, getting out of her seat. Grudgingly, he got up, too, and that's when her facial expression changed. Mike knew exactly what that look meant. Mike, at 5'4", was a few inches shorter than she was. His prospects of dating this woman had just shrunk, all due to his stature. After their second cup of coffee, Mike didn't even have the heart to ask for her phone number, and she didn't offer.

"Maybe I'm selling myself short, but in my experience, it just wouldn't work," he says. The one time he did date a taller woman who claimed she didn't mind the height difference, Mike admits that it made him a little uncomfortable. When they kissed, *she* had to bend over, which was a huge blow to his ego. At parties, strangers would shoot the couple a quizzical look that said loud and clear, *What are those two doing together?* At least she didn't mind wearing flats; with her in heels, they'd have looked downright ridiculous. Mike was almost relieved when they broke up.

The hurdles Mike faces in the height department aren't all in his head. In one study of newlyweds' bank records—which often note couples' heights for identification purposes—only one in 720 couples consisted of a wife taller than her husband, when this should have been the case for 18 couples if men and women were paired randomly. Typically, women prefer to look up to the men they date, literally and figuratively. Height is synonymous with strength and power.

On the bright side, there are ways short guys can even the playing field. For one, having a successful career can actually make men look taller. To illustrate how this optical illusion works, psychology professor Paul Wilson brought in a guest lecturer to his classes named "Mr. England," in some cases introducing him as a "student from Cambridge" and other times as a full-fledged professor. Afterward, Wilson asked his students to estimate Mr. England's height. Professor England was estimated to be a full two and a half inches taller than England the undergrad, even though it was the same gentleman both times. Men with less imposing statures can also compensate by making more money. In a 2006 study of 30,000 online daters, Günter Hitsch at the University of Chicago calculated that a 5'6" man making $237,500 is just as likely to be pursued as a six-foot man making an average salary of $62,500 per year.

Finally, height isn't the only aspect of a man's physique that factors into a woman's attraction levels. Another crucial measurement is his waist-to-shoulder ratio (WSR). In studies where women were asked to rate the attractiveness of various physiques, a waist-to-shoulder ratio of .60 was deemed ideal, which means a man's waist is 60 percent the diameter of his shoulders. And while women may *say* they prefer tall guys in an abstract sense, in one study where they were presented with actual photos of men of varying heights, they gravitated more toward men of medium height (5'9" to 5'11"). Some researchers argue that tall men overestimate their desirability as a dating partner, while shorter guys underestimate their appeal, so to a certain extent an attitude adjustment rather than elevator shoes may be in order.

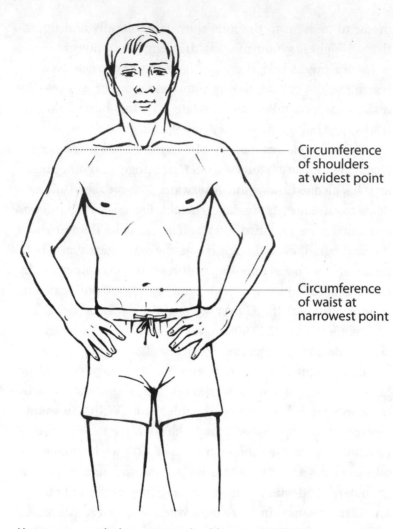

Circumference
of shoulders
at widest point

Circumference
of waist at
narrowest point

How men can calculate waist-to-shoulder ratio (WSR). Using a measuring tape, measure the circumference of your waist at its narrowest point. Then, measure the circumference of your shoulders at their widest point. Divide the circumference of your waist by the circumference of your shoulders. According to studies, a waist-to-shoulder ratio of .60 is considered ideal.

Women Like Beards. Really.

Paul Bunyan–style beards may have fallen out of fashion, but oddly, recent studies suggest that while women *say* they hate that hairy look, deep down, they secretly love it. Robert Pellegrini at San Jose State University handed ten bucks to students with beards willing to shave them and have their pictures taken at each stage in the process. The resulting photos showed men fully bearded, with moustache and goatee, moustache alone, and clean-shaven. When these photos were shown to women, they rated the fully bearded men as the most attractive, mature, confident, dominant, courageous, and creative. The more hair men shaved, the lower their ratings. Researchers theorize that women may be subconsciously responding to the fact that facial hair advertises high testosterone levels.

Symmetry: A Genetic Seal of Approval?

Can beauty be boiled down to a mathematical formula? According to Tommer Leyvand, the answer is yes—and he's invented a computer program called "beautification engine" to illustrate the results. To create this software, Leyvand and a team of researchers asked a group of men and women to rate photos of faces, assigning attractiveness ratings between one and six (six being most attractive). Researchers then located 84 facial feature points on these photos and measured 234 distances between them—distance between the lips and chin, width of the forehead, size of the eyes, and otherwise—to come up with an algorithm of which dimensions were deemed ideal. Send a digital photo of your own face through the beautification engine, and it will make slight adjustments to these distances, creating a modified version of your face that, according to this engine's algorithm, is more alluring than the original (for before-and-after photos, see page 45).

"The adjustments boil down to a few millimeters here and there," Leyvand explains, adding that which features this program tweaks varies by individual. Some people need more chiseled chins, others wider-set eyes. There is, however, one factor that the beautification engine corrects across the board: symmetry. According to Leyvand's and other researchers' studies, the more symmetrical the face, the more attractive it will appear to others.

Symmetry can also be measured in the rest of your body, including the length and width of your ears, hands, and feet. In 1994, Steven Gangestad and Randy Thornhill at the University of New Mexico published a study in the journal *Ethology and Sociobiology*, in which they measured these and other dimensions on seventy-two men and women. After showing their photos to a panel of judges, Gangestad and Thornhill found that those deemed most attractive were also highly symmetrical, meaning their left-to-right asymmetries were as low as 1 to 2 percent. Meanwhile, the lowest attractiveness ratings went to more lopsided folks, where asymmetries can be as high as 5 to 7 percent.

The benefits of balanced proportions don't end there. In further studies, symmetrical people were rated better dancers, had two to three times as many sexual partners in their lifetimes, and gave their partners more orgasms than asymmetrical sorts. Research shows that we don't even need to *see* people to gauge how symmetrical they are, since we can hear it in their voice and smell it on their clothes. When study subjects were asked to sniff T-shirts worn for two days straight by

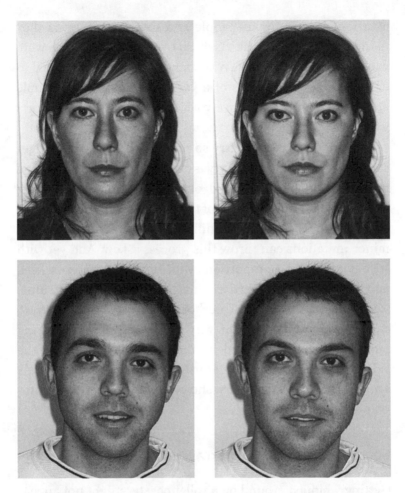

A mathematical makeover? The faces shown left are real; the ones on the right have been through the "beautification engine," a software created by Tommer Leyvand that makes subtle adjustments based on a mathematical formula involving 234 facial measurements (such as the width of the forehead and distance between the eyes). One feature that gets corrected across the board is symmetry. According to studies, the more symmetrical the face, the higher its attractiveness ratings.

a variety of anonymous people and to pick the scents they found most appealing, shirts worn by symmetrical sorts were chosen more than others. When study subjects were asked to listen to voice recordings of a variety of anonymous people and pick the most attractive voices, again, symmetrical sorts won the most votes.

Why do we like symmetry so much? According to Gangestad and Thornhill, symmetry is a sign of good genes. "As you grow—inside the womb and out—ideally your cells divide evenly, resulting in each side of the body being a mirror image of the other," explains Thornhill. Sickness, malnutrition, and minor mutations can throw this process askew. And yet with strong genes, your proportions will remain on an even keel, and serve as a clear advertisement that you're worth pursuing. According to Nancy Etcoff, author of *Survival of the Prettiest*, small asymmetries explain why some people prefer being photographed from one side or the other in order to hide the side with the "flaw." Even Marilyn Monroe wasn't entirely symmetrical, which is why she was almost always photographed from the right.

Scared, Angry, or Embarrassed? Good.

Getting whipped around on a roller coaster might not appear to do much for your looks. Ride a roller coaster with your date, however, and scientists swear it will make you look hotter to the person in the seat next to you. In a study titled "Love at First Fright," published in the *Archives of Sexual Behavior*, a team of researchers led by Cindy Meston at the University of Texas in Austin stationed themselves in front of a roller coaster ride at Six Flags. As a sea of visitors got on and off the ride, researchers approached, asking if riders would mind rating the attractiveness of people shown in a series of photos. Passengers exiting the ride rated the photos as more ravishing than those waiting to get on did.

The reason is a phenomenon called "excitation transfer," which, true to its name, transfers excitement from one source to another. Here's how it works: By most people's standards, riding a roller coaster is as exciting as it gets. Pulses race. Adrenaline surges. Hopefully, that cheese dog you ate earlier stays put. Once we stagger off the ride, there's a spillover effect: Any lingering feelings of giddiness get transferred to whatever sexual prospects are in sight. When riders looked at the photos they thought, *Wow, these photos are breathtaking*, when in reality they were just catching their breath. However, a living, breathing human being can also catch the overflow— and roller coasters are hardly the only excitement bank worth borrowing from.

Take bridges. Not any old bridge, but the kind that sway and wobble in the breeze like they do in the *Indiana Jones* movies. One day, men crossing such a bridge in Vancouver, Canada were intercepted in the middle by a woman named "Gloria" (who was actually an attractive research assistant). After chatting for a while, Gloria handed over her phone number, then headed home to wait by the phone. Of the twenty-three men Gloria met on the shaky bridge, nine ended up calling—a pretty impressive success rate. And yet, when the experiment was repeated on a nearby sturdy bridge, only two of sixteen men ended up dialing her digits. This experiment, devised by Donald Dutton and Arthur Aron, suggests that unsettling circumstances can intensify our attraction to others.

Fear isn't the only emotion that can act like an aphrodisiac. In other studies, people were subjected to feelings of anger by being chewed out by a professor, stress in the form of painful electroshocks, and even disgust by being trapped in a room polluted with ammonium sulfide. In all cases, attraction levels skyrocketed between fellow sufferers. The emotions stirred up didn't even need to be real, as was proved in another study where men were told to pretend they were soldiers being tortured by a female interrogator (who was yet another attractive research assistant). As the men were "tortured"—which entailed dropping "acid" (actually water) into their eyes, some screamed so convincingly the female interrogator had to be coaxed to continue. Afterwards, these men expressed a higher-than-average desire to kiss their captor and end their harrowing saga on a happy note.

Viewing violent scenarios on a movie screen can also breed some warm-and-fuzzy feelings. In one study, Brett Cohen at the University of South Florida kept tabs on how physically affectionate couples were upon entering and leaving a movie theater. Pairs who had bought tickets to *52 Pickup*, a thriller packed with blackmail and murder, left the theater hanging all over each other. By comparison, duos who'd seen the documentary *True Stories* about middle-class life in America acted as indifferent toward each other coming out of the theater as they had heading in.

Even feelings of embarrassment can lead to bonding. Consider an experiment by Barbara Fraley and Arthur Aron at the University of New York in Stony Brook, who paired volunteers together to learn some dance steps. To up the awkwardness factor, Fraley blindfolded one partner and stuck a drinking straw in the mouth of the other, who had to mumble out dance instructions from a sheet of paper. These pairs might not have won any dance contests, but they did win over each other. Squashed feet and unintelligible instructions aside, these dance partners rated each other as more attractive than pairs who were allowed to learn their steps without any impediments.

Flaws can be endearing, a fact that was underscored in another study where volunteers were asked to estimate the attractiveness of various quiz show contestants by listening to audiotapes of each contestant answering some questions. Two contestants answered nearly all the questions perfectly; two didn't. Of the two who aced the quiz, one also spilled coffee all over his new suit. In spite of this blunder—or, more accurately, *because* of this blunder—this contestant was rated as the most attractive, since, rather than being perfect, he'd become something better: *almost* perfect.

Your Nose Knows Who's a Catch

Alan Hirsch, head of the Smell & Taste Treatment and Research Center in Chicago, has devoted his career to studying noses. Hirsch has studied the impact of scent on everything from space perception (the smell of cucumber, for example, makes rooms seem more spacious) to hand-eye coordination (a noseful of jasmine raised study participants' bowling scores).

In 1995, Hirsch decided to pinpoint which scents put us in an amorous mood. How, exactly, could he measure which scents turned us on or off? The solution was two gadgets that are staples in many sex researchers' labs: the penile plethysmograph, a.k.a. the Peter Meter, a blood pressure–like cuff that wraps around the penis, and the vaginal photoplethysmograph (sorry, no cute nicknames here), a tampon-like contraption that gets inserted in the vagina. Once properly in place, these devices accurately measure blood flow down below, a fairly reliable index of arousal levels. After finding male and female volunteers willing to try on the equipment,

Hirsch got to work, wafting various fragrances their way to see which ones revved their responses below the belt.

Surprisingly, the scents one might assume would get a rise out of people—i.e., perfume and cologne—had little impact on study subjects' arousal levels. However, Hirsch found that something else really fired their loins: food. Men, it appears, really like pumpkin pie. In Hirsch's study, the smell of this dessert combined with lavender boosted penile blood flow by 40 percent. A doughnut-and-licorice combo came in second, triggering a 31.5 percent surge. For women, the most arousing aroma was Good & Plenty mixed with cucumber, which perked up vaginal blood flow by 14 percent. While Hirsch isn't sure why these specific scents revved our sexual motors, he says the allure of food smells in general makes sense from an evolutionary perspective. "Perhaps our earliest ancestors only felt they could reproduce when provisions were plentiful," Hirsch reasons, adding that it may also explain why dinner is such a common date-night activity. Hirsch also found that scent can affect more specific aspects of someone's appearance. Women wearing a spicy/floral scent ("It smelled like a combination of Herbal Essences shampoo and Old Spice aftershave," Hirsch recalls) appear twelve pounds lighter than their actual weight, while the smell of pink grapefruit will shave six years off their age.

Grapefruit, Good & Plenty, and pumpkin pie aside, people's own personal bouquets can also draw us closer or drive us away. When Diane, an office administrator in Ames, Iowa, first started dating Kyle, one of the first things she noticed was that she was mesmerized by the way he smelled. "I would get a whiff of him while we were making out and it would put me over the edge," she says. "I would even search for his scent on his pillow after he'd left. I loved wearing his sweatshirt because then I could breathe it in constantly. For a while, it drove me crazy trying to figure out where this scent came from. He didn't wear cologne. His soap was nothing special. Eventually I settled on the fact that it was just him. His scent hits me right in the gut. It's comforting, sweet, and a turn-on all at once."

If you've ever been smitten with someone but been mystified as to why, it could be your nose talking, and that ineffable smell infiltrating your nostrils could be MHC. Short for major histocompatability complex, MHC is a sequence of genes that helps your immune system fight disease. Everyone's MHC is a little bit different, and generally, the more different your MHC is from your mate's, the better, since that means any offspring you produce will have strong immune systems that can fight a broader range of disease. At the dating service ScientificMatch.com, you can actually mail in a sample of your DNA (attained from swishing a cotton swab in your mouth), have it analyzed, and get set up with MHC compatible partners, although it'll cost you (currently it's $995 for a lifetime membership). The cheaper option, of course, is to let your nose filter through prospects. If someone's MHC complements your own, your nose will say *Mmmm, this person smells good.* If your MHCs are too similar, your nose will say *Back off and search elsewhere.* To test the accuracy of these olfactory hunches, Swiss biologist Claus Wedekind handed out new T-shirts to forty-four men who had agreed to wear them while they slept for two nights in a row. After collecting their dirty laundry, Wedekind asked forty-nine women to take a whiff and pick which shirts they liked best. By comparing their choices to the men's DNA samples, Wedekind found that women were drawn most to men whose MHCs were distinct from their own.

While both men and women sniff out compatible partners, women have a more finely tuned sense of smell. Women on the Pill, though, are a glaring exception. Hormonal contraceptives scramble a woman's MHC radar and make her internal man-compass go haywire; in Wedekind's study, women on oral contraceptives were drawn to the *wrong* men—in other words, men with similar MHC. Due to this olfactory glitch, women who are shopping for a possible father for their children are better off using non-hormonal forms of birth control until they've found a keeper. Meanwhile, women who were already on the Pill when they meet a great guy should keep in mind that they may find their attraction levels waning if they go off oral contraceptives. Either way, MHC compatibility is nice, but it's by no means the only ingredient to a great relationship and healthy kids. It's a bonus, but it shouldn't be a deal breaker.

MHC may not be the only aroma affecting our attraction levels. Pheromones may also be sending out come-and-get-me signals. The effects of these odorless chemicals are easily seen in many animals; pheromones from butterflies can pull in potential mates from as far as six miles away. In humans, there's no hard proof so far that pheromones hold sway over our behavior, although that hasn't stopped scientists from creating synthetic versions we can dab behind our ears for a little extra luck when we're on the prowl. In the mid-1990s, Winnifred Cutler, a reproductive biologist credited with co-discovering human pheromones ten years earlier, created a synthetic version for women called Athena Pheromone 10:13 (in honor of her birthday) and Athena Pheromone 10X for men. To test their effectiveness, Cutler asked seventy-four men and women to add a few drops to their perfume or aftershave, then report the daily frequency of up to seven "socio-sexual behaviors" such as dating, kissing, and sex. Seventy-four percent of female pheromone users (verses 23 percent of placebo users) happily reported an increase in three or more sociosexual behaviors. Forty-one percent of the male phero-mone users (verses 9.5 percent of placebo users) noted the same, which suggests that Cutler's concoctions can make a difference.

Why Women Like Jerks

Theater tickets. Candlelit dinner. Flowers. Roy, an accountant living in Eugene, Oregon, had pulled out all the stops to impress Rachel on their first date, and it seemed to be working. That is, until Rachel happened to mention her ex.

"Thank god I got him out of my system," Rachel said, rolling her eyes. When Roy asked why, Rachel reeled off a litany of complaints: For one, her ex was an alcoholic. Plus he'd borrowed money from her and hadn't paid her back. To top things off, he never called, barring the few sloppy 3 a.m. entreaties to crash at her place, which Jennifer always refused. Well, almost always.

"That relationship, if you could call it that, was going nowhere," Rachel said. Thankfully, she added, Roy wasn't anything like her ex. Roy was . . . nice.

Hearing this, Roy had to steel himself so as not to wince. Scores of women before Rachel had also raved about how "nice" Roy was, and while they meant it as a compliment, from Roy's perspective it was the kiss of death. Roy was what women deemed "relationship material," and while this had earned him a decent number of girlfriends over the years, he kind of envied guys like Rachel's ex, who could treat women like crap and *still* swing by their place for a booty call at their convenience. What did Rachel see in this guy? Was she truly over him, or would she cave the next time he called, even if Roy was in the picture?

Daniel Kruger, another self-professed nice guy, was also puzzled that women would ever give bad boys the time of day. "In high school, I'd hear these guys bragging about their conquests in the locker room and wonder what women saw in them," he says. Years later, working as a research fellow at the University of Michigan, he got an inkling of the answer. While attending a conference on Darwinian literary criticism—which interprets books through the lens of evolutionary theory—Kruger noticed that many of literature's most memorable male characters fell into one of two camps when pursuing a mate: They were either cads (jerks) or dads (nice guys who'd make model fathers). Literature's most memorable female characters always seemed to be torn between the two.

After pouring over the pantheon of British literature, Kruger found a variety of characters who epitomized the cad and dad ideal. Here are two examples:

George Staunton, from *The Heart of Midlothian*

His carriage was bold and somewhat supercilious, his step easy and free, his manner daring and unconstrained . . . those eyes that were now turbid with melancholy, now gleaming with scorn, and now sparkling with fury—was it the passions of a mere mortal that they expressed, or the emotions of a fiend who seeks, and seeks in vain, to conceal his fiendish designs under the borrowed mask of manly beauty?

Waverley, from *Waverley*

His real disposition seemed exclusively domestic . . . As one of his acquaintances said of him, "High and perilous adventure is not his forte . . . I will tell you where he will be at home and in his place—in the quiet circle of domestic happiness, lettered indolence, and elegant enjoyments of his family's estate. And he will refit his old library in the most exquisite Gothic taste, and garnish its shelves with the rarest and most valuable volumes; and he will draw plans and landscapes, and write verses, and rear temples, and dig grottoes; and he will stand in a clear summer night in the colonnade before the hall, and gaze on the deer as they stray in the moonlight, or lie shadowed by the boughs of the huge fantastic oaks; and he will be a happy man."

After showing these passages to over 250 female undergraduates, Kruger asked them the following question: If you could date, marry, or go on a road trip with either of these fellows, which one would you pick? The women didn't hesitate. Waverly was by far the better choice. And yet, there was one occasion when the women admitted they'd ditch Waverly and give surly Staunton a call: if they were in the mood for a no-strings-attached one-night stand.

Kruger says his research supports an evolutionary theory known as the "sexy son hypothesis," first proposed in 1979 by noted biologists Patrick Weatherhead and Raleigh Robertson. This theory deems that a nice guy is perfect for marriage, companionship, and raising a family, but he doesn't necessarily have the best genes to pass on to the kids. Those belong to the bad boy, who, thanks to his more aggressive, risk-taking ways, is often successful, powerful, and (here's the clincher) pretty suave with the ladies. A son born by this man, women assume, would also be successful, powerful, and pretty suave with the ladies. This sexy son would bear many grandchildren and guarantee her genes will get spread far and wide in the future. The downside, of course, is that fathers of sexy sons rarely stick around to help change the diapers or pitch in with the grocery bills. As a result, women are forced to choose what's more important: superior genes from a sleazeball, or so-so genes from stable marriage material?

Now, before all you nice guys start thinking, *Wait a minute, who says my sons will end up less sexy than those from some jerk?*, keep in mind, the sexy son hypothesis is only a theory. No one has tested it on humans, and in animals, they've found evidence to the contrary. Lars Gustafsson, a Swedish ecologist, noticed that female flycatchers often chased after "bad boy" males who were polygamous but attractive—which, in flycatcher terms, meant that they sported a wide, white patch of feathers on their forehead. Gustafsson decided to observe these birds generation after generation to see if the sexy son idea held water. Twenty-four years later, Gustafsson had his answer: no. Offspring of philandering males might have had the right genes to develop a wide, white forehead patch, but this feature's development is highly dependent on receiving adequate nutrition while young. Given that promiscuous fathers were too busy mating to deliver food to the nest, their offspring failed to acquire this highly desirable trait, and went off to sire fewer grandchicks than flycatchers who had been raised by less attractive but monogamous males who took better care of their young. Nice guys might not finish last, provided they can convince women to stop mooning over the jerks and give them a chance.

"My advice to nice guys is this: wait," says Kruger. "Bad

boys might be successful in their twenties, but later on, they're going to be that jerk, sitting in a bar, alone. Eventually, women wise up and the tables will turn."

Age Does a Number on All of Us

Samara, a divorcée in her forties who owned her own catering business in Cape Coral, Florida, was surfing online dating profiles one evening when she spotted a guy who seemed right up her alley. "Runningman305" was also in his forties, an avid triathlete, and lived a mere five-minute drive from her house. There was only one problem, which was summed up in his description of whom he was seeking: women aged twenty-five to thirty-five.

"It's not fair," she says. "I look great for my age, but past forty, it's as if I've magically turned into chopped liver." Pretty much every online dating profile Samara views indicates that men are seeking women younger than they are. Once, as an experiment, she changed the age on her profile to thirty-eight. Within days, interested suitors started filling her once-empty inbox. Meeting these men for dates, though, was a nerve-wracking ordeal. Even if Samara looked younger than her years, the ruse was up the instant they got a look at her driver's license—would her fib or her forties scare them off?

To add insult to injury, Samara's ex-husband had married someone who was a decade younger than Samara. To console herself, Samara found plenty of disparaging ways to explain her ex-husband's behavior. He was superficial. Immature. Clearly going through a mid-life crisis (what would be next, a red Audi and a gold earring?). And yet, now that she'd made the rounds online, it was beginning to dawn on her that nearly all men fell in this camp. Were Samara's dating days truly over? Should she just give up, get a cat, and while away the rest of her days with all the other divorced female forty-somethings she knew who seemed to be in the exact same boat?

Marriage records paint an equally grim picture of the premium men place on youth. On average, men marry women who are three years younger than they are. Which doesn't sound that bad, but it gets worse once divorce enters the picture. On average, men's second wives will be five years younger. Wife #3? Eight years younger. Then, of course, there are those couples with Grand Canyon–sized age gaps between them that make onlookers whisper, "She could be his *daughter!*" Point and cluck all you want, but remember we're at the mercy of our need to pass on our genes.

Our bodies are wired to want to procreate, and we gravitate toward those who can deliver. A woman's fertility levels soar in her twenties, decline in her thirties, and disappear in her fifties (the average age of the onset of menopause is fifty-one). It's no accident that men's attraction levels for women tend to mirror this trajectory. According to a study of more than 5,000 Swedish couples published in *Biology Letters*, men will have the most offspring when their wife is six years younger than they are.

Scientists have discovered that men, too, have biological clocks—and they're winding down faster than we might think. In one review of the medical literature of the past twenty years published in the journal *Fertility and Sterility*, Sharon Kidd at the University of California at Berkeley found that men over the age of fifty suffered up to a 22 percent drop in semen volume, 37 percent drop in sperm motility, and up to a 38 percent lower chance of pregnancy compared to men under age thirty. According to Harry Fisch, author of *The*

Male Biological Clock, of the six million American couples seeking help for fertility problems today, a full 40 percent will find out that the complication is due to the man's reproductive system, 40 percent of problems are due to women, and 20 percent are due to both partners or unknown causes.

The Oldest Dad Award Goes to . . .

The oldest father on record is an Australian mineworker named Leslie Colley, who sired a son at age ninety-two in 1992.

So which is more important in attracting a mate, beauty or youth? George Fieldman of Buckinghamshire Chilterns University presented a photo of a ravishing thity-six-year-old woman alongside photos of slightly less alluring women as young as twenty. When men in their twenties were asked which woman they'd most like to date and marry, across the board, they picked the thirty-six year old. Even when Fieldman lied and informed the men the woman they liked was forty-five years old, the men weren't fazed. At thirty-six or forty-five, the woman was attractive.

And the Oldest Mom . . .

Dawn Brooke of Guernsey (a British dependency off the coast of Normandy), who gave birth to a son in 1997 at the age of fifty-nine. Throw IVF treatments into the mix, and the oldest mom is Omkari Panwar of India, who gave birth to twins in 2008 at the ripe old age of seventy.

Women: Lemmings in Love?

Matt hated grocery shopping. The Charlotte, North Carolina, computer programmer's reason for this was simple: It always made him feel so undeniably, pathetically single. As Matt brought his basketful of frozen burritos, pizzas, and other easy-to-make items up to the counter, he could swear that the checkout ladies felt sorry for him, based on the look in their eyes and the tone of their voice as they shuttled his purchases through the scanner. Even the cute ones he'd consider hitting on seemed to regard him as a sad, lonely bachelor. Which is all the more reason why Maryann, meandering through the organic vegetable aisle, caught his eye one evening. She, too, seemed to be shopping for one.

"I don't get it," Matt said as his opener. "What makes organic tomatoes so much better than regular ones?" Matt was displeased, but not surprised, to see the woman eye him and his frozen food–filled basket suspiciously. Sensing that he wasn't totally bombing, Matt managed to segue into introductions, and eventually "Would you like to meet for coffee sometime?" Somewhat reluctantly, Maryann wrote down her e-mail address.

Flash forward five months: Matt and Maryann, now a couple, go grocery shopping together. While it could be his imagination, Matt could swear the checkout ladies look at him differently. One cashier who, during his single days, would barely deign to make eye contact now smiles and says hello. The women at his office also seem to have warmed up since he started mentioning his girlfriend in passing. Not only are women acting more friendly, occasionally Matt can sense they are being flirty. Fine, maybe they feel it's safe to flirt, since it won't (or at least shouldn't) lead to anything serious. Still, that alone can't explain this sudden onslaught of attention. One night, a female coworker told Matt, "If you and Maryann ever break up, I'd snap you right up." After processing this, Matt asked why she'd never made a move when he was single. She couldn't say.

"That's when I started seriously wondering whether women were crazy," Matt says. "When I was single, I was a pariah. Women avoided me like an STD. Now that I'm taken, women throw themselves at me. It makes no sense. I'm still the same guy. Does a girlfriend on my arm make me look like less of a reject, or what?"

Science has an explanation for Matt's dilemma, and it's called "mate-choice copying." The basic premise is that women's opinions are contagious. Once a man has won one woman's stamp of approval, others will also find him appealing. A man lacking favorable female attention, on the other hand, will probably stay that way. In one telling experiment, Benedict Jones at the University of Aberdeen in Scotland showed female study subjects photos of men where nearby women were either smiling or looking bored. When Jones asked the study subjects to rate each man's attractiveness, they consistently judged the guys flanked by smiling women as far more appealing than the men surrounded by indifferent onlookers. The fact that women cave so easily to the opinions of their peers might seem woefully wishy-washy, but there's actually a very good reason women swoon as a group.

When it comes to having sex, females must choose carefully, and separating the good guys from the bad can be a long, tedious process. That's where mate-choice copying comes in. By picking a guy who's been pre-approved by others, women can gauge a guy's quality quickly. Mate-choice copying is a time-saver, plain and simple—not that there aren't occasionally some messy side effects. Some women end up falling for men who are already in relationships, a phenomenon known among researchers as the "wedding ring effect." Typically, the mistresses of married men defend their decision by lamenting that "all the good men are taken." And yet, in a study titled "Are All the Taken Men Good?," Kevin Eva at McMasters University and Timothy Wood at the Medical Council of Canada turned this maxim on its head by showing that women merely *perceive* men in relationships as more of a catch. They asked thirty-eight women to rate the attractiveness of men in photos accompanied by a description of the individual—some married, some single. More often than not, women rated the married men as more magnetic than the single ones.

Is It Love? Who Can Tell?

When seeking a second opinion about whether you and your amour are a match, ask your single friends rather than the married folks. In one study, psychologist Frank Bernieri at Oregon State University asked 168 volunteers to watch video clips of couples and rate how smitten they were with each other. Married people, perhaps because of their rose-tinted view of the world, often declared the couples were in love when they weren't all that committed. Single people, on the other hand, were able to gauge where the relationship stood fairly accurately.

Do men adhere to mate-choice copying and ape the opinions of their male peers? To a small extent, but the effects are minimal, and certainly not enough to get them mooning over married women. Men, unlike women, don't face dire costs (i.e., pregnancy) when they pick a partner who ends up being a dud. As a result, gathering information through their pals to avoid bad decisions isn't all that important.

We All Get Prettier When We Play Hard to Get

Country music: Love it or hate it, you've gotta hand it to its song titles. Not only are they memorable (who can forget "Drop Kick Me, Jesus, Through the Goal Post of Life"? Or "I Don't Know Whether to Kill Myself or Go Bowling"?), many contain insights into the human condition. Consider the following: "Don't the Girls All Get Prettier at Closin' Time." This gem, by Mickey Gilley, has no question mark at the end because, well, it's not a question. Of *course* the girls all seem prettier at closing time. Why? And how much prettier are we talking about? Can a two turn into a ten and send you home with someone you'd never dream of sleeping with had you met over an afternoon coffee?

James Pennebaker, a professor at the University of Virginia, sent his research team out to three college-town bars at 9 p.m., 10:30 p.m., and midnight (closing time was 12:30). During their visits, researchers asked bar patrons to rate the attractiveness of the romantic options before them. By the end of the night, it was obvious that Mickey Gilley was right: Both the girls *and* the boys appeared better-looking to potential mates, although the results weren't as extreme as we might think. On average, ratings slid from five to six on a ten-point scale. In other words, no matter how many Alabama Slammers people drank, chances were slim they'd head home with someone they really didn't find attractive.

A lot of the reason we find others more appealing late at night is booze-related. In one study by Barry Jones at Glasgow University, students who had downed the equivalent of just two pints of beer rated photos 25 percent more attractive than sober students did. The reason beer goggles adjust our lens so radically is because alcohol stimulates an area of the brain called the nucleus accumbens, which is used to judge facial attractiveness. It's even given rise to its own country song–worthy saying: Beauty is in the eye of the beer holder.

Alcohol, however, isn't the only thing pickling our judgment. Another phenomenon to blame for the bump in ratings is "reactance theory." Essentially, when we're told we can't do something, we react by wanting to do it more. Sure, it's immature, but that's just how our minds work. To illustrate this point, Pennebaker conducted another study where he placed two different signs on college bathroom walls. One read *Please don't write on these walls*, the other *Do not write on these walls under any circumstances*. In two weeks, the wall with the latter sign was covered in graffiti. Bathrooms aren't the only place where you'll see reactance theory in action. In bars, as the clock ticks and the writing on the wall starts reading *There's no way you're getting lucky tonight!*, the desire to find someone grows stronger—and, for better or for worse, our standards loosen to accommodate those needs.

Reactance theory doesn't just dictate our pickup decisions in bars. It also comes into play when parents disapprove of their child's choice of mate. Researchers call this the Romeo and Juliet Effect, and have found that the more stridently parents disapprove of a certain liaison, the stronger the attraction levels. What's more, the harder star-crossed lovers work to surmount their parents or whatever obstacles are in their way, the stronger their feelings for one another become as a result. All those fairy tales had it backward: True love doesn't inspire heroic effort, heroic effort inspires true love. Work hard, and you appreciate the prize more.

So is playing hard to get really the way to go? To test this long-held belief, Elaine Hatfield conducted an experiment where she set up men with women who had been trained to respond in one of two ways when they came a-calling. The first group of girls eagerly accepted the men's invitations to go on dates. The second group hemmed, hawed, said they were busy, then eventually gave in. After their dates, Hatfield checked in with the men to see which women they liked most. While she assumed the hard-to-get gals would pique their interest, surprisingly, they proved no more alluring than the easy-to-get ones. Hard-to-get women, while highly desirable, also threatened men's confidence levels. Meanwhile, the easy-to-get gals were a quick ego boost, but men also worried they were *too* easy. In truth, "Each woman was uniquely desirable and uniquely frightening," Hatfield wrote in her study, comparing the men's dilemma to that of sailors from Greek mythology forced to navigate between the sea monsters Scylla and Charybdis. Were women fated no matter what to come across as picky or slutty? Or was there some way they could borrow the best from both and appear friendly but not desperate, particular but not hard to please?

In her next experiment, Hatfield pinpointed the winning formula by setting up a fake dating service where men submitted profiles with photos, then came in to the lab to review women's profiles and pick the ones they found most desirable. Along with the women's profiles, the men got to see whom these women were willing to date. Some of the women were willing to date many men (this was the easy-to-get group). Other women weren't all that impressed with any of the men, including the guy in question (this was the hard-to-get group). A third group of women, however, indicated that they weren't all that impressed with most of the men's profiles, but they were willing to make themselves available to the guy in question. Overwhelmingly, this last group won the most favorable ratings. We like people who like us, but we like them even more when they like *only* us. By acting *selectively* hard to get, these women made the men they did pick feel special, by far the biggest ego boost of all.

Money Can't Buy Love . . . or Can It?

"So what do you do?"

Anne was at a singles mixer in Los Angeles. It was a decent-looking crowd, but Anne wasn't there for the eye candy. Anne was on the market for marriage material—and that meant popping the profession question as soon as she could smoothly sneak it in.

"I'm an actor," one man said. Given this was L.A., no surprise there. Anne quickly moved on.

"I'm a screenwriter—or, at least, I hope to be as soon as I sell my script." Anne smiled, then extricated herself from the conversation as quickly as possible.

"I'm an entertainment lawyer." This time, Anne stuck around. Fine, so the conversation that ensued about electronic copyright law wasn't all that scintillating, and he wasn't as cute as the other men she'd met. But he had passed the one bar Anne had set for herself, and that was that he made decent money.

"I know this sounds terribly materialistic, but I swear, it's not so I can kick back and play tennis all day," says Anne, an executive at an advertising firm who makes a sizable six-figure salary. "It's because I want kids, and for them to have every opportunity I can give them. Maybe I'd even quit my job and raise them myself. A man without money just doesn't fit into that picture." On another note, Anne has to admit that there's just something sexy about a man with money, and something unsexy about a man without it. Once when she did go on a date with a struggling actor, his sex appeal dipped considerably when he marveled at the price of the appetizers and paid the tip with a pile of change. "It just made me feel sorry for him," she says. "Can I help it that dinner at Spago is more of a mood-setter?"

Even in a day and age when women earn their own income, a man with money is magnetic. Resources matter even more than a man's looks, as was illustrated in one 1996 study where Erich Goode at New York State University in Stony Brook posted fake personal ads in newspapers sporting a variety of professions. The "handsome cabdriver," while handsome, gleaned only fifteen responses from women, while the "average-looking" male lawyer amassed 64 interested parties. Meanwhile, the "average-looking" female lawyer received 240 responses from men while the "beautiful" waitress hit the attraction jackpot with 668 male suitors. Men, it appears, don't really care how much money a woman makes as long as she's cute. And yet, other studies suggest that men's blasé attitude toward women's earnings may be changing.

In 2003, Donald Strassberg at the University of Utah published a study in which he had placed his own phony "women seeking men" personal ads on Internet dating sites. The ads were almost identical, except that one ad described the woman as "lovely . . . very attractive and slim," another that the woman was "financially independent . . . successful [and] ambitious." As responses rolled in, Strassberg was surprised to find that the wealthy, successful woman attracted 185 responses, while the slim, attractive woman fetched only 129 responses. How can this be, given seven years earlier, the men in Goode's study preferred beauty over ambition? One possibility is that Goode's ads appeared in newspapers, while Strassberg's ads were online, which might attract males with higher education levels who place greater value on a woman's intelligence and earning potential. Or, given that the career woman's ad didn't say she was *un*attractive, perhaps the male respondents assumed (or at least hoped) she'd be attractive *and* be able to pick up the tab for dinner. Either way, men who chase brains and ambition over beauty may end up very glad they did. In one Australian study of more than 5,000 men and women by economist Shane Mathew Worner, a man's likelihood of being "very happy" increases by 8 percent for every extra year of education his wife has, most likely because of her added earning potential, says Worner.

Who, You? Marry for Money?

In 2007, research firm Prince and Associates asked more than a thousand men and women, "How willing are you to marry an average-looking person that you liked if they had money?" Two thirds of women and half of men said they would be "very" or even "extremely" willing to tie the knot if the price was right. How much was enough? On average, men and women said they'd walk down the aisle for $1.5 million.

As for men and women who aren't rolling in dough, there's hope for them as well. In 1996, Michael Cunningham at the

University of Louisville, Kentucky, presented men and women with written descriptions of a variety of potential partners. One candidate was a successful surgeon who made $500,000 per year but wouldn't have much free time to devote to a spouse and kids. Another was a high school teacher who made only $20,000 per year but had plenty of spare time to devote to a spouse and family. When Cunningham asked which person was better dating and marriage material, the high school teacher won among both men and women. All things being equal, a wealthy partner tends to be more appealing than a poor one, but if that wealth detracts from the quality of the relationship, most people will find that an attentive, nurturing partner trumps cold hard cash.

Like Likes Like

At the Face Research Lab at the University of Aberdeen, scientists experiment with faces. Not in a nip/tuck kind of way, but by altering digital photos with computer programs. They turn round faces oval, big noses button-sized, widen jaws, then show the results to volunteers, who pick their favorites. In one experiment by Lisa De Bruine, viewers confessed that one face looked especially trustworthy, although they couldn't put their finger on why. De Bruine, however, knew exactly why: Her volunteers were viewing altered photos of their own faces. Essentially, De Bruine had taken photos of her viewers and digitally altered them to appear like the opposite sex. The changes were so subtle that study subjects couldn't quite catch on that they were essentially staring in a mirror and admiring their own mugs.

What De Bruine's study suggests is that in a vast world filled with infinite choice, we're going to find comfort in peo-

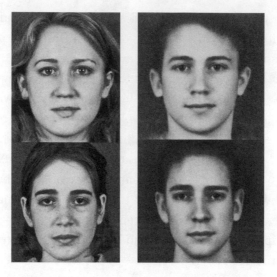

What do these men and women have in common? Here's a hint: A lot more than you think. That's because the facial features in the women shown left were used to create an opposite-sex version of their own faces, shown right. In one study, people found faces with features that mirrored their own to be the most trustworthy.

Adapted from Penton-Voak, I., D. I. Perrett, and J. Pierce (1999). "Computer graphic studies of facial similarity and judgements of attractiveness" *Current Psychology* 18 (1): 104–18. For face transformations and experiments, see http://www .perceptionlab.com.

ple who look and act a lot like us. The old "opposites attract" maxim might make for great sexual chemistry in movies, but in real life, differences just make life difficult. These similarities may not always be as specific as a passion for knitting or a love of the Sci-fi channel, but in terms of broad strokes, what couples have in common—education levels, life goals, and otherwise—often outweigh what they don't. Similarity is such a cornerstone of compatibility that in one study by David Novak at Duke University, men and women rated an emotionally disturbed person who was otherwise similar to them as more attractive than someone who was emotionally stable but different.

In a similar vein, we also tend to be attracted to people who look like our parents. Scientists call this phenomenon "sexual imprinting," and it occurs in many animals, often with some bizarre results. Ducks brought up by geese, for example, will try to mate with geese. Goats raised by sheep will mount sheep rather than their own species. In humans, studies have shown that we tend to date people whose race, hair, and eye color match that of our opposite-sex parent, and that people raised by older parents find older faces more attractive, while those raised by younger parents prefer a more youthful appearance in their romantic partners.

But doesn't our love of all things similar sound a little incestuous? Aren't we supposed to *avoid* sexual partners who are carbon copies of ourselves because of the genetic problems those offspring might inherit? To a certain extent, yes. Remember the MHC discussion? That's why people will produce offspring with strong immune systems by mating with someone whose immune system is genetically dissimilar to their own. On the other hand, though, some researchers suggest that mating with someone whose overall genetic makeup is *too* different could be its own type of liability, since this could break up locally adaptive gene complexes that can help offspring survive in a certain environment. Taken together, this evidence suggests that we should ideally be drawn to mates who are similar, but not *too* similar, and studies on facial attractiveness bear this out. In one study by David Perrett, subjects' ratings of photographs increased the more the photos looked like them, but dipped once the faces became extremely similar to their own. While people in De Bruine's study deemed opposite-sex versions of their own faces the most trustworthy and decent marriage material, for short-term flings, their preferences veered toward faces that looked different. Which makes sense: For people you trust and marry, similarity is an asset since it portends that things will run smoothly far into your future. For random flings, similarity is a moot point, since you probably won't be spending that much time together. As a result, we're more willing to tolerate differences and dabble beyond our comfort zone.

So what does this mean if you're dating someone who *is* different? Are your long-term prospects doomed? Thankfully, no, since whatever differences you start out with, stick together and over time, many of them will disappear. Spending time with anyone for extended periods will cause your viewpoints to converge, as was proved in one study where roommates who had known each other for seven months were asked to watch a variety of movies together. Results showed that more so than strangers, the roommates' emotional reactions to the films, even their facial expressions, were nearly mirror images of each other. Stranger still, people who spend tons of time together eventually begin to *look* like each other as well. In another study, Robert Zajonc showed his study subjects some old high school yearbook photos of students who had graduated twenty-five years earlier. All of these former students, Zajonc said, ended up marrying someone else in that pile of photos. Could they guess who? Not surprisingly, most study subjects were unsuccessful in matching up the couples. But when Zajonc presented them with *present*-day photos of the people in question, it was a cinch matching up who'd married whom. No matter how different couples are at the get-go, over time they tend to eat the same foods, get out-doors or hole up in front of the TV for similar amounts of time, and do other things in tandem that would affect their appearance.

Another phenomenon that helps get us in a groove with someone new is called "the mere exposure effect," which has been used by advertisers for decades, but it also works with people, too (which explains why so many people end up mar-rying their coworkers). In one study by Zajonc, subjects were shown a rotation of photos of twelve different people. While certain people were shown only once, others popped up two, five, ten, or twenty-five times. When Zajonc asked his study subjects how they felt about the people they viewed, he found that the people flashed more frequently were liked more than those who made fewer appearances. In another study, sub-jects were asked to pick from a group of photos the person they'd most want to marry. Then, the images were flashed on a screen, some more often than others. Afterward, volunteers were asked again whom they'd like to marry. Oddly, many changed their original picks to someone whose photo had gotten more screen time.

The Confidence Game

On certain days, Sara Kiesler and Roberta Baral instructed their female research assistant to dress to kill. On other days, they told her to dress downright ugly—Coke-bottle glasses, frumpy outfit, the works. Then, Kiesler and Baral instructed their research assistant to approach certain men who were sitting having coffee in the cafeteria at Carnegie-Mellon Uni-versity. Her mission: To find out which disguise inspired in-terest in the men she met.

While one might assume that the research assistant got hit on when she was dressed to the nines, this turned out to be right only half the time. That's because the men in question had just taken an I.Q. test. Regardless of their actual performance, Kiesler and Baral had informed certain men that they'd aced the test, and told others that they were blowing it—all a ruse to temporarily raise or lower their confidence levels. As predicted, the men who were told they'd aced the test were feeling pretty good about themselves and, as a result, had the guts to chat, flirt, and ask for the attractive research assistant's phone number. Men who'd been told they'd botched the test, on the other hand, could only muster up enough confidence to hit on the research assistant in her frumpy state.

"Our results indicate that self-esteem will affect which romantic partners are chosen: low self-esteem will lead to choice of a partner lower in attractiveness than will high self-esteem," Kiesler and Baral concluded. How we feel about ourselves determines where we set the bar when seeking others. Even if you possess the most appealing assets on the planet, they won't do squat for your dating prospects unless *you* believe you're pretty hot stuff yourself.

Flattery Can Be a Self-Fulfilling Prophecy

She was shy, homely, and utterly undateable. She was perfect.

In his 1938 book *The Psychology of Human Conflict*, behavioral psychologist Edwin Ray Guthrie recounts the story of this unfortunate young woman who caught the eye of a few of her more popular classmates. They decided to conduct an experiment: By treating this ugly duckling like a semi-celebrity, could they give her a makeover from the inside out?

Tricks to Attract a Mate (All Scientifically Vetted, of Course!)

Get a handle on their hands. A firm handshake is a hallmark of genetic fitness, and a quick glance at someone's fingers contain further clues. Long fourth fingers are linked to more outgoing personalities in men; long index fingers suggest a woman has more feminine sensibilities.

Schedule your dates around ovulation. Single women who want to drive men wild should plan their outings when they're fertile, which occurs anywhere from nine to fifteen days after the start of their last period. Men will benefit, too, since women who are ovulating tend to advertise this fact by dressing in skimpier clothes and being aggressive in bed.

Unlock the secret of scent. If you're assessing someone's relationship potential, lean in and breathe deep. If you like what you smell, that's a sign you're genetically compatible. More surprising still, the odor of pumpkin pie (for men) or cucumber (for women) may increase genital blood flow and prime them for a good time.

Home in on what you two have in common. Similarity is a sign you two will see eye-to-eye, in bed and otherwise. So try to highlight your common interests, whether that's your mutual addiction to YouTube or your love of all racket sports. We even prefer people who look like us and who have similar-sounding names. So if you're name's Jason, find a Jane. If you're Sally, find a Sam to increase the odds that sparks will fly.

Get your date's heart racing—literally. Get on a roller coaster. Go for a hike. If a movie's more your speed, pick a horror or action flick. Any activity that gets your pulse pounding and blood pumping are great date-night ideas, since your partner may mistakenly attribute that surge of fluttery feelings to being with you.

Don't let height or weight hold you back. Heavy women and short guys may feel disadvantaged in dating, but it's actually not as bad as you think. In studies, men picked women of average weight as ideal rather than rail-thin gals. Likewise, women picked men of average height as better dating material than tall guys. Men who are hungry or low on cash also prefer women with a little more meat on their bones, so if you fit that description, consider scheduling the date before dinner (and, ideally, pre-payday) to appear more attractive. Short men who are successful are assumed to be a few inches taller than they actually are.

Quit playing hard to get. While some relationship guides suggest waiting three days to return phone calls or pretending to be "busy" when you're asked out on a date, the reality is, you're just discouraging the person you're trying to impress, so stop playing games. If you like someone, show it—and to drive home that you've got high standards, make it clear you think your date is a cut above the rest. We like people who like us, but we *really* like people who like only us.

Recruit a wingwoman. Women tend to go for guys who are already receiving some favorable female attention. That means men should leave their male buddies at home and hit the pickup scene with a female friend, which will make female onlookers think, *Hmmm, what's he got that she's so into?* and swing by for closer inspection. This also works for men (although the effects aren't quite so strong), so women should consider heading out with a male pal versus their female friends.

Lack model looks? Time is on your side. People seem more attractive the more often we see them. So if at first some cute stranger from your spinning class doesn't seem all that interested in you, keep attending and your fellow cyclist may warm up as the weeks go by.

Stick around until closing time. That old country western song had it right: People really do get better looking the later it gets. Hang in there until the wee hours and the odds you'll head home with someone will improve.

Shower your date with compliments. People tend to live up to whatever expectations we place on them, so if you tell your date "you're so smart/funny/confident," he or she will actually *become* more smart, funny, or confident. Never underestimate the power of this self-fulfilling prophecy to bring out the best in your date.

"They treated her by agreement as though she were the reigning college favorite," Guthrie writes. The students made sure that at least one of them always sat next to her in class or the cafeteria, and that she was invited to every social event and asked to dance at parties. At first, the woman was baffled by all the attention. But over time, she started enjoying it, and cultivated a newfound self-confidence. To live up to her new-found social status, she started paying more attention to the way she looked and dressed. Her appearance and personality improved. Men began pursuing her in earnest.

Eventually, the students who had devised this experiment stopped making any deliberate effort to boost this woman's confidence. But at this point, she didn't need it—the flattery she'd received initially may have been artificial, but it had affected the rest of her life in a permanent and positive way. While contemporary ethics would never allow a scientist to sign off on such an experiment today, there's a valuable lesson to be learned from this story: Finding a dream date is largely in our hands. Think of yourself as a catch, and you will try harder to live up to these expectations and become a catch.

Now that you understand the invisible forces that draw two people together, the dance of seduction begins. The next chapter will give you a quick primer on how to flirt your way into someone's good graces.

A Field Guide to Flirting

John and Jane were on their second drinks. So far, neither of them had spoken a word to each other. And yet silent come-and-get-me signals were flying back and forth between them. Jane fiddled with her hair. John fidgeted with the straw in his drink. Jane hiked up her skirt, scratching an imaginary itch on her thigh. John stretched, puffing out his chest. Jane looked at John, but when John looked back, she looked away, then the game of eye tag repeated itself in reverse. Jane was getting frustrated. What was taking John so long to take the hint? Was his interest in her purely a figment of her imagination?

John was also wondering whether the signals coming from Jane's direction were just his own wishful thinking. He'd mis-read women before, and hated being shot down, so he sat and waited, praying for a clear sign. As if on cue, Jane walked up to the bar, put her hand on John's arm so that she could scoot by him and get the bartender's attention. "Excuse me," she apologized to John. "Crowded in here tonight, isn't it?"

Even then, John was torn. Did that touch mean Jane was merely craving another Stoli and soda, or was that a ploy to break the ice? Was Jane just being friendly, or flirty? To find out, John looked Jane in the eye. This time, when their gazes met, Jane held it for a beat longer than usual and smiled. John smiled back. Finally, it clicked: They'd both been flirting with each other all night.

"Can I buy you a drink?" John asked.

To his relief, Jane accepted.

J ANE'S THIGH SCRATCHING, John's chest puffing . . . these weren't random nervous gestures. They were classic cues in the ancient human ritual known as flirting. What are the steps to this subtle dance? And what makes certain people better flirts than others? In the 1980s, Monica Moore, a grad student at the University of Missouri, decided to pin down some answers by hitting countless bars, clubs, and parties to spy on men and women in action.

To blend in with the crowd, Moore dressed the part: dark eyeliner and black attire on Goth night, cowboy boots and jeans on Western night, bed sheet on toga night. To avoid getting hit on herself, Moore typically brought along a male colleague. "We would look like we were on a date," she says. "Which was great, because single people rarely pay much attention to couples." Once Moore and her "date" had scoped out the scene, Moore would pick her study subject out of the crowd, sit back, and watch, mumbling her target's every move into a tiny tape recorder stashed under her clothes. *Hair flip . . . eyebrow flash . . . head toss . . . neck presentation . . . Type I glance . . . Type II glance . . . smile . . . woman approached.*

Moore's first discovery on the front lines of flirting was that human courtship is far more complex than a little eye batting. She cataloged a total of 52 flirtatious tactics (shown on pp. 82–83). Moore's second discovery was even more surprising: People who rack up the most attention aren't the best looking, but the best flirts. On average, someone sending out 35 come-hither cues per hour will be approached by four people during that time period. "I made this discovery one night while watching two women who were flirting pros," Moore recalls. "They were average-looking, and yet men were approaching them left and right. It proved that being attractive was only part of the equation. What you do with what you've got is equally important."

Sending out a flurry of hair flips and eyebrow arching is only half the battle. The other half is recognizing when someone's attempting to flirt with you. To the untrained eye, this can be a difficult task, says Timothy Perper, author of *Sex Signals*, who has clocked 3,000 hours sitting in singles bars, airports, and church socials taking notes on people's behavior. The majority of men, he found, were essentially blind to the signals women were sending them, which suggests that flirting is a language we would all stand to learn better.

You Lookin' at Me?

When Yvonne met Henry at a party, she looked into his eyes and saw . . . something. "I still don't know *what* I saw," she admits. "Henry has beautiful blue eyes, but still, I don't think that was it. All I know is that the moment we locked gazes seemed to last forever, even though I'm sure it was just a second."

Yvonne and Henry chatted for a while about what they did for a living (Yvonne was a high school counselor, Henry a contractor) and what they enjoyed doing in Salt Lake City, Utah, where they had both lived since college (they were both ski addicts who hit Snowbird on a regular basis). And yet Yvonne considered all this conversation mere window dress-

Room encompassing glance (Type I)

Short darting glance (Type II)

Gaze fixate (Type III)

Eyebrow flash (raised eyebrows)

Head toss

Neck presentation (head tilted 45 degrees to the side)

Hair flip

Head nod

Lip lick

Lipstick application

Pout

Smile

Coy smile

Laugh

Giggle

Kiss

Whisper

Face to face (looking straight at someone at a range of
approximately 5 cm)

Arm flexion (wrist and elbow bent in toward own body)

Tap

Palm reveal (palm of hand is presented toward target)

Gesticulation

Hand hold

Primp

Hike skirt

Object caress

Caress (face/hair)

Caress (leg)

Caress (arm)

Caress (torso)

Caress (back)

Buttock pat

Lean forward

Brush (hand placed on someone else while passing by)

Breast touch

Knee touch

Thigh touch

Foot to foot

Placement

Shoulder hug

Hug

Lateral body contact

Frontal body contact

Hang on someone

Parade (walking by with exaggerated hip roll)

Approach

Request dance

Dance (acceptance)

Solitary dance

Point/permission grant (as in "you can sit here")

Aid solicitation (request for help)

Play (pinching, tickling, or sticking your tongue out)

From Moore, M. (1985). "Nonverbal courtship patterns in women: Context and consequences." *Ethology and Sociobiology* 6 (4): 237–47. Reprinted with permission from Elsevier.

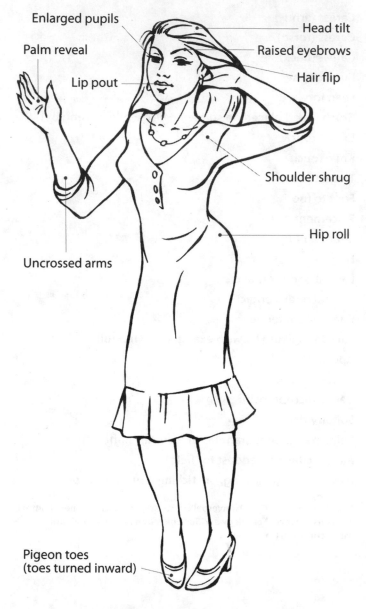

Enlarged pupils

Palm reveal

Lip pout

Head tilt

Raised eyebrows

Hair flip

Shoulder shrug

Hip roll

Uncrossed arms

Pigeon toes
(toes turned inward)

Your head-to-toe guide to flirtatious signals

ing for whatever it was she saw and felt when she stared into his eyes. And clearly, Henry saw something, too, since he asked for her number and they've been dating ever since. "I was never one to believe in love at first sight until that night," Yvonne says. "I can't explain it. Did we know each other in a former life? Were we soul mates? I have no idea. All I know is that it was powerful."

There's a reason why scores of people sense the first stirrings of sexual attraction when staring into each other's eyes. According to MRI scans of people's brains, eye contact causes an area called the ventral striatum, otherwise known as the reward center, to light up like a slot machine. Essentially, that means we're wired to interpret someone gazing deep into our eyes as a great pleasure. Eye contact feels so fantastic, in fact, that in experiments where study subjects were shown photos of people staring straight at them in disgust, as well as photos of people with a pleasant expression looking off to the side, the disgusted faces were rated as more appealing than the pleasant ones, all due to a little eye contact.

While established lovers can stare into each other's eyes for ages, for two strangers straight out of the flirting gates, it's a much more tentative process. Couples take turns looking at each other for a while until they screw up the courage to meet each other's gazes head on. Even then, it lasts only two to three seconds on average, although even that will seem like an eternity (in nonromantic situations, people lock eyes for only 1.18 seconds on average). After that point, one party, usually the woman, will look away. The game repeats itself as many times as necessary until someone, usually the guy, gets the hint and starts circling his quarry. Moore, who actually counted the number of look-then-look-away games it took for a guy to pick up on the fact that a woman had laid out the welcome mat, found that just one or even two times usually doesn't cut it. It took a total of three times before men got the hint.

Once two people get comfortable with each other, longer bouts of eye contact settle in—and some curiously strong feelings ensue. To study the effects of eye contact on intimacy levels, body language experts Allan and Barbara Pease told clients at a dating agency that the person they were being set up with had a lazy eye that could be spotted if they looked closely enough. During the date, this prompted both people to stare into each other's eyes more often than they usually would—and, as a result, they were four times more likely to meet again than the dating agency average. Stranger still, in another experiment where James Laird at Clark University asked 96 men and women who didn't know each other to stare into each others' eyes, stare at each other's hands, or some combination thereof (she stares at his hands and he at her eyes, for example), those who'd engaged in a mutual gaze confessed to feelings of "passionate love" for one another. In another study where Arthur Aron at Stony Brook University New York asked men and women to stare into each others' eyes for four minutes, they also admitted that they felt unusually attracted to each other. Six months later, rumor has it that two of these study subjects got married.

Eye contact is such a powerful force, it has even produced its own version of speed dating called speed gazing, where participants spend three minutes with a variety of romantic prospects, but the catch is, you can't talk. All you do is stare into each others' eyes. At first, many speed gazers can't help but giggle, fidget, or make faces to break the tension. By the end, though, once the staring contests are wrapped up and participants are allowed to mingle, their conversations are often much more profound as a result. As Ryan Parks, a twenty-six-year-old hedge fund research analyst described the questions that the eye gazing sparked: "Why are you sad? Why are you optimistic? You start asking yourself all these deep questions about the person you're looking at," he told the *New York Times*. "They're all so much better than the dumb questions of normal small talk."

My, What Large Pupils You Have

Centuries ago, prostitutes used eye drops containing belladonna, a plant tincture containing atrophine, to enlarge their pupils and appear more attractive to clients. Unfortunately, prolonged use led to vision problems and even blindness.

Another reason why we love eye contact may boil down to the clues contained *in* someone's eyes—like the pupils. One night in bed, as psychologist Eckhard Hess at the University of Chicago watched his wife read a book, he noticed that her pupils grew and shrank in size as she poured over certain passages. Since then, studies of pupillometry have shown that our pupils constrict to pinholes when looking at photos of politicians we hate, widen a little when looking at photos of politicians we like, and widen further if the person in the photo is naked (thankfully, researchers didn't test the effects of viewing naked politicians). Enlarged pupils not only signal we like what we see, but prompt people to like us back. Like tiny black holes, pupils draw people in, as researchers found out by administering a drug to study subjects that artificially widened their pupils for a while. Set loose among a larger group of volunteers who were then asked to pick a partner to

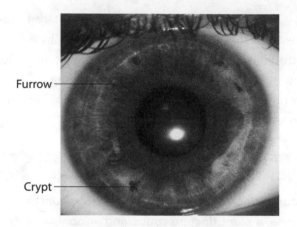

Furrow

Crypt

What the iris reveals. The colored part of the eye often contains crypts (discolored depressions) and furrows (curving lines around the outer edge) that are correlated to certain personality traits. People with crypts are more likely to be friendly and affectionate; people with furrows are more likely to be spontaneous and hedonistic.

From Larsson, Mats, Nancy L. Pedersen, and Håkan Stattin (2007). "Associations between iris characteristics and personality in adulthood." *Biological Psychology* 75: 165–75. Reprinted with permission from Elsevier.

work with on an experiment, the people with bigger pupils were picked far more often than the rest. Our love of large pupils may explain why many people find blue and green eyes more attractive than brown ones, since on these lighter backgrounds, pupil dilation is easier to see.

Whatever eye color is your favorite, that little Lifesaver of color surrounding the pupils also contains clues to compatibility. That's because the iris contains crypts (discolored de-

Why Men Talk to Women's Breasts

Ever notice how a man's gaze tends to wander over a woman's anatomy mid-conversation? Believe it or not, studies show that women also eyeball a guy's goods, even more often than men do theirs. The reason guys don't catch women looking has to do with variations in each gender's powers of peripheral vision. Typically, "women's peripheral vision extends to at least forty-five degrees to each side, above and below, which means she can appear to be looking at someone's face, while, at the same time, she is inspecting the goods," Alan and Barbara Pease write in their book *The Definitive Book of Body Language*. Meanwhile, men's peripheral vision is much narrower in scope—which is great for spotting targets far in front of them (hello, hunting), but not so great when you're trying to sneak a peak at something hovering along the outskirts. To illustrate the peripheral vision discrepancy between men and women in the most obvious way possible, the Peases accompanied a group of men and women on their first field trip to a nudist colony. As visitors frolicked with the locals, the Peases' videotapes of their interactions clearly showed the men staring agog at people's privates, even though the men swore up and down they tried to do so in secret. Women, meanwhile, claimed they were constantly sneaking peaks but never once looked like they were.

pressions) and furrows (curving lines around the outer edge). Crypts and furrows form due to irregularities in the density of cells in the iris, and may contain clues to whether someone's worth flirting with. In 2007, Swedish psychologist Mats Larsson examined the eyes of 428 college students and counted the number of crypts and furrows in each set. He also gave his study subjects personality tests. He found that people whose irises contain a lot of crypts were more likely to be warm, tender, and trusting. People with a high number of furrows were more likely to be impulsive and prone to indulge their cravings. The more crypts and furrows, in other words, the better—at least, if you want to be bantering with someone who's tender, warm, trusting, impulsive, and prone to enjoy the good things in life.

So, Um, Come Here Often?

"Is your daddy a thief?" "Did it hurt when you fell from heaven?" "Is that dress felt? Would you like it to be?" With lines like these out there, no wonder most people hate pickup lines. Still, to begin seducing someone, the conversation needs to start somewhere. Michael Cunningham at the University of Louisville gave his students a mission: Get out there and start hitting on people. Cunningham provided them with an array of canned come-ons that fell into one of three categories: direct, innocuous, and cute/flippant. Direct approaches, it turns out, were most successful. The opener "I feel a little embarrassed about this, but I'd like to meet you" scored highest with an 82 percent success rate ("success" was defined as the recipient being willing to continue the conversation). The innocuous approach came in second, with the line "What do you think of the band?" scoring 70 percent. Even a simple "Hi" scored 55 percent. Meanwhile, cute-flippant gambits bombed badly. "Bet I can out-drink you" only got the conversation rolling 20 percent of the time, "You remind me of someone I used to date" only 18 percent. Not surprisingly, really cornball openers—e.g., "I may not be Fred Flintstone, but I can make your bed rock!"—might seem hilarious to your friends, but when uttered to complete strangers, they're so not funny, and should be avoided at all costs. The above results apply to men hitting on women; women, on the other hand, got a positive response from men 80 percent of the time no matter what opening line they used.

If the direct approach is too scary, consider these alternatives, tested by Christopher Bale at the University of Edinburgh in Scotland. Suitors will fare well if they use opening lines that offer help ("Want me to carry that for you?"), ask for help ("Could you help me pick out a gift for a friend?"), or display intelligence ("It amazes me that Van Gogh painted this at Saint-Rémy"). Women hitting on men are better off taking a direct approach. "Since we're both sitting alone, would you care to join me?," "I'd really like to get to know you," and even a classic "Hi" made it into men's top-five favorite overtures from women.

As flirters continue talking, they can solidify their bond by seeking out common interests ("You ski? _I_ ski! What a coincidence!"), although that doesn't mean you should bask in your similarities nonstop. In one study at the University of Oklahoma where pairs of participants were told to talk about certain topics, those who agreed with their partner 100 percent of the time were found to be less likeable than those who disagreed at the outset, then later yielded to the other person's opinion. Putting up a fight at first can also work wonders with compliments, as researchers at the University of California in

Tongue Tied?
Top Ways to Break the Ice

Type of line	Percent rating line as good or excellent
INNOCUOUS	
Want to play Frisbee? (at a beach)	68 percent
Do you want to dance?	64 percent
Hi.	60 percent
Hi. My name is . . .	59 percent
I haven't been here before. What's good on the menu?	58 percent
Can I bring you anything from the store?	56 percent
What do you think of the band?	50 percent
The water is beautiful today, isn't it? (at a beach)	50 percent
DIRECT	
Can I help you to the car with those bags? (at a grocery store)	61 percent
Want to go have a beer or cup of coffee while we're waiting? (at a laundromat)	57 percent
I feel a little embarrassed about this, but I'd like to meet you.	56 percent
Would you like to have a drink after dinner?	55 percent
That's a very pretty (sweater, dress, etc.) you have on.	52 percent
Can I buy you lunch?	52 percent

Would you like to join me for coffee
    when you've finished your meal?   51 percent
Since we're both eating alone,
    would you like to join me?   51 percent
You have really nice (hair, eyes, etc.).   50 percent

CUTE/FLIPPANT

It took a lot of nerve to approach you,
    so can I at least ask what your name is?   52 percent

Adapted from Kleinke, C. L., F. B. Meeker, R. A. Staneski (1986). "Preference for opening lines: Comparing ratings by men and women." *Sex Roles* 15 (11/12): 585-600. Reproduced with kind permission of Springer Science and Business Media. There are instances where we have been unable to trace or contact the copyright holder. If notified, the publisher will be pleased to rectify any errors or omissions at the earliest opportunity.

Santa Cruz found out when conducting a study where participants were able to "overhear" what other participants were saying about them. In certain cases, the comments were positive from beginning to end. In other cases, the comments started out negative but became positive over time. Afterward, when these study subjects were asked to evaluate the people they had overheard, they preferred those who trashed them then turned nice over the ones who had gushed constant accolades.

Whatever you say, the way you say it is also important. Alex Pentland at the Massachusetts Institute of Technology analyzed nearly 60 speed-dating conversations. Instead of focusing on the content, Pentland examined the tone, pitch, pacing, number of interruptions, and length of time spent talking by each party. Pentland found patterns that could help him predict with 75 percent accuracy who was attracted to whom. One factor important in women was pitch. The more a woman varied the pitch of her voice, the more attractive she appeared to potential prospects. Another important factor for men and women was the number of short interjections such as "I see" or "go on" peppered in the conversation. Some people used as many as thirty interjections in five minutes, others as few as five. And while grunting "wow" or "uh huh" might not sound all that impressive, it's actually *more* impressive than a soliloquy you might be tempted to trot out about finishing med school or crossing the Sahara on camelback. Interjections encourage others to trot out their *own* stories, which makes you something even better than a great talker: a good listener.

"He Gave Good Text"

Flirting need not even occur face-to-face, as millions of online daters can attest to after having exchanged a flurry of friendly e-mails and text messages before even meeting for coffee. This can create a sense of "virtual intimacy," says Paige Padgett, a researcher at the division of epidemiology and disease control at the University of Texas School of Public Health. This may explain why, in her study, nearly one third of online daters end up having sex on their very first date. In comparison, only 15.1 percent of people in a nationwide sample have had sex with someone they've known for only a day or two.

Conversation can be so telling, Pentland and his colleagues have developed a software for cell phones that, based on the number of interjections tallied on the other end of the line, reveals whether someone is hanging on your every word or only half listening. Called the Jerk-O-Meter, this software is not yet commercially available, so for the meantime you'll just have to listen closely and perform your own mental calculations. Are your comments met with exclamations such as "No way!," or with dead air? Keep tabs, and you'll soon know if you should carry on or stop calling—permanently.

The Mona Lisa Effect

Which person would you be more likely to sleep with if they made the following statements:

Person #1: "I really enjoy helping people."

Person #2: "Old people bore me and I find children irritating."

Person #1 is the more appealing partner any day, right? Andrew Clark at the University of Bristol in England begs to differ. In 2007, he showed animated line drawings of faces to study subjects, asking which face they found most attractive. He also dubbed in prosocial and antisocial statements. When offensive declarations were paired with smiles, raised eyebrows, and other positive facial expressions, viewers rated these faces as more attractive than those drawings that didn't smile but made more admirable statements. Clark's conclusion: What we say doesn't matter all that much, provided we smile when we say it.

In flirting parlance, all smiles are good. But certain smiles—and humans have eighteen types total—are better than others. Scientists who know this owe thanks to French neurologist Guillaume Duchenne, who began experimenting with heads acquired from the French guillotine. These heads, though dead, still responded to electrical impulses, which allowed

Duchenne to jolt certain facial muscles and see which expressions ensued.

One day while tinkering with his heads, Duchenne discovered that smiles were controlled by two distinct sets of muscles. The first set, the zygomatic major muscles, pull the corners of the mouth back in a U-shaped grin. The second set, the orbicularis oculi, make the eyes squint and cause crow's feet. Duchenne also found that the zygomatic majors are linked to our voluntary nervous system and, as a result, can be consciously willed to whip up a fake smile when a situation calls for one (like when we say "cheese" to a photographer). The orbicularis oculi muscles, however, are linked to our autonomic nervous system and aren't under our conscious control; they'll only react when we're genuinely happy. Why should you care which nerves are connected to what? Because

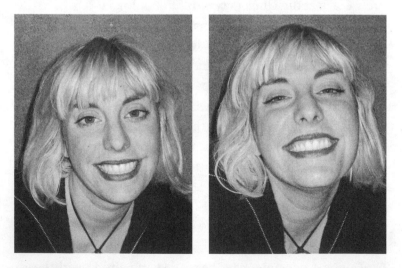

Which smile is real? The smile on the left is fake, but the one on the right is genuine because of the squinting around the eyes, which is a muscular reaction beyond our conscious control.

if you're wondering whether that smile someone's giving you is for real, check for crinkling around the eyes. If it's there, this person's truly glad to see you. If not, you're just being tolerated until your victim can plan an escape.

If, on the other hand, your friendly entreaties are being greeted with a poker face, consider stepping up to the plate and smiling yourself. Smiles are contagious. In one Swedish study, neurologist Ulf Dimberg hooked up people's faces (live ones, not guillotine castoffs) to equipment that detects subtle electric signals from muscle fibers. Then, Dimberg showed his subjects photos of happy and angry faces, simultaneously instructing his subjects to smile or frown at what they saw. Occasionally, Dimberg instructed them to smile at photos of frowning faces, or frown at photos of smiling faces. Easy, right? And yet, the electric signals coming from their facial muscles told a different story. No matter what Dimberg said, when faced with a smiler, facial muscles automatically twitched upward to smile in kind. When faced with a frowner, the mouth crept downward. Our natural impulse is to mirror what we see, so try a smile when you want someone to smile back.

Laughter: The Best Medicine?

No flirtatious exchange would feel complete without lots of laughter in the mix. But surprisingly, most laughter occurs when nothing funny is said. Robert Provine, a professor at the University of Maryland and author of *Laughter: A Scientific Investigation*, knows this all too well. He and a team of researchers skulked around campus surreptitiously listening in on students' conversations, recording what prompted a giggle. A full 1,200 "laugh episodes" later, Provine found that only 15 percent of laughter is generated by anything remotely recognizable as a punch line. The majority of laughter followed surprisingly mundane statements, such as "May I join you?" or "It was nice meeting you."

Why do we laugh when nothing's funny? According to Provine, it's to bond with others. That's why we're thirty times more likely to laugh around company verses when we're alone. Even nitrous oxide, or laughing gas, triggers few giggles when taken in solitude. Jane Warren and Sophie Scott at the University College in London performed MRI scans of people's brains while they listened to audio recordings of laughter as well as upsetting sounds like screaming and retching. The laugh tracks activated the brain's pre-motor cortical region, which, in turn, triggered the muscles of the face to crinkle in their own fit of chuckles. When we hear someone laugh, we're programmed to laugh right along with them (and thankfully, this copycat tendency doesn't hold true when we hear people screaming or retching).

Any laughter is good laughter when you're trying to spread the love, but laughter about funny stuff is best—which makes having a sense of humor a major asset. According to Eric Bressler at McMasters University, each gender defines a sense of humor differently. To a woman, a man with a sense of humor is someone who "produces" humor (i.e., jokes). To a man, a woman with a sense of humor is someone who "appreciates" humor (translation: *She* laughs at *his* jokes). Bressler found that men like women who "produce" humor as pals, but this wasn't an important factor when picking women to date. The reason may lie in how men use humor: as a means to mock other men. Putdowns are par for the course in male circles, as was proved in an experiment where Sam Shuster, a professor at Norfolk and Norwich University Hospital in England, rode a unicycle through town and tallied the comments he received. Women were encouraging. Men shot snide remarks like "Lost your wheel?" Given men wield humor as a weapon, it's understandable they'd be leery of taking a comedian to bed. What if she turns his penis or some other personal foible into the butt of her next joke?

The ABCs of Body Language

"We've got to get out of here—now."

David Givens was in a van, parked in the southeast section of Seattle, Washington. He and a wildlife photographer had been surreptitiously snapping pictures of a group of people at a bus stop. It was a rough section of town, and while Givens and his cameraman tried to maintain a low profile, clearly a few of the men they'd been observing through a telephoto lens had caught on, and weren't too happy about it. As the men started toward the van, Givens scrambled for the keys and peeled off. "Studying human courtship behavior in their natural habitat can be a dangerous profession," he admits. "It's like watching wildlife. If a rhino charges, you'd better have the key in your ignition for a quick getaway."

Givens has spied on people flirting in a variety of venues, from bus stops to bars, airplanes to college cafeterias. Jotting down notes in a leatherbound notebook, he rarely listens in on what people are saying. In studies examining videotapes of people conversing about their feelings and attitudes on a variety of topics, researchers have found that only 7 percent of what we mean is based on what we say. Another 38 percent is based on how we say it. The rest—by far the majority at 55 percent—is based on an entirely different language. Body language, of course.

Every part of our bodies, from head to toe, speaks volumes

about our interest levels. Among the easiest to spot immediately, Givens says, are someone's hands. The phrase "talk with your hands" exists for a reason. In particular, take note of whether the palms are facing upward or downward as they move around or rest on the table. Palms up is a sign that someone has nothing to hide, a way to say *See? I'm not holding a rock, Mace, or anything else that will hurt you.* Palm-down gestures, on the other hand, are a sign of dominance. Think back to how your grade school teachers would attempt to calm unruly students by patting the air palm-down in front of them (not that it worked, but hey, they tried). Generally, dominance is not something you want to display in any kind of seduction scenario, although men may occasionally direct a gesture of dominance (from palm-down air-patting to chest-puffing) toward nearby rivals to say *I've got dibs—go hit on someone else.*

Clearly, arms crossed over the body are a way to say *Back off, bud,* but not all arm barriers are easy to see. People sitting at a table facing you, for instance, might erect their deadly force field a bit farther out. For an easy tip-off, check where they've placed their coffee cup, martini, or water glass. If the cup is on the right and they're right-handed, then you're barrier-free. If the cup's on their left, that means they'll have to reach across their body to grab it, perhaps even leaning their elbow on the table and using their forearm to form a more permanent blockade. To the average observer, it's just two people having coffee. Look closer, and you'll see two people with zero chance of sharing a bed later. On the bright side, if you see a shoulder shrug, you're getting warmer. This bashful, aw-shucks gesture is known among biologists as the "cute response," and crops up unconsciously when we meet babies or puppies. In a seduction scenario, the shoulder shrug says basically the same thing: *Let's cuddle.*

Which woman is open to your advances? If someone's drink is placed so that her arm has to reach across the table to grab it, that's a hidden arm cross— a protective maneuver which signals she's not all that into you. If her drink is placed on the same side of the table as the hand she uses to grab it, that's open stance—and a sign she might want to get closer.

While staring at someone's feet may not be the wisest move soon after having met someone, if you glance down occasionally you might get a glimpse of what may be the most reliable indicator of which way the wind is blowing. The farther away a body part is from our brain, the less aware we are of what it's doing. Most people are aware of their facial expressions and can fake them when necessary, which can come in handy when you want to look thrilled opening a gift from Grandma that turns out to be yet another ugly sweater. Down below, though, the feet dance to their own drummer. Generally, they'll point in the direction we most want to go. If someone's feet are pointed toward you, that's good. If they're pointed away from you, that's bad. If they're pointed toward the door, that means they really want to get the hell out of there. If the toes are pointed in toward each other? While these so-called "pigeon toes" might not seem like a very sexy gesture, feet arranged this way reveal a subconscious attempt to shrink in size and say *I'm harmless. I'm helpless. Take me home.*

Legs can also talk, especially when someone's sitting so the limbs are free to roam. Legs spread open convey dominance and openness, while crossed legs convey submissiveness or defensiveness. Crossed legs where you rest an ankle on the knee can be the best of both worlds. This posture is dominant, and yet relaxed. Cavalier, but in control. This pose is especially common among Americans, which is why it's been nicknamed the "American Figure Four." (In World War II, Nazis were told to keep an eye out for people sitting this way, since chances were high it was an American spy.) Crossed ankles, whether standing or sitting, are the mental equivalent of biting one's lip. They're a sign someone's holding back opinions, whether about your silly sideburns or your suggestion to see the movie *Beverly Hills Chihuahua.* So if you spot an ankle lock, it might be worth asking, "Is something bothering you?" Your perceptiveness may glean some brownie points and allow you to redeem yourself.

Body language doesn't just communicate how we're feeling or whom we'd like to take home with us. It can also brag—by flaunting our assets. That's why women will fiddle with and flip their hair even if it's short and doesn't need flipping, tilt their heads to expose their necks, walk with that boom-chiga strut to accentuate their curvy hips, and lick their lips—which, supposedly, remind men of another set of lips. Meanwhile, guys stretch or stick their hands in their pockets, which conveniently broadens their chest into a wedge shape that says *I am man, hear me roar.* If those pocketed hands are situated so that the thumbs are visible and pointing inward, that's called a "crotch display," which serves to draw our eyes to the prize. Crotch displays are pronounced among other primates as well.

Dominant baboons will all but parade their penises before on-lookers, fondling them constantly to remind everyone that yes, they really are all that. Human males also engage in "crotch adjustments," although usually on a more subtle level.

You Can Flirt *Where*?!

Flirting is so natural an impulse we don't reserve all our efforts for Happy Hour. A full 62 percent of drivers say they've flirted with someone in a different vehicle during their morning commute, and 31 percent of those flirtations have resulted in a date (thus the success of Flirtingintraffic.com, a Web site on which you can purchase a sticker with a unique ID, which drivers can jot down when they see you and send you a message via the Web site).

In the same way that people search for things they have in common during conversation, we also seek out common ground through body language, a practice known as isoprax-ism, or the chameleon effect. To a certain extent, this happens naturally, as Tanya Chartrand and John Bargh at New York University found when they enlisted volunteers to complete a task paired up with research assistants who had been instructed to either shake their foot or rub their face throughout the interaction. By the end of their ten-minute session, video-tapes showed that the volunteers were also shaking their feet and rubbing their faces in a subconscious attempt to get in sync with their partner. Next, Chartrand and Bargh turned the tables and instructed their assistants to mimic the movements of volunteers they were paired with. Afterward, volunteers who had been aped reported liking their partners much more than volunteers whose partners made no effort to mirror their actions.

Getting In the Zone

Givens was on an airplane, observing flirting unfold at 40,000 feet. *Saturday, p.m. November 23—Aboard Southwest Airlines flight 358, Oakland to San Diego*, he jotted down in his leather notebook. In the row in front of him, a man and woman had just taken their seats in 11D and 11E and buckled their seat belts. Givens couldn't see much in terms of their facial expressions, but he didn't have to. Even the backs of their bodies were communicating plenty.

"What do you do?" the man asked the woman, leaning toward her.

"I work in real estate," the woman replied, leaning back—and farther away—from her friendly seat mate. Realizing he'd crossed some invisible threshold and made her uncomfortable, the man straightened his posture. Only after a drink, more conversation, and some flirtatious hair-fiddling on her part did he again venture closer. This time, she did not lean away. This time, Givens noted, she had allowed him into her personal space.

Whether you realize it or not, there's a bubble of air surrounding you that you consider your space. For most Americans, this "intimate zone" extends for eighteen inches around your body. Only your closest allies—spouses, lovers, children, pets—are allowed past this invisible barrier. Beyond that, from eighteen to forty-eight inches out, lies the "personal zone," which is the area we reserve for acquaintances at cocktail parties. From four to twelve feet out lies the "social zone," reserved for your postman, plumber, and other people you

1 Intimate zone
Distance: 0 to 18 inches
Who's allowed in:
Lovers, spouse, family, pets

2 Personal zone
Distance: 18 to 48 inches
Who's allowed in:
Friends and acquaintances

3 Social zone
Distance: 4 to 12 feet
Who's allowed In:
People we don't know well

4 Public zone
Distance: Over 12 feet
Who's allowed in:
Anyone

A map of the invisible barriers we have around our bodies, and whom we're comfortable allowing in each area.

don't know very well. Anything beyond twelve feet is the "public zone," where anything goes. These barriers also vary by culture. In Japan, the "intimate zone" extends only eleven inches, which is why the Japanese will often stand too close to Americans, who back off, which in turn prompts the Japanese to take another step closer. When video recordings of Japanese and American businessmen are played at high speed, it often looks as if duos are waltzing around the room.

Chances are, you and potential paramours will meet and mingle in each other's "personal zones," hovering eighteen to forty-eight inches within each other's orbits. Getting intimate involves breaking into their "intimate zone." Do it too soon, however, and you're bound to make them uncomfortable. Find an excuse to step *briefly* into someone's intimate zone— to allow someone behind you to pass or grab an appetizer off a wandering tray—then step back out again. If that person is drawn to you, he or she will respond by stepping in closer after you've backed off. Once that happens, you're ready to get even closer. How? Through touch.

At first, most people will reach out and touch . . . themselves. It's called "self-grooming." They stroke their own neck, or rub their own knee, since what they really want to do is stroke *your* neck or knee. Eventually, people will tentatively try grooming each other, an activity called "lint-picking." She whisks an imaginary speck from his lapel. He brushes a crumb from her sweater.

One option is to head for the elbow. This pointy appendage is so used to getting jostled, a tap from you will seem friendly but not *too* friendly. Give it a try, and feelings of good will may start magically moving in your direction. In one experiment, a team of researchers led by Joel Brockner at Tufts University placed a dime on the ledge of a telephone booth, then waited

Lay on the eye contact. Start out with what's called a Type I glance (your eye sweeps the room, passing by your prospect), then move on to a Type II glance (short, darting glance), then a Type III (you hold someone's gaze for a second then look away). The longer you can look, the stronger your feelings may grow for each other—provided, of course, that all that eye contact is mutual. Otherwise, staring at someone who's not staring back will just come off as creepy.

Widen your pupils. The pupils in our eyes dilate when they see something they like; it can also make you look more alluring to others. To take advantage of this fact, pick dimly lit places for your dates, which will force your pupils to dilate so you two can drink each other in.

Separate the real smiles from the fakes. Unsure whether someone's genuinely overjoyed to see you or has plastered on a fake smile for the sake of being polite? Shift your focus from the mouth to the eyes. If the corners of the eyes are squinting (perhaps you'll see crow's feet), then the smile is the real deal. You're welcome company.

Say something—anything. While you may feel tongue-tied, pretty much anything you say will get the conversation rolling. Just avoid cheesy pickup lines, which will only make you seem insecure. While women often wait for men to break the ice, women who do so are almost guaranteed to get a positive response.

Encourage people to keep talking. During conversation, try to sprinkle in around six short interjections per minute, such as "I see," "Go on," "Interesting," or "What happened next?" This indicates that you're interested in what someone is saying, which encourages people to open up and will encourage bonding.

Mirror your date's movements. If he crosses his legs, cross yours. If she takes a sip of her drink, do the same. This will convey that you two are on the same wavelength, further enhancing rapport. One caveat: Don't be so obvious about it that you get caught having to explain why you two just happen to be scratching your left ear at the very same time. That would be weird.

Keep an eye on the feet. The direction people's toes point can be very telling. If the toes are pointed toward you, that's good. If they're pointed away from you, that means your target would rather be elsewhere. If the toes are pointed in toward each other, see our next point.

Reassure people you're harmless. To advertise your friendly intentions and that you have nothing to hide, present an upturned palm mid-conversation or shrug your shoulders in an "aw-shucks" gesture. These tactics work well for both sexes, although they work especially well for women, since appearing small and helpless can inspire men to take care of them. To really lay it on thick, women can turn their toes inward toward each other to further shrink in size and emphasize that they need protecting.

Enter the zone. The area extending eighteen inches around someone's body is someone's "intimate space"—a no-go zone when you first meet someone. But as things get more intimate, find some excuse to step into this zone (to allow someone behind you to pass, for example) then step back out. If someone likes you, he or she will respond by taking a step closer to you.

Reach out and touch something. Early on, flirters will often fiddle with their hair, stroke their arm, or rub their knee. Take it as a good sign, fueled by a subconscious desire to be touched by someone else. When you first attempt to initiate physical contact with an acquaintance, try tapping a forearm, an elbow, or the back of a hand—all safe options to get things started without coming on too strong.

for unsuspecting subjects to walk in and find it. At this point, a researcher approached and asked, "Did you happen to see my coin in that phone booth?" On average, 66 percent of people returned the coin. And yet when the researcher's question was accompanied by a light touch on the stranger's arm, 78 percent returned the dime.

A touch on the back of the hand can also work wonders. In another experiment, librarians who touched book borrowers on the hand were rated more positively, and borrowers were also more likely to remember the librarian's name. In another study, waitresses made significantly higher tips by touching the customer's forearm when handing over the menu. Touch warms people up, which can come in handy if you're hoping to one day transition to the grand finale: heading to bed together.

CHAPTER 4

So . . . Want to Have Sex?

It was 2 a.m. John and Jane were still at the bar, talking up a storm. They both knew it was late, but how could they part ways when they were having so much fun? John was overjoyed to see Jane laughing at his goofball sense of humor, while Jane liked the fact that John wasn't cagey about discussing his past relationships. As the conversation flowed, their bodies inched closer and closer together. She patted his knee. He brushed a stand of hair off her face. It was clear they were into each other. Now what?

John, of course, was dying to invite Jane back to his place. But coughing up the necessary words to propose such a plan seemed all but impossible. What if Jane said no? Worse yet, what if Jane said, "Hell, no," and threw the rest of her drink in his face? While John pondered how to phrase his invitation, Jane was wondering how she'd respond if he did pop the question. Would he think less of her if she accepted? If they did head home together, would that doom their chances of a relationship down the road?

Jane's silent deliberations were interrupted when John mentioned he had planned to spend the evening catching up on episodes he'd TiVo'd of South Park.

"South Park!" Jane gushed. "I love that show."

Without thinking, John blurted, "How about we go back to my place to watch it?"

Against her better judgment, Jane said yes.

W ANT TO COME UPSTAIRS for a night cap?" "Want to see my etchings?" "Want to meet my cat?" No matter how someone pops the question, we all know what it really means: Want to have sex? After a night of eye batting and drink clinking that moves two people closer and closer to the brink, what prompts us to make the leap? Our levels of attraction can tip the scales, as can the amount of José Cuervo coursing through our systems. But what else convinces us to cave in to temptation? And for that matter, why do some of us cave in to just about anyone, while others are pickier than four year olds faced with a plateful of Brussels sprouts?

The number of people you sleep with matters, although not exactly in the ways you might think.

The Coolidge Effect

Imagine, for a moment, that you're sitting in Starbucks minding your own business when a stranger sits down next to you and says, "I've been noticing you around town and find you very attractive. Would you go to bed with me tonight?" What would you say? Two psychologists—Russell Clark at Florida State University and Elaine Hatfield at the University of Hawaii—sent spies to a variety of cafés to see who would accept such an offer. As you might have guessed, most of the takers fell squarely on the male side of the gender divide. Seventy-five percent of men approached were happy to head straight to bed (and in case you're wondering what happened then, the spies revealed it was just an experiment and made graceful exits). Meanwhile, none of the women approached accepted. When those same spies toned down their approach and asked, "Would you like to go out on a date?," 56 percent of the women accepted, while only 50 percent of the men did. Men are out for one thing, women another. It's the quantity versus quality debate, otherwise known as the Coolidge Effect.

Why You Should Wait to Have Sex

If you're hoping to meet marriage material, there's something to be said for waiting to get to know each other. According to a poll by the National Opinion Research Center, only 1.4 percent of married couples had sex within the first two days of meeting.

President Calvin Coolidge didn't do all that much while in office, which may explain why one of his biggest claims to fame is a rumored visit he took to a chicken farm with his wife. During this countryside jaunt, Mrs. Coolidge—who was clearly craving a little more action from Mr. Coolidge—learned that the rooster had sex dozens of times every day. "Please tell that to the President," Mrs. Coolidge quipped. When he was told, President Coolidge asked, "Same hen every time?" When he found out the answer was no, he quipped back, "Tell *that* to Mrs. Coolidge." True or not, this story has stuck around, most likely because it pegs men's and women's sexual habits so well. According to a 2005 survey of over 12,000 Americans by the National Center for Health Statistics, men will typically have sex with six to eight partners by their mid-forties, women four.

When asked how many partners they'd *like* to have, the numbers diverge even more. In one study by psychology professors David Buss and David Schmitt, men said they would prefer to bed down with eighteen partners, while women said they would be content with four or five.

The Numbers Never Lie . . . but We Do

How many people have you slept with?

When students at Ohio State University came across this question in a survey they'd agreed to fill out for class credit, no doubt it made many squirm in their seats. Certain students squirmed more than others, since they'd been assigned to one of three very different testing scenarios. The first group of students was left alone in a room to complete the survey and place it in a locked box, and were thus guaranteed anonymity. The second group was told to hand their survey directly to the attendant waiting outside the room, which led study subjects to believe this person would be able to see their responses—not exactly the most comfortable circumstances. A third group—the group with greatest reason to squirm—completed the survey while hooked up to a lie detector.

"The lie detector was actually a fake," admits Terri Fisher, who conducted the study. "Nonetheless, we went through this big charade to convince the students it was real. The polygraph ran, the needle moved, the students were pretty impressed." This method of scientific inquiry is known as a "bogus pipeline" because it suggests the experimenters have access (or a pipeline) to the truth. "And as long as people *think* you have a pipeline to the truth, they're more likely to tell the truth," explains Fisher.

Fisher had set up the experiment in such a manner because

when it comes to discussing our sexual pasts, we tend to fudge the facts. How much we fudge would depend, Fisher theorized, on how students were asked the question. Those hooked up to polygraphs, for example, might feel more pressure to stick to the facts. Those handing in their questionnaires to an actual person, on the other hand, might feel more pressure to fib and give an "acceptable" number in case the truth wasn't so acceptable. After all, what if the attendant—a student at their school—spilled the results to his friends, ruining people's reputations for good? (In actuality, the attendant wasn't allowed to peruse people's answers, but was merely there to give the illusion that this was a possibility.)

While the number of partners men reported remained about the same across the board, women's answers varied significantly based on how they were asked the question. When an attendant was hovering nearby, women reported a relatively low number of only 2.6 partners on average. When women were left to answer the question anonymously, they reported 3.4 partners. And when hooked up to a lie detector, women 'fessed up to 4.4 partners—just as many as the men in the study. Fisher's conclusion: Even today, the double standard exerts pressure on women to downplay their sexual experience levels.

Another study by Norman Brown at the University of Alberta suggests that men lie, too, but their fibs lean in the other direction: If they've slept with two women, they say ten. Social pressure to come off as a stud could be one explanation for why men inflate their totals, says Brown. "In lab slang, we call this the macho-and-maiden hypothesis," he says. And yet, Brown believes another theory may hold more water. This new theory, which Brown dubbed the men-are-pigs hypothesis, posits that men aren't deliberately boosting their tallies. They just can't remember every woman they've slept with.

To prove the men-are-pigs hypothesis holds water, Brown asked 1,787 college students how many people they'd slept with in the past month, past year, and in their entire lifetime. For the past month and past year, men and women reported sleeping with an equal number of people. Over a lifetime, though, men's and women's numbers diverged. Women reported an average of 6.2 partners, men 11.9. How do you explain such a spread? "Most likely these men weren't lying," Brown argues, "since they would have also exaggerated their numbers across the board for the past month and year as well." To dig a little more into this discrepancy, Brown asked his pollees another question: Can you actually remember each and every person you've slept with? Two thirds of women claimed they did. That's how they knew that their lifetime partner tally was accurate. Most men, however, claimed they couldn't recall each and every woman they'd brought to bed. Rather than dredge through their murky, Jägermeister-addled memories for an accurate count, men resorted to a different method to tally their total: They made an estimate.

Is It Time to Have Sex?

If you're wondering when you're going to get laid, take a peek at the clock. According to a survey by the Andrology Institute, 10:34 p.m. is the moment couples are most likely to be going at it.

"In all areas of life, estimates tend to be overestimates," says Brown. We round up on everything from how much money we spend on gas to how often we go to the gym—that's just how our brain works. As a result, men fumbling for a ballpark figure of how many women they've slept with are bound to overshoot the mark. While college-age men may *say* they've slept with 11.9 partners, that's just a guess. If one were to sit them down and force them to make a list, the number would be lower.

Does Promiscuous = Problem?

Ben and Stacy had been dating for six months when it dawned on Ben that Stacy had a ton of ex-boyfriends. "She'd told me about this boyfriend and that boyfriend and the boyfriend before this and that boyfriend, and then the *other* boyfriends, and then this and that fling. I was pretty sure I'd heard about everyone," he says. Then, one night, Stacy mentioned *another* boyfriend. That's when Ben felt compelled to ask, "How many people have you slept with, anyway?"

"A lot!" was Stacy's response. "I don't even know if I remember all of them."

Ben was flabbergasted. A newspaper reporter in his midthirties living in the liberal enclave of Austin, Texas, Ben considered himself to be a fairly tolerant and open-minded guy. He had no problem dating a woman who'd had her share of fun. Still, Stacy had had a little more fun than he was comfortable with. "I had met my ex-wife in college, and we were together for fifteen years, so the whole idea of sleeping with more people than you can count was entirely foreign to me," he says. The fact that Stacy was a woman didn't make a difference; if a male friend had said he'd slept with a hundred women, Ben would have thought that was weird, too. At the same time, it got Ben wondering if maybe he'd missed out— and whether his skills in bed measured up to Stacy's high standards.

When Ben confided this concern to Stacy, she tried to comfort him. "I'm with you now," she said. "That's all that matters." Still, her occasional remarks about past lovers were hard for Ben to hear. Eventually they broke up, and while Ben doesn't think Stacy's sexual past was to blame, combined with other aspects of her personality, they seemed to suggest she had an insensitive streak that didn't mesh with what Ben was looking for. In the back of his mind, he couldn't help wondering: Was he merely guy #72, soon to be forgotten like the rest?

Fair or not, promiscuous people worry us. Aren't they plagued with low self-esteem, commitment issues, and STDs? Scientists who have studied them say the answer isn't quite so simple. Let's take a look at the self-esteem issue first. In studies comparing people's number of sex partners to their scores on psychological tests (such as Rosenberg's Self-Esteem Scale), whether promiscuous sorts feel good or bad about themselves depends on the era in which they live. In the 1960s, when sexually permissive attitudes were in their infancy, promiscuous people scored low for self-esteem. And yet, tests from the 1970s onward show that promiscuous people have *higher* self-esteem than their sexually conservative peers. In 1991, the most recent study to date from the journal *Sex Roles* determined that women with low self-esteem had 5.5 partners, women with high self-esteem 8.8 partners. Meanwhile, men with low self-esteem had 8.8 partners, those with high self-esteem 16 partners.

As for other personality traits such as sociability and empathy, people who sleep around fall into one of two camps. They're either extremely warm and friendly, or they're total cold fishes. Promiscuity can be fueled by different motives. Warm people, for example, are promiscuous simply to express their affectionate nature. Cold people, however, may aim to avoid that same intimacy by sleeping with as many people as possible. A creative streak can also boost the number of notches in someone's belt. One study of 425 men and women by Daniel Nettles at Newcastle University in England found that people in creative fields such as art or poetry have five to eight partners on average, while people in more straight-laced professions have typically slept with three to four partners.

To a certain extent, promiscuous people are at greater risk for having sexually transmitted diseases (which, for the record, are also called sexually transmitted *infections*, or STIs, since *disease* implies noticeable symptoms or health problems, whereas many sexually transmitted infections are asymptomatic). In a nationwide study by the National Opinion Research Center, people with one partner in the past year had a 1 percent chance of having an STD. Of those with two to four partners, 4.5 percent had an STD. Of those with five or more partners, 5.9 percent had an STD. It's simple math: More partners = greater risk. Still, even if someone's sexual history isn't littered with lovers, that doesn't necessarily mean this person *doesn't* have an STD, either. Unconvinced? Take a tour through the hallways of Jefferson High.

The World Wild Web of Sex— and How to Stay Safe

Jefferson High (not its real name) is a mid-size, midwestern high school that's about as typical as it gets. More than half of its students have had sex, which is comparable to the national average. This made Jefferson the perfect petri dish in which to perform an ambitious experiment, led by Peter Bearman, director of the Institute for Social and Economic Research and Policy at Columbia University. Over 800 students participated, sitting down with researchers and spilling the names of every person they'd slept with over an eighteen-month period from 1993 to 1995. Researchers promised the students their confessions would remain confidential.

After getting an earful about these high schoolers' hookups, Bearman constructed a "sex network" connecting partners past and present. The resulting picture looks a lot like an airline route map. In the diagram, promiscuous people resembled a bustling airline hub like Chicago with many flights convening there. Meanwhile, sexually conservative sorts looked more like a small town where very few flights traveled at all. Bearman found that a golden rule seemed to govern students' dating decisions: Never, ever sleep with your ex's ex's ex (which, if you're a guy, would be your ex-girlfriend's ex-boyfriend's ex-girlfriend). Why? Because a loss of status may result. Due to this unspoken rule, promiscuous hubs couldn't easily form at Jefferson, since once a few people had "traveled" to a certain city, the destination quickly lost its appeal to others. Instead, at Jefferson, a "chain" model reigned, where student A slept with B, and B with C, and C with D, and so on down the line. Most hadn't slept with more than one or two people, but if you put them all together, this network spread far and wide. In the largest web, linking a web of 288 students, the two most distant individuals connected through past partners were a full thirty-seven steps apart.

This web of 288 interconnected students isn't merely interesting from a parlor game perspective. It's also an epidemiological nightmare. Consider if one student in this web had chlamydia. That would mean anyone who sleeps with him after he contracted the disease—as well as the students *they* sleep with—could catch chlamydia, too. Making matters even more complicated, these long chains made it all but impossible for students to see all the way down the line and get a sense of everyone they'd "slept with" indirectly. Even scarier to contemplate is the fact that this was merely an eighteen-month window at a midwestern high school. What about your own long, drawn-out sexual history? If you were to track every single person your current partner has slept with, and every single partner *those* partners have slept with, how far and wide would your own network spread?

Combine the interconnected nature of modern-day social groups with unsafe sexual practices, and it's no surprise that, according to a 2006 report by the Guttmacher Institute, the United States has the highest STD rate of any industrialized country. More than half of Americans will have an STD at some point in their lifetime, with 19 million new cases occurring each year. According to the Centers for Disease Control and Prevention, almost half of new STD cases will hit young people age fifteen to twenty-four, with HPV being the most common, followed by trichomoniasis and chlamydia. Given the severity of these statistics, practicing safe sex is paramount. Nothing, not even condoms, will keep you 100 percent safe, but there's plenty you can do to lower your risk (for more advice, see "Steps to Take for Safer Sex" on pp. 122–123).

Your New Lucky Number

Now that we know (more or less) how many people the average American has slept with, how many *should* we sleep with before settling down? Peter Todd, a professor at Indiana University, may have found the answer by exploring the modern-day applications to a problem from probability theory called the Dowry Problem.

A sultan, wishing to test the wisdom of his advisor, arranges

Steps to Take for Safer Sex

Consider the big picture. When you sleep with someone, it's not just your partner's sexual past you need to take into account, but your partner's *partners'* pasts, and *their* pasts, and so on down the line. That can add up to a lot of people. If any one of them had an STD, you might get it, too, which is all the more reason to take some precautions.

Keep in mind people lie to get laid. In one study of 665 Southern California college students published in *The New England Journal of Medicine*, one in three men admitted that in their past, they'd told at least one bald-faced lie in order to convince someone to have sex. Twenty percent of men said they would lie about having taken an HIV test. A significantly smaller portion of women lied (or at least admitted to it).

Condoms can offer some protection. In one study, researchers tracked couples where one partner was HIV positive and the other was not. Of the 123 couples who always used condoms, not one uninfected partner caught the virus; among 122 couples who used condoms inconsistently, 12 became infected. While regular condom use can lower your risk of STD transmission, it doesn't offer fail-proof protection, since condoms can break or slip off during use. The latex in condoms will also disintegrate if it comes in contact with oils (like massage oil), so make sure any lubrication you're using is water-based (like K-Y Jelly) or silicone-based, which is used on lubricated condoms but also sold by the bottle.

Sexual intercourse isn't the only risky activity. Certain STDs such as herpes can be transmitted through oral sex, which is why you should use dental dams as a barrier. Anal sex is also extremely risky, given blood vessels in the rectum can tear and serve as an easy pathway for transmission of an STD like AIDS (here, condoms can help protect both partners). Finally, cuts and tears on the hands can expose you to disease if they come in contact with the genitals or anus. Latex or rubber gloves can help curb the risk.

Don't assume your relationship is monogamous—ask. Even if your partner calls every night, sees you every weekend, and says he's fallen hard for you, that doesn't mean he's not sleeping around, or might in the future. The only way to know you're in a monogamous relationship is to ask. Sure, broaching the "Are you seeing anyone else?" question is awkward. And yet it's a lot *more* awkward to assume you know the answer, then realize later you're wrong when your partner gives you an STD. So no matter how secure your relationship looks, sit down and have the monogamy talk to ensure you're on the same page.

Get tested. If you've had unprotected sex, it's best to get tested even if you don't notice any symptoms, since many STDs are asymptomatic. Some people assume they get tested for STDs automatically during routine medical exams like physicals and pap smears, but that's not true; you have to request the test. You can go to your regular doctor or log on to Plannedparenthood.org and enter your zip code to find a clinic in your area. If you want your partner to get tested, steer clear of accusatory statements like, "You've slept around a lot and I'm worried you might have an STD." Instead, try phrasing your request in positive terms like, "I'd really like to take our relationship to the next level, and was hoping you'd be open to getting tested for STDs."

to have him meet a hundred women in his kingdom, from which he must pick the one with the highest dowry to marry. The wise man only gets to meet each woman once, and can ask the size of her dowry, but then must decide on the spot whether to accept or reject the woman, and can't return to her later. Plus the advisor has no idea what a typical dowry size is. What strategy should the wise man use that will optimize his chances of picking right? The solution is a concept called *satisficing*, a combination of satisfy and sufficing. In a pool of a hundred prospects, the wise man should meet and automatically reject the first 37 women purely for information-gathering purposes, making a mental note of the highest dowry in the bunch. Then, he should marry the very next woman whose dowry not only satisfies but exceeds that amount. This strategy strikes the best balance between seeing what dowries are out there while minimizing the risk that the advisor will pass over Mrs. Megdowry by dragging out his search longer than would be ideal, based on his sample size.

Of course, the rules for modern-day dating are different from those faced by the sultan's advisor. For one, our options aren't lined up for quick and convenient picking; plus they also have a say in whether they want to marry us, too. Still, the same basic principle applies: When it comes to picking the best partner out of the many people you meet, your chances of choosing well improve the more people you check out—up to a point. Settle down with your first or second sweetheart, and the fact that you have so few points of comparison means chances are high you've settled for someone subpar. Mow through thirty potential soul mates, though, and you've probably passed over someone who could make you very happy and are just being too picky.

So how do you strike a balance between shopping around

Do Your Own Numbers Add Up?

Don't believe what people say about their sexual pasts. Studies suggest that women downplay the number of sexual partners they've had, and that men exaggerate the number of notches in their belt. So if you do find out how many people someone has slept with, take their tally with a grain of salt.

Try the twelve-bonk rule. Curious how close you are to finding Mr. (or Mrs.) Right? Add up the total number of people you've slept with, dated, or gotten to know romantically in some manner. If you're under the twelve-person mark, perhaps you should keep looking. If you're way over (like thirty or more), then that might mean you've already met someone who would make you happy, and perhaps you should consider giving an ex from your past a second chance.

but not losing out because you were too particular? To find out, Todd made a few adjustments to the formula. For one, it's probably not realistic or necessary to hold out for *the* best mate out of the bunch; most people would probably be happy with someone who ranks in the top tenth-to-twenty-fifth percentile of whom they would deem ideal. Based on these adjustments, you should sleep with twelve people, then pick the best after that. If you're lucky, it will be number 13. Of course, if whoever's next in line *doesn't* pass muster, by all means move on to numbers 14, 15, and so on until you find someone you do deem a catch based on your prior experiences.

Todd's solution has been dubbed the "twelve-bonk rule"—which is catchy, Todd admits, although not what he'd have called it. "And it doesn't have to involve 'bonking,' either," he points out. You don't have to actually *sleep* with twelve people; dating twelve is also fine. The point is to get to know them well enough to develop a sense of which qualities you like and loathe in a long-term mate—then use that baseline to satisfice your way to a successful relationship.

CHAPTER 5

This Is Your Body on Sex

The minute John got June back to his apartment, they kissed for the first time. In that instant, Jane knew this was going to be good. Not only was John an amazing kisser—passionate but not too aggressive—but there was something else. For lack of a better way of putting it, John tasted great. There was no other way to explain it. All she knew was that she liked kissing John, a lot.

As for the sex? That ended up being a little anticlimactic.

The first problem kicked in once their clothes came off. Jane wondered whether her thighs looked huge. John worried whether his penis looked huge enough. Self-consciousness turned to confusion as they reclined on his bed and started exploring. John went in search of Jane's G spot, but came up empty. Jane was dismayed when John's erection lost altitude, even though he swore the beer was to blame. There were some pleasant surprises, too. John nearly hit the roof when Jane introduced him to the pleasures of his perineum. Meanwhile, Jane was blown away when John headed down and started sucking on her big toe. She'd always heard the big toe was an erogenous zone, but thought that was just a myth (at least until tonight).

127

"The sex was . . . interesting," Jane recounted to a coworker the next day. "But it was hardly earth-moving."

"What do you expect?" her coworker pointed out. "It was your first time. First-time sex is always awful. Your bodies aren't in tune with each other yet."

Jane knew her coworker was right. Still, she couldn't help wondering: If John called, was there anything she could try next time in bed that would really knock his socks off? At that moment, John was sitting in his own office, staring at Jane's business card perched on his computer keyboard, wondering the exact same thing. He decided to find out. He picked up the phone and gave Jane a call.

JOHN AND JANE ARE hardly the first couple to stumble across a few surprises once they stripped down and started exploring. While most of us know more or less how sex works, plenty of its mysteries remain unsolved. Why, for example, can some of us have orgasms by having our earlobe nibbled, while others can't? Why do erections rise when we least want them to, or stay down for the count in spite of our best efforts? Our bodies baffle us. And yet, piece by piece, part by part, scientists have begun putting this puzzle together.

Many of the world's greatest thinkers have pondered what happens when we join at the hip, and the first man to hazard a wild guess may have been Leonardo da Vinci. In 1493, he unveiled *The Copulation*, a sketch that depicts the internal anatomy of a man and woman engaged in sexual intercourse. At first glance, this X-ray style rendering of the penis inside a vagina—complete with tubes, testicles, uterus, and other relevant body parts—looks amazingly accurate. A closer look, though, shows that da Vinci didn't quite get everything right.

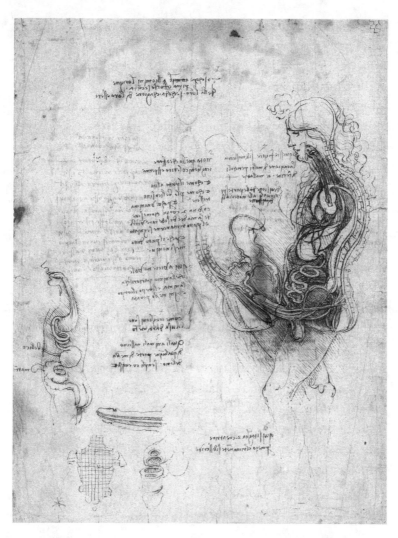

Leonardo da Vinci's *The Copulation*. With permission from The Royal Collection © 2008, Her Majesty Queen Elizabeth II is gratefully acknowledged.

Take the penis. In *The Copulation*, the penis contains two tubes: one for semen, one for urine. Another tube extends from the penis up to the brain, based on the widely held belief at the time that semen originated in a man's head. There's also a tube winding from the woman's right breast down to her vagina, because of the popular belief that breast milk was formed from menstrual blood. Da Vinci might have been a genius in many areas of life, but clearly, sex was not one of them.

We've come a long way in our understanding of sex since then. Today, scientists, like skilled paparazzi, have devised an array of ingenious ways to infiltrate our nooks and crannies and snap a few photos that reveal what's going on beneath the surface. Now that MRI machines can provide true X-ray-style photos of our innards, couples have trouped into labs and copulated inside them as scientists snapped photographs. Other researchers have attached tiny video cameras to penises then set them loose inside women's vaginas to fetch some footage. Still others have used infrared cameras to pinpoint which areas of the body heat up, literally, when two people tango. Taken together, these scientific snapshots can shed some light on many of the body's biggest mysteries so that you can spend less time in bed scratching your head and more time feeling fantastic.

Why We Kick Things Off with a Kiss

By the time Heidi finished the last bite of the jambalaya Doug had served her in his kitchen, it was clear to her that Doug fulfilled her 3 C's. He was cute. He could cook. (Heidi, who worked eighty-hour weeks as a corporate lawyer in Atlanta, Georgia, was completely useless in the kitchen.) Last but not least, he was a great converstionalist. Although they hadn't kissed yet, Heidi decided tonight was the night. Rounding the kitchen counter, Heidi leaned in toward Doug and planted one.

To Lock Lips, Lean Right

What should you keep in mind as you pucker up and lean in to seal the deal? If you want to avoid an incredibly awkward nose bump, you're better off tilting your head to the right than to the left when you lean in. So says German psychology professor Onur Güntürkün, who, for two and a half years, spied on 124 couples canoodling at airports, railway stations, beaches, and parks around the world. Twice as many people leaned their heads to the right when locking lips than to the left. Güntürkün theorizes this is due to a "head-motor bias" that's observed even in the womb. Nurture may also have an influence, since as many as 80 percent of mothers cradle their infants on their left side, which means the little tykes turn their heads to the right to nurse or nuzzle. Brain chemistry may also play a role, since those who lean to the right have activated the right, more emotional hemisphere of the brain. Some scientists even say that people who lean to the left when they kiss are cold fish, since this activates the left, rational side of the brain.

The moment their lips met, though, Heidi was surprised and dismayed to sense that something was off. "For lack of a better way of putting it, I felt like I was kissing my brother," she admits. "It was really weird." Hoping her reaction was a fluke, Heidi continued dating Doug, but had the same exact reaction during their next make-out session. Rationally, she couldn't find a good reason to call this relationship quits, but her body was sounding some sort of alarm bell. Eventually, she broke up with Doug, although she often wonders whether she made a mistake. Science, however, would argue that her instincts were right on target.

There's a reason why that first kiss is such a pivotal, make-or-break moment. The secret may lie in a string of DNA known as the MHC, or major histocompatability complex. As you might recall from the previous chapter, MHC serves as the blueprint for our immune systems. People whose MHCs are distinct from each other produce offspring with stronger immune systems. A DNA test can determine if your MHC profiles are compatible, but your body has designed its own method: swapping spit. If your MHCs aren't compatible, that first kiss may prove so distasteful it may very well be your last. In one survey by Susan Hughes at Albright College in Reading, Pennsylvania, 59 percent of men and 66 percent of women confessed they'd experienced initial kisses that were so bad they lost interest in the person. But if, on the other hand, your MHCs are a good match, you'll want to keep kissing.

First Things First: Does Size Matter?

When men strip down, the first issue to rear its head is the question of penis size. In one survey of over 25,000 men titled "Does Size Matter?" by Janet Lever at the University of California in Los Angeles, only 55 percent of men were satisfied with their size, while 45 percent wished they were bigger. Still other men think their penises are getting smaller day by day. This mental disorder, known as Koro, or Genital Retraction Syndrome, can even be contagious, turning into a more widespread phenomenon known as Penis Panic. Most men won't ever experience size issues of this magnitude, but it does illus-

Penis Panic!

Genital Retraction Syndrome, or Koro, a psychological disorder where men think their penises are getting smaller, has led to a more widespread phenomenon known as Penis Panic. Here's where it has hit:

1967: An outbreak of Penis Panic struck Singapore, as thousands of men swarmed hospitals based on rumors that poisoned pork was causing shrinkage. Home remedies for preventing the penis's disappearance included using clamps or gripping the penis constantly (family members were often recruited for this purpose). The outbreak died down after the Singapore Medical Association stated that Koro was a mental disorder rather than a physiological one.

2001: A mild wave of Penis Panic hit U.S. shores, according to one report in the medical journal *Addiction* documenting three cases of men who believed their penises were shrinking while smoking marijuana.

2003: Penis Panic struck Sudan. Rampant cell phone text messages claimed that victims' penises would melt away if they shook hands or shared a comb with strangers who practiced black magic.

trate just how concerned men can get about their dimensions down below.

In an effort to assuage men's concerns on this front, researchers have tried to pinpoint exactly how big penises are on average, but quickly found that it's a tricky process. First off, there's the question of who's doing the measuring. In surveys that trust men to measure their own penises and report the results, the average size ranges around six and a quarter inches erect. Bring in the doctors with the white lab coats and rulers, however, and it becomes clear that men are exaggerating—by a quarter- to a half-inch on average. In 2001, when over 400 men at the Dady Rock nightclub in Cancun, Mexico, agreed to take a break from their partying to have their erect penises measured by medical staff, the average length was found to be 5.877 inches, with 54 percent measuring between 5.5 inches and 6.3 inches.

Big Shoes, Big Nose, Big . . . ?

While rumors abound that the size of a man's nose, hands, or feet offer clues to the size of his genitals, there's no proof any of these theories hold water. In one study "Can shoe size predict penile length?" in *BJU International*, two urologists measured the stretched penile length of 104 men and found no correlation to their shoe size. Their final conclusion: The only way to know what a guy's packing is to check.

Is bigger really better in bed? In the 1960s, research team William Masters and Virginia Johnson decided to test this bedroom wisdom by measuring the length and girth of 312 male study subjects and comparing that to their performance. Size, they found, bore no relation to how many orgasms a penis could give or to the recipient's satisfaction levels in bed. Lever's study has underscored these findings, with 84 percent of more than 26,000 women polled saying they were completely happy with the size of their partner's package. Men should also keep in mind that a penis in repose bears no relation to how big it can get once it's risen to the occasion. In Masters and Johnson's most telling comparison, one man's penis measured 7.5 centimeters flaccid but grew to 16.5 centimeters at attention—the same final length achieved by a flaccid 11-centimeter-long specimen. Men truly can be growers, not showers.

Size Matters for Women, Too

Men aren't the only ones with size insecurities. Women have their own worries when they disrobe. With breasts, the bigger-is-better philosophy also rules, although why men care is a bit of a mystery. Some evolutionary experts theorize men consider big breasts best because they can serve as fat storage containers during tough times. Another odd theory is that these bouncing orbs of flesh are merely a second-place stand-in for a similar-looking body part out back: the butt. Way back in our cave-dwelling days, the theory goes, humans had sex like most animals—from behind. One day, a few enterprising Neanderthals decided to try it face-to-face. This was nice from an intimacy standpoint, but sorely lacking in eye candy, which was once provided for by the butt. To compensate, women's breasts ballooned in size to mimic the view men missed. Problem solved. Most evolutionary experts consider this breasts-mimic-butt theory tenuous at best, and stand by the more credible theory that large breasts advertise a woman's youth and fertility.

Large breasts certainly turn heads, but if you ask men what they prefer on their partners, more moderately-sized models actually do best. Chris Kleinke at Wellesley College snapped photos of fairly flat-chested women who then progressively stuffed their bras with cotton to make them appear larger . . .

and larger . . . and larger. Then, men reviewed the photos and were asked which bust they liked best. Rather than gravitating toward the biggest breasts in Kleinke's sample (which measured 36.8 inches), men picked a pair on the small side of average (34.8 inches). Meanwhile, another study suggests that breasts, big or small, may not mesmerize men as much as we think. When Richard Lerner at Eastern Michigan University asked more than a hundred men to rank the importance of twenty-four physical characteristics, a woman's chest came in ninth on the list, well behind face, teeth, and overall weight distribution.

Women who aren't all that jazzed about the size of their breasts or other body parts may be relieved to know that men actually don't spend that much time ogling women's curves once the clothes come off. When Kim Wallen at Emory University showed naked pictures of women to men whose eyes had been rigged up to a tracking device that measured where their gaze lingered, men dwelled very little on the expected areas such as breasts, butt, and genitals. So what were they paying attention to? Oddly enough, women's faces. Wallen was surprised. Even the men rigged up to the eye trackers were surprised. Men may like looking at breasts, butts, and genitals, but Wallen learned that their primary concern when presented with a naked woman is something else entirely: *Is she turned on?* For that, his best gauge is to home in on her face, which contains far more cues to her arousal levels than her breasts, butt, or genitals.

So what are women checking out on guys? When Wallen repeated his eye-tracking experiment with women looking at nude photos of men, they spent most of their time staring straight at his genitals, the most obvious indicator of his

Fun Facts About Your Body

Biggest organ on the body . . . Your skin. The average adult has six pounds of skin from head to toe.

Biggest penis . . . The largest penis belongs to Jonah Falcon, a New York actor whose penis measures 9.5 inches flaccid and 13.5 inches when erect. Guinness World Records is too proper to have a record for longest penis, so Falcon holds the honor because of the lack of any outspoken rivals.

Smallest penis . . . The smallest penis on record measures 1 centimeter in length.

Biggest breasts . . . The largest natural breasts belong to Atlanta, Georgia, native Norma Stitz. According to Guinness World Records, Stitz boasts a bra size of 48V. Each breast weighs 28 pounds.

Why it's called a "blow job" . . . The term "blow job" may have actually begun as "below job."

What else grows in anticipation of sex . . . A man's beard grows fastest when he anticipates sex.

Strangest theory about the genitals . . . Scientists since the second century assumed that the vagina was just a penis turned inside out. This belief was held to be true until the sixteenth century.

Strangest way to say hello . . . Men of the Walibri tribe in Australia greet each other by shaking penises instead of hands.

arousal level. Once we're naked, it looks like none of us are all too concerned with whether our partners have six-pack abs or Pamela Anderson proportions. We just want to know our bedmates are having a good time.

You Got Turned On *How*?!
Erogenous Zones, Explained

"When it comes to turning a woman on, I have one word for men out there to think about: neck."

Ron, a dermatologist living in Mesa, Arizona, came to this conclusion during a date with a girl who had invited him back to her place. "We didn't even know each other very well, so we were still playing it cool," he says. "We were just watching TV, with her head on my chest and my arm around her. At one point, I reached over and lightly stroked my thumb on her neck, just below the jawbone." After two or three strokes, Ron was surprised to feel her whole body tense with sexual excitement. She turned and pounced. "I didn't even have to try to kiss her because *she* kissed *me*," he says. "And it literally took about three strokes of my thumb on an area that usually isn't given much attention. From then on, I saw the neck not just a place to end up as an afterthought, it's the place I go to get the night started. Another girl I dated would almost climax when I kissed her collar bone. It was as if I were going down on her, it was that good. I have no idea why, but it works."

Nearly everyone has—or, at least, has heard—a story or two much like Ron's. *She went crazy when I started nibbling her inner thigh. I had an orgasm when he French kissed my navel.* Things start getting even stranger once you hear from the sex researchers themselves. Barry Komisaruk, a professor at Rutgers University who has been studying the neurological underpinnings of sexual pleasure for decades, was once chatting with a colleague in a conference room when he heard his own eyebrow-raising story. "A colleague of mine was describing how one night, while smoking marijuana at home, he placed a battery-powered vibrator on the tip of his nose," Komisaruk recalls. Within minutes of going nose-to-vibrator, Komisaruk's colleague sneezed. But this was no ordinary sneeze. The sensation was so intensely pleasurable, it could only be called one thing: an orgasm. A nose orgasm, to be exact.

"I was surprised, but curious," Komisaruk admits, but after in-depth questioning, Komisaruk believed his colleague and published his findings. In 1998, readers of the medical journal *Psychoneuroendocrinology* got a shock when they encountered the study by Komisaruk describing his colleague's nose orgasm in detail, complete with the drug-induced imagery that accompanied it:

> *The imagery evoked was described as starting as a small point of light then approaching closer and closer, getting brighter and larger, as if flying directly into the face. At the moment when the irritating sensation was unbearably intense, which was just before collision of the bright light against the face, a sneeze occurred, blowing away the light.*

As if the nose orgasm wasn't weird enough, Komisaruk's colleague also described having a "knee orgasm" and a "hand orgasm" by placing his vibrator on the aforementioned body parts until the muscles spasmed in pleasurable bursts. Komisaruk's conclusion: "While the genital system is particularly well-organized to mediate the orgasmic process, other body systems evidently manifest at least some of the same properties, and consequently, under appropriate stimulus conditions and sensitization may exhibit comparable activity."

While one might think Komisaruk's report might have provoked snickers and wisecracks from his peers, the letters and feedback he received indicated the opposite. "No one said 'you're crazy,'" he says. "I heard from some people saying they'd had similar experiences." Browse through the scientific literature, and there's more evidence that just about any body part can become an erogenous zone when rubbed just right. According to Alfred Kinsey, individuals he interviewed had "been brought to orgasm by having their eyebrows stroked, or by having the hairs on some other part of their bodies gently blown, or by having pressure applied on the teeth alone." Virginia Johnson pointed out in a 1979 *Playboy* interview that "the total body is a potentially erotic 'organ.' It is very possible to choose a completely asexual part of the anatomy and develop it as the source of sexual stimulation to orgasm. There can be back-of-the-neck orgasms, bottom-of-the-foot orgasms and palm-of-the-hand orgasms."

Why do particular body parts respond to pleasurable input more than others? To a certain extent, it's simple math: More nerve endings = greater pleasure potential. To locate the most nerve-rich areas, scientists have used a technique called two-point discrimination thresholds, which involves poking the skin with two metal points that are anywhere from mere millimeters to several inches apart. If the skin is sensitive enough, the recipient will perceive being poked by two points; if the skin is less sensitive, the subject will perceive it as one point. "On the calf, back, upper arm, and upper thigh, the points must be more than forty millimeters apart before we can perceive them as two points, whereas on the fingers and lips, they need be only less than five millimeters apart before they can be perceived as two points," says Komisaruk. "I demonstrate this in my classes and the students are always amazed."

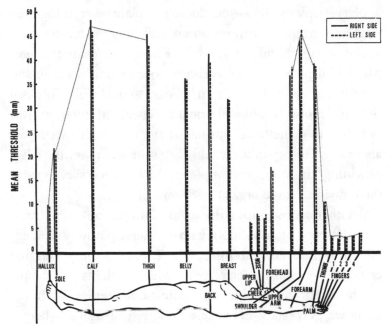

Figure 10-4. Two-point discrimination thresholds for males.

Skin sensitivity from head to toe. Scientists have mapped out the sensitivity of various body parts using two-point discrimination thresholds, where the skin is poked by two metal points of varying distances apart. If the area being poked is sensitive, the person will perceive two points. If it's less sensitive, it will feel like one point. On the fingers and lips, these two points can be as close as five millimeters apart and still be perceived as two points, which means these areas are extremely sensitive. On the back of the calf, these two points must be 45 millimeters apart before they're perceived as two points, thus proving this area is less sensitive.

From Weinstein, S. (1968). "Intensive and extensive aspects of tactile sensitivity as a function of body part, sex, and laterality." *The Skin Senses: Proceedings of the First International Symposium on the Skin Senses,* edited by D. R. Kenshalo, 195–222. Courtesy of Charles C. Thomas Publisher, Ltd., Springfield, Illinois.

Nerve density, however, doesn't explain everything. For starters, certain erogenous zones will only switch on once you're already highly aroused. In Kinsey's cases, individuals who had experienced the eyebrow orgasm, hair orgasm, and teeth orgasm had already been brought to the brink of orgasm through more traditional means. Then, stimulation was switched to something unusual at the very point when just about *any* sensory input would have sent them over the edge, providing "the additional impetus which is necessary to carry the individual on to orgasm," Kinsey noted.

Another neurological quirk to take into account is crosstalk, where electric signals shooting up one nerve pathway accidentally stray onto a neighboring path. "It's well documented that crosstalk can cause 'referred pain,' which explains why people feel heart attacks in their arm," points out Komisaruk. In the same way, crosstalk may cause "referred pleasure" where a hand on the knee can be felt in the genitals. Within the brain, even more mix-ups can occur. In women, nipple stimulation activates an area of the brain known as the paraventricular nucleus of the hypothalamus—an area that's also activated during stimulation of a woman's genitals. This may explain why some women can reach orgasm through breast stimulation, and why many more women find it highly arousing.

Neighboring neurons in the brain can also influence each other, which might shed light on one of the most puzzling erogenous zones of all: the big toe. There's a good reason why this tiny appendage plays a starring role in many highly erotic encounters. It's because in the brain, the area that receives sensations from the toes sits right next to the area receiving sensations from the genitals. Fire up one area, and it can spread to the other. This reflex also works in reverse, where stimulation of the genitals can ricochet down to your toes (thus the popu-

How to Explore Your Erogenous Zones

Take your time—really. While it's a running joke that women are constantly lobbying for more foreplay but that men view foreplay as a chore, this stereotype isn't true. Andrea Miller and Sandra Byers at the University of New Brunswick asked 152 couples how much foreplay they typically had during sex, as well as how much they'd like. In a perfect world, women reported they'd ideally indulge in nineteen minutes of foreplay, although they only engaged in eleven minutes on average, assuming that was as much as their husbands could take. Ironically, though, men said they craved eighteen minutes of foreplay—about the same amount as their partners.

Engage in sensate focus. Sensate focus, an exercise recommended by William Masters and Virginia Johnson, encourages couples to step on the brakes and explore all the pleasures foreplay has to offer. They recommended couples spend an hour or so on each stage of this process over days, weeks, or however felt best.

Stage 1: Taking turns, one partner caresses the other, only the real hot spots (breasts and genitals) are off limits.

Stage 2: Taking turns, one partner touches the other anywhere, including the breasts and genitals. Still, intercourse and orgasm are off limits.

Stage 3: Couples can touch each other simultaneously, but must still steer clear of intercourse and orgasm.

Stage 4: Couples can touch and rub up against one another, but still hold off on intercourse and orgasm.

Stage 5: Finally! Anything goes.

Masters and Johnson insisted this painstaking trek was worth the effort. Here's why: Many of the couples they were treating were simply too focused on sex. Women worried about reaching orgasm. Men worried about getting it up, and keeping it up. These anxiety-inducing scenarios only made it harder for couples to relax and become aroused. By taking sexual intercourse out of the equation entirely, couples could shift their focus from performance to pleasure. This gave couples time to get in tune with each others' bodies so that once they did have sex, they were ready and raring to go.

Not everyone needs to indulge in this marathon foreplay scheme in its entirety. Instead, you could consider trying bits and pieces à la carte. For example, one night you try telling your partner to not lift a finger because you're going to focus entirely on his pleasure (he can return the favor later). Or, maybe you set your alarm for a half hour and agree to turn each other on like crazy but not jump into intercourse until you hear the alarm go off. Devise even small ways to step on the brakes, and you'll be amazed what you discover.

Dwell on the sensations you receive. Ever notice how a food tastes better when you take the time to savor every mouthful versus just wolfing it down before your one o'clock meeting? The same is true for every inch of skin on your body. Take the time to appreciate how amazing that foot massage or ear nuzzling feels, and you might be surprised how this tiny shift in focus can change the experience.

Adjust based on your gender. We often touch people the way we want to be touched ourselves, but that's not always a good gauge of how we should treat others. Men's skin is generally thicker and less sensitive than women's; as a result, men often find a woman's touch too soft, while women will find men's caresses too rough for their tastes. Take note and adjust your efforts accordingly.

Mix tried-and-true turn-ons with new tactics. Bring your partner to the brink of orgasm through the usual means, then switch to something unusual. Caress her genitals, then move further out to stroke her thighs or breasts. Give him oral sex, then switch to fellating his fingers. Given your partner is already highly aroused, just about any sensory input might send him over the edge, and you might win major points for creativity.

Keep in mind that everyone's erogenous zones are different. Our taste buds, which are also nerves, provide a perfect analogy for our erogenous zones. Some people's palates go wild for Tabasco sauce, while others can't handle the stuff. Some of us have a raging sweet tooth, while others would rather reach for potato chips. In the same way our taste buds enjoy different tastes, there are different strokes for different folks. In one study of over 300 men and women published in *The Journal of Sexual Medicine,* 82 percent of women reported that they found breast and nipple stimulation arousing. And yet, 7 percent of women said it decreased their arousal levels. Meanwhile, 52 percent of men also said they found nipple stimulation arousing. And yet, their partners rarely toured these two tiny landmarks, assuming guys weren't into it.

larity of the term "toe-curling orgasm"). Drugs like marijuana and LSD can further blur neurological boundaries by breaking down inhibitory pathways in the brain and allowing sensations that usually remain separate to freely associate. This phenomenon, known as synesthesia, explains why people on LSD claim they can taste colors. It might also explain why people on drugs often report some pretty unusual orgasmic experiences, like that nose orgasm noted by Komisaruk.

Finally, there's the fact that people don't just get turned on by tactile sensations, but also by visual ones. According to anthropologist Desmond Morris, author of *The Naked Woman*, "It is well known from many psychiatric studies that, at moments of sexual arousal, certain parts of the body easily become 'anatomical echoes' of other organs. Lips become labia, the mouth cavity becomes a vagina, stiff fingers become a penis and breasts become buttocks inside the sexually excited brain." If someone sucks on your fingers or toes, it can serve as an arousing reminder of what your partner could be doing to your genitals.

Rev Up Your Engines: What's Happening Under the Hood

Once the body becomes aroused via any variety of strokes and squeezes, more changes are afoot beneath the surface. Some of you may be well aware of yourself. Hearts beat faster. Sweat glands get sweatier. Blood flows in directions that make certain body parts larger, or more lubricated. These changes, however, aren't the half of it. Scientists have found that just about *every* part of your body from head to toe undergoes some changes during sexual activity. Masters and Johnson noted that women's breasts get 25 percent bigger, a man's tes-

Sex Changes Things

How your body changes once sexual arousal enters the picture:

Pupils dilate

Earlobes swell in size

Nasal and salivary secretions increase

Erectile tissue in the nose swells in size

Facial muscles contort

The chest reddens in a "sex flush" due to increased circulation

Breasts increase in size by up to 25 percent

Heart rate increases up to 180 beats per minute

Blood pressure rises

Fingers curl or spread

Penis increases in length and diameter

Clitoris increases in length and diameter

Vagina lubricates and expands in a tent-like shape

Uterus elevates

Testicles increase in size by 50 percent and rise toward the body

Contractions occur in the prostate, Bartholin's, and Cowper's glands

Reduced bleeding (menstrual and from open wounds)

Neurological blocks are alleviated (stutterers will often stop stuttering)

Reduced sensitivity in hearing, smell, taste, temperature, and pain

Toes curl or spread

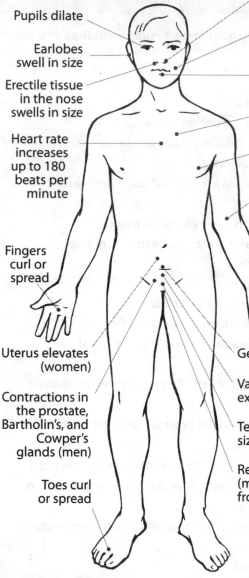

Pupils dilate

Earlobes swell in size

Erectile tissue in the nose swells in size

Heart rate increases up to 180 beats per minute

Fingers curl or spread

Uterus elevates (women)

Contractions in the prostate, Bartholin's, and Cowper's glands (men)

Toes curl or spread

Nasal and salivary secretions increase

Facial muscles contort

Reduced sensitivity in hearing, smell, and taste

Chest reddens in a "sex flush"

Breasts increase in size by up to 25% (women)

Blood pressure rises

Reduced sensitivity to temperature and pain

Genitals increase in size

Vagina lubricates and expands (women)

Testicles increase in size by 50% (men)

Reduced bleeding (menstrual and from open wounds)

How sex affects the body from head to toe

ticles 50 percent bigger. Our earlobes swell in size, stutterers often stop stuttering, and sometimes our salivary glands start salivating to the point that, if our mouth is open, "saliva may be spurted some distance out of the mouth," Kinsey noted. (For a full rundown of these physiological changes, turn to "Sex Changes Things" on page 147.)

While it's commonly thought that men get turned on far more quickly than women, infrared cameras tell a different story. These cameras measure temperature gradients through-out the body, with red areas being hottest, slowly fading to yellows and blues around the edges. When Irv Binik at McGill University used infrared cameras to film men and women as they watched a variety of pornographic film clips, he found that men reached their peak temperature in 665 seconds (which is roughly ten minutes). Women, however, weren't far behind, reaching their peak temperature at 743 seconds, which goes to show that both genders get revved for sex at surprisingly similar rates.

The Penis: Ground Zero of Erogenous Zones

At the Marriott Hotel, women were seated staring at their dinner plates. Attached to the surface (via suction cup) of each plate was a penis—or dildo, to be precise. Lou Paget, who has been dubbed the Martha Stewart of sex advice, was hosting one of her infamous sexuality seminars, where women would learn an array of sophisticated manual and oral techniques to try in bed. "The hotel staff will often ask, 'Will you be eating anything?' " Paget says. "I tell them 'Not really.' "

Paget's classes are a testament to the fact that in spite of its easy-to-please, user-friendly exterior, a man's package is far more complex than meets the eye. Scientists have conducted experiments like monofilament touch tests, where they poke the penis with tiny wires of varying diameters to figure out what feels good where. The thinner the wire, the less pressure it exerts, but if the patch of skin being tested is sensitive enough, a man will feel it nonetheless. Scientists weren't only satisfied with seeing how many nerve endings various parts of the penis possess; they also wanted to know what kind of nerve endings were buried within. And so, to get an even closer look, some took pieces of penises (which are available after male-to-female transsexual surgeries), sliced them into razor-thin pieces, stained them with dye, then examined them under a microscope.

Many people see the penis as one giant hot spot that responds with equal enthusiasm wherever it's rubbed. But the nerve network suggests certain parts of the penis will appreciate attention more than others. For one, for all the time we spend traveling up and down the shaft, this column contains some of the least sensitive skin. A far more sensitive area is the glans, or head of the penis. According to German anatomist Zdenek Halata, the glans is not only rich in nerves, but different kinds of nerves. The majority are called "genital corpuscles," but you'll also find other nerves called Pacinian and Ruffinian corpuscles sprinkled throughout the mix. Some of these corpuscles respond to light strokes, others to heavy pressure, while still others pick up subtle vibrations. The entire glans is rich in corpuscles, but these nerve endings tend to crowd around two areas in particular. The first is the coronal ridge, that tiny precipice where the glans meets the shaft. The second is the frenulum, a vertical notch located on the bottom side of the corona at six o'clock.

Once the penis gets petted in a pleasurable way, it will typically respond by swelling in size—a hydraulic feat that's

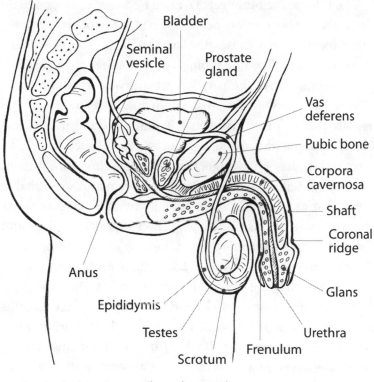

Bladder

Seminal vesicle

Prostate gland

Vas deferens

Pubic bone

Corpora cavernosa

Shaft

Coronal ridge

Glans

Anus

Epididymis

Testes

Scrotum

Frenulum

Urethra

The male genitals

uniquely human. Most male mammals in the animal kingdom achieve erections via the assistance of a bone in the penis called a bacula. In spite of the popularity of words like "boner" and "boning," there are no bones in the human penis. Human hard-ons derive their strength from a much more ethereal source: a gas known as nitric oxide (NO), not to be confused with its cousin nitr*ous* oxide (N_2O), or laughing gas. Nitric oxide might not appear very imposing or impressive, and yet, in 1998, the discovery of its function in the human body led to a Nobel Prize in Medicine. Here's how this chemical works its magic.

The minute the brain gets riled up by a sexy sight or a hand down the pants, it orders nerve endings in the penis to release nitric oxide, which causes the arteries in the area to dilate. Blood rushes in, flooding spongy tissue in the penis called corpora cavernosa. As the corpora cavernosa starts swelling in size, it compresses veins that drain the area known as the venous plexus, much like you'd flatten a soda straw. As less blood seeps out and a deluge pours in, you've erected, well, an erection—which, on average, contains eight times the amount of blood the flaccid penis usually does. Men may also be glad to know that their erections are actually twice as long as meets the eye. That's because the corpora cavernosa extends deep into their groin area, branching out at the base and attaching to the front of the pubic bone. Like a tree with a strong root system, this helps anchor the penis so it doesn't wobble. Once the penis is in a vagina, many people assume a man's penis remains straight as an arrow while it moves in and out during intercourse. And yet, according to MRI images, the penis actually bends like a boomerang, as much as 120 degrees, to accommodate the vagina's natural curvature. It's firm, but flexible.

Given that good circulation is key to getting an erection to roar to life, men should keep in mind that whatever health habits are good for their heart—more gym trips, fewer Big Macs—are also good for their hard-ons. Not all exercise, however, is beneficial to getting blood flow down below. According to a study of more than 1,700 men published in the *International Journal of Impotence Research*, riding a bike more than three hours per week may increase a man's risk of erectile dysfunction. Bicycle seats can press on arteries leading straight into a man's groin; luckily the problem can be alleviated with wider "noseless" seats which allow riders to bear their weight on their sitz bones, as they do when sitting in a

What's Your Penis Up To Tonight?

If you're curious whether you're getting nocturnal erections that keep your penis healthy, you can perform your own at-home test with a strip of postage stamps. Just lick one end of the strip so you can overlap the ends and seal the ring, wrap it snugly around the base of your penis, then go to bed (snug underwear will also help keep the stamps in place). Come morning, check if the stamps are broken along a perforation. If they are, congratulations, your penis is in top form. If not, then both your penis and your overall cardiovascular health could stand improvement.

regular chair. Men can also keep their lovemaking machinery running smoothly by using it, often (finally, a health habit that's actually fun to do). In the same way cars run best when they aren't parked in a garage for months on end, penises run best when they're regularly taken for a spin, whether that's through intercourse with a partner or going solo. Keeping blood moving in and out of the penis helps wash away plaque that could otherwise cake itself onto the arterial walls and cause trouble. Clogged arteries not only shunt blood flow to the heart, but can stem the tide to your privates, making erections slow to rise or preventing them entirely.

Regular erections are so important to keeping the arteries debris-free, in fact, that the penis conducts its own complimentary pipe cleaning when you're not even aware it's happening: at night. On average, men experience four to five erections while sleeping. These are different from the wet dreams most men had in adolescence in that (thankfully) they don't ejaculate four to five times per night. Rather, the penis just rises and falls. These nocturnal erections are not only important for penile health, they're also a reliable indicator of overall cardiovascular fitness. Doctors even offer (and health insurance often covers) Nocturnal Penile Tumescence (NPT) Testing, where they give patients a snap gauge—a plastic ring that men wear around the penis while they sleep, either at home or in a sleep lab. When an erection occurs, the snug-fitting snap gauge breaks, indicating the penis is in tip-top shape.

Foreskin, or Against?

Another erogenous zone on the penis worth mentioning is one that many men don't even have anymore: the foreskin, a layer of tissue that covers the glans like a skullcap. The foreskin contains yet another type of corpuscle called Meissner's corpuscles, which respond to an extremely fine, feathery touch. This makes the foreskin exquisitely sensitive; plus it can serve as a protective covering for the glans, which can receive *too* much stimulation and become desensitized as a result. Many assume circumcision happens for the sake of health and hygiene, but if you dig back to this procedure's origins, you'll find that the original goal of circumcision was actually to reduce sexual pleasure. Moses Maimónides, a renowned Jewish rabbi and physician from the twelfth century, made no bones about the pleasure-dampening purposes of this procedure. As he explained in his work *The Guide of the Perplexed*, a treatise on Jewish theology, "The fact that circumcision weakens the faculty of sexual excitement and sometimes perhaps diminishes the pleasure is indubitable." And yet, Maimónides goes on to say this is a good thing, adding, "This commandment has not been prescribed with a view to perfecting what is defective congenitally, but to perfecting what is defective morally." Circumcision was introduced to English-speaking countries in the late 1880s, and quickly caught on as a way to prevent and cure masturbation.

Grow Your Own Foreskin?

Jim Bigelow—a college professor, therapist, and clergyman—restored his own foreskin by slowly stretching the skin that was left up and over the glans, taping it down to keep it in place. Bigelow was so pleased with the results, he wrote a book titled *The Joy of Uncircumcising* for men who would like to follow in his footsteps.

But what about those supposed health benefits? While there is some evidence that circumcision lowers the risk of urinary tract infections, STDs, and penile cancer, some scientists argue that these benefits are so minimal, the pain doesn't justify the gain. According to a cost-benefit analysis of circumcision by Frank Lawler, a professor of family medicine at the University of Oklahoma, circumcision will add only about ten days to a man's life. Currently, the American Academy of Pediatrics finds that the pros and cons of circumcision largely cancel each other out, and as a result, does not recommend routine neonatal circumcision, leaving the decision up to parents. So far, studies on the sexual side effects of circumcision remain inconclusive. In one 2006 study published in *BJU International* of 255 men who were circumcised after the age of twenty, 48 percent of respondents said that masturbation had become less pleasurable. Eight percent, however, said masturbation had become more pleasurable. Twenty percent said their sex life had gotten worse after circumcision. Six percent noted improvements.

The Family Jewels: A Few Pearls of Wisdom

The penis, like the front man in a rock band, gets tons of attention. But its backup singers—the testicles—also deserve some respect. For one, while most people rarely pay them a visit, the testicles are rich in nerve endings, which make them a highly underrated erogenous zone. And while most people know that the testicles are responsible for sperm production, few are aware just how delicate and intricate this process is. That requires a closer look.

Within each testicle is a wad of tubing that, if untangled, would stretch for a half mile on average. Deep in its core, sperm cells are multiplying at a rate of one thousand per second. From there, though, they play a game of hurry up and wait. Given sperm traffic exits via that half mile of tubing, all sperm can do is get in line and inch forward. On average, it takes sperm two months to get to the front of the line.

During their journey, a lot can go wrong along the way. For one, even small fluctuations in temperature can prove ruinous. The testicles hang the way they do for climate control, since the optimal temperature for creating sperm is 94 degrees Fahrenheit, which is approximately four degrees cooler than the rest of the body. When the temperature is too cold, a reaction called the cremasteric reflex kicks in, reeling the testicles closer to the body to conserve heat. Most times, though, too *much* heat is the problem, causing the whole sperm production assembly line to grind to a halt. Whiling away hours in a Jacuzzi, for one, can have this effect. In one study in the journal *Clinical Urology*, infertile men who were spending an average of 149 minutes per week in a hot tub were able to boost their sperm counts by 491 percent by abstaining. Another lesser-known culprit could be laptops. In one study published in *Human Reproduction*, researchers took the scrotal temperature of men who were seated holding laptops and found it creeped up by approximately three degrees, which might impact sperm count down the line for men who perch their iBooks on their laps on a regular basis.

Rumors abound that a man's underwear choice can also impact his scrotal temperature and sperm count, with snug-fitting briefs doing the most damage. And yet, in one study titled "Are Boxer Shorts Really Better?" in the *Journal of Urology*, Robert Munkelwitz and Bruce Gilbert at New York State University at Stony Brook concluded that the tighty whities' bad rap is largely unmerited. They performed scrotal temperature checks and semen analyses on 97 men—some who wore boxers, others briefs, and others who had made the switch from one style to another. Men wearing tighter underwear, they found, were only 0.3 degrees warmer down below, which was not enough to impair their sperm count or motility significantly.

Heat isn't the only threat testicles have to watch out for, and any guy who has ever been kicked here knows this all too well. Why does even the slightest swat here hurt, well, everywhere? One reason is that even though the testicles hang on the outskirts of the body, they actually have much more in common with your innards, meaning your visceral organs, such as your stomach, liver, and kidneys. Visceral organs feel sensations differently than nonvisceral organs like your skin and skeletal muscles. If you were to place your hand on a hot stove, for example, nerves would send a message up to a part of the brain known as the sensory cortex, which would pinpoint exactly where the pain was coming from and prompt you to move your hand, pronto. Visceral organs, on the other hand, are connected to a more primitive pain system, sending messages up to the brain stem instead. This, in turn, triggers a diffuse sensation of pain throughout the body, which is why a kick in the testicles (not to mention a stomach ulcer or kidney stones) will cause men to double up, throw up, and all in all be put down for the count. In one study of 179 infertile men, endocrinologist Wolfram Nolten found that thirty had suffered "blunt testicular trauma," which, in laymen's terms, means a major wallop to the groin. Most times, these injuries had occurred back in high school while playing contact sports like football or wrestling without wearing the right below-the-belt protective gear.

So what happens if a man's sperm manages to avoid the dangers of Jacuzzi jets, laptops, or getting walloped by a hockey stick? Once sex commences, 300 million sperm get shuttled into a three-centimeter-long waiting area known as the prostatic urethra. Once there, three nearby glands—the prostate, seminal vesicles, and bulbourethral glands—kick into high gear and start contracting, squeezing their own ingredients into the mix. Fructose, a type of sugar, serves as food for sperms' journey. Zinc, vitamin C, amino acids, and other compounds also help sperm get where they need to go. Meanwhile, compounds called prostoglandins act to suppress a woman's immune response to destroy foreign invaders, sperm included. While these final preparations are being made, men will feel a warm, tingling sensation deep in their groin. Scientists call this phase of the arousal process "intromission," but most guys will recognize it as the Point of No Return. Within seconds, a flurry of muscular contractions known as an orgasm come barreling through, sending its cargo of sperm shooting up and out the urethra into the world.

Believe it or not, there was a time when, rather than placing a hand on the Bible, people in courtrooms took oaths on their testicles instead. In Genesis, for instance, when Abraham asked his servant to swear to him he said, "Put your hand on my thigh, and I will make you swear by the Lord, the God of heaven and earth." Translators euphemistically used the word *thigh* rather than *testicles*. In either case, the word "testify" comes from this ancient practice.

The Sweetest Taboo?

Few people ever venture anywhere near the back door—which is a shame, since when not performing its janitorial duties, the anus can play a pivotal role in great sex. Except for the genitals, the anus contains more nerve endings than any other area of a man's body. And more nerve endings = greater pleasure potential.

The anus also offers access to the prostate gland, another erogenous zone first identified by sex researchers in the 1980s. Researchers Beverly Whipple and John Perry, who had already made waves announcing their discovery of a woman's G spot, dubbed the prostate gland "the male G spot" with similarly pleasurable benefits when stimulated. Ironically, the prostate's pleasure potential was common knowledge well before any of these scientists extolled its powers. During World War II, medics would often treat sexually deprived soldiers for a vague ailment called "pelvic congestion"—what's known today as plain old horniness—by giving them a prostate massage through anal penetration (hard to imagine this treat-

How to Handle a Man's Hot Spots

Focus on the most sensitive parts of the penis. The shaft of the penis may be the most obvious destination, but the most nerve-rich areas are up top. During manual or oral maneuvers, pay special attention to the glans (or head of the penis), the coronal ridge (where the glans meets the shaft), and the frenulum (the vertical notch on the bottom side of the corona at six o'clock). During sex, try shallow thrusting to concentrate sensations near the tip of the penis.

Try an array of stimulating activities. While a straight up-and-down motion is the most common way to please a penis, there are plenty of ways to mix things up. During manual stimulation, try twisting your wrist clockwise or counterclockwise to rub nerve endings in a new way. During oral sex, try humming or moaning—the vibrations from your vocal cords will reverberate throughout the area. Or, take a swig of coffee or put an ice cube in your mouth to tantalize temperature-sensitive nerve endings down below. On extra-sensitive areas, keep in mind that less is more. Try some light tongue swipes around the corona, or tickling the frenulum with one finger. Or, during oral sex, take a break from your oral ministrations, pucker your lips, and blow on the head. Even this slight breeze will give him chills.

Enhance the sensations he's receiving. While stimulating him manually or orally, or during intercourse, you can kick things up a notch if you encircle the base of the penis with thumb and forefinger then pull down toward his body. This will tug the skin of the penis taut, thereby exposing even more nerve endings. That means that anything you do will feel even more intense.

Don't expect a raging hard-on the whole time. Sometimes, men's erections come and go of their own volition. As a result, they're not necessarily a reliable barometer of a man's arousal levels. So if your partner's not rising to the occasion, don't take it personally. Firm or flaccid, the penis contains the same number of nerve endings and will appreciate attention in either state. When in doubt, ask your partner for guidance.

Pay the twins a visit. Many people steer clear of the testicles fearing that any stimulation here is overboard. And yet, when handled with care, this area is packed with pleasure potential. Try stroking, tickling, or rolling the testicles gently between your fingers and see what happens. If, at some point, his testicles rise and hunch closer to the body, congratulations—that means he's enjoying it. That's because you've triggered a reaction in the cremaster muscle, which coils tighter like a spring and pulls the testicles upward to prepare for the orgasmic finale.

To prolong the fun, give the testicles a tug. If he's quickly approaching orgasm but you want to delay his grand finale, wrap your thumb and forefinger around the base of his scrotum and gently pull downward toward his feet. The testicles tend to hunch closer to the body in preparation for orgasm, so by pulling them away from their locked-and-loaded position, you can delay climax for a while.

Press up on the perineum. The perineum is the patch of skin between the scrotum and the anus (which, you've no

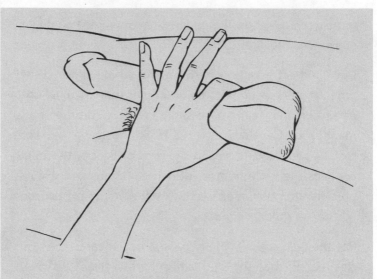

How to delay ejaculation

doubt heard, has been quaintly nicknamed the 'tain't since "'tain't one or the other"). Press on this area with the pads of your fingers, and you'll indirectly stimulate the prostate— a gland located within the pelvic cavity that's exquisitely sensitive to stimulation.

Explore the back door. The anus is often avoided, but is well worth a visit provided you take a few precautions. For one, lube isn't just nice, it's a necessity. The anus, unlike the vagina, doesn't lubricate in response to sexual arousal. That means that store-bought lubricant like K-Y Jelly should definitely be on the premises before you start exploring. Once you head in, make sure to take it slow. Start small (use just one finger, covered in a rubber glove or condom if you wish), proceed at a snail's pace, and keep the lines of communication running nonstop, asking things like *Should I move forward, back up a little, or stay put?* Every millimeter you move counts, so take your time to ensure you get in safely and comfortably.

Reach for the prostate. Located within the pelvic cavity, this gland can be stimulated by pressing up on the perineum (see above) or through the anus. To try the latter option, insert a finger in the anus and feel around for a walnut-sized bump along the front wall of the rectum around three inches in. Then, massage the area by gently crooking your finger in a come-hither motion. If all goes well, the prostate may swell in size, and if things are going really well, it may actually contract in small bursts.

ment would fly in today's military). Even earlier, at the turn of the twentieth century, a steel device called a prostate massager was marketed to women as a way to make a man very happy in bed.

History of the Clitoris

Packed with 8,000 nerve endings—twice as many as are in the entire penis (read it and weep, fellas)—the clitoris is the center of many a woman's sexual universe. And yet, scientists have been slow to catch on to this fact.

The first man to "discover" the clitoris was one Realdo Columbus. In 1559, after peering beneath the petticoats of over a hundred female patients, the Italian anatomist concluded that women possessed a tiny "protuberance" that, if touched, would become "a little harder and oblong to such a degree that it shows itself as a sort of male member," he reported in his book *De Re Anatomica*. At that point, Columbus did what pretty much any self-respecting scientist would do in his situation: mark his territory. "If it is permissible to give names to things discovered by me," he wrote, "it should be called the love or sweetness of Venus." Columbus even made an effort to enlist his most famous patient, Michelangelo, to collaborate with him on an illustrated anatomy text, but Michelangelo refused, so no clitoral masterpiece ever came to pass. Soon after Columbus reported his discovery of the clitoris to the dean of the university where he worked, he was arrested, put on trial, and imprisoned for blasphemy, witchcraft, and Satanism.

After that, the clitoris continued to maintain a low profile. *Gray's Anatomy*, the classic textbook of the human body first published in 1858, made no mention of the clitoris until its 1901 edition, only to delete this label in 1948. In 1966, psychiatrist Mary Jane Sherfey put the clitoris back on the map with her publication of *The Nature and Evolution of Female Sexuality*; *Gray's* soon followed suit. Still, the full size and complexity of the clitoris remained muddled until a group of feminists decided to take on the challenge of figuring it out.

In 1975, nine women at the Federation of Feminist Women's Health Clinics (FFWHCs) decided to write a book on women's reproductive anatomy. Undeterred by their lack of formal medical training, they gathered for consciousness-raising seminars, where they would take off their pants, sit in a circle, masturbate, and compare their privates to illustrations in the available literature. One member, an artist named Suzann Gage, took an anatomy course at UCLA and began drawing the clitoris—all eighteen parts of it. Some parts, like the tip, known as the clitoral glans, were easily visible, as were the clitoral hood (the equivalent of the foreskin in men). Others parts, like the clitoral shaft, could only be felt by pressing down on the area or pressing up inside the vagina. Still other parts, including muscles, blood vessels, and nerves, couldn't be seen or felt, but were all part of the package as far as the FFWHCs were concerned. The results were published in a book, *A New View of a Woman's Body: An Illustrated Guide.*

Since then, MRI scans of the area have confirmed that the clitoris is much larger than meets the eye. "It's actually about the size and shape of a turkey wishbone," says Ken Maravilla at the University of Washington in Seattle. Like the penis, the clitoris becomes even larger when aroused due to the same cascade of chemical changes that occur in the penis (quick recap: there's a poof of nitric oxide, vessels dilate, and blood rushes in). There is, however, one difference. While the venous plexus veins draining the penis get clamped shut so men can build one monumental erection, the clitoris lacks this airtight mechanism. Blood flows in, then back out. As a result, a clitoral hard-on is nowhere near as firm as that of a penis. And that's actually fine and dandy—preferable, in fact—for a number of reasons. One, unless you're really creative, the clitoris probably won't be penetrating anything, so there's no reason to pump it to full capacity. Two, in certain sexual positions the clitoris is bound to get squashed a bit, so all the better it has the consistency of a pencil eraser rather than a snub-nosed bullet. Three, the clitoris's ability to rise and fall explains why women have an easier time reaching multiple orgasms.

The clitoris and penis may have their differences, but the same plumbing principles and problems apply to them both. As a result, while it might not be as noticeable as when a guy can't get it up, clitorises can also fail to rise to the occasion due to insufficient blood flow. Again, poor cardiovascular condi-

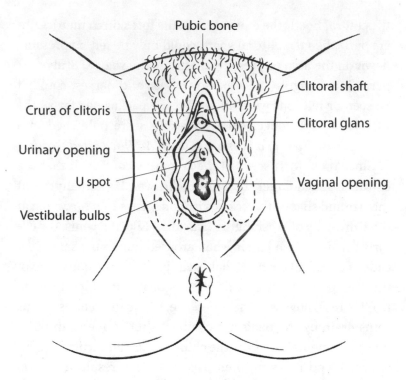

Pubic bone

Crura of clitoris

Urinary opening

U spot

Vestibular bulbs

Clitoral shaft

Clitoral glans

Vaginal opening

Internal anatomy of the clitoris

tioning and clogged arteries are often the culprit, a problem that can be curbed with proper exercise and diet. As a further artery-unclogging measure, when women sleep, their clitorises undergo the same series of three to five nocturnal erections that penises do (which wasn't easy to measure, but Ismet Karacan at the University of Florida managed to confirm this with miniscule erection-measuring equipment in a sleep lab).

Even those who recognized the clitoris's existence early on, though, tended to discount the pleasurable perks it could bring to its owner. Sigmund Freud, for one, argued that an orgasm brought on by clitoral stimulation was "immature," as if the clitoris were a toy that women should eventually outgrow. Real women had vaginal orgasms. And if they didn't? They had a psychological hang-up known as frigidity, which—conveniently—Freud claimed he could cure with psychoanalysis. Frigid women far and wide started filling Freud's waiting room, hoping he could fix this puzzling new problem.

In the 1960s, Masters and Johnson argued that *all* orgasms were clitorally-based, and that these mythical vaginal orgasms Freud was talking about were actually caused by indirect stimulation of the clitoris during intercourse. Still other scientists, however, have argued that the vagina does have its own set of orgasm triggers. To settle the debate, many have gone searching within the vaginal environs for proof. And they found plenty.

The Controversy over the G spot

In 1944, a German anatomist named Ernst Gräfenberg stumbled across an extrasensitive area inside the vagina located along the front wall, anywhere from one to three inches in. Today, we know this area as the G spot. Gräfenberg dubbed it "a primary erotic zone, perhaps more important than the clitoris" in his writing, and discovered that if you rubbed this area just right, women wouldn't only reach orgasm, but do something long felt to be the sole sexual stomping ground of men: ejaculate. How could this be? Gräfenberg never found a plausible explanation, and his discovery of the G spot never made headlines as he'd hoped. The medical community, incredulous that such an erogenous zone could exist, didn't bite. As a result, news of the G spot got buried, only to resurface thirty years later.

In 1981, Beverly Whipple and John Perry published a study

in *The Journal of Sex Research* saying that Gräfenberg was right. They had witnessed (and videotaped) their first case study—a married woman in her late thirties. "With the aid of the subject's husband, [we] were able to observe her response to digital massage of her Gräfenberg spot, which led to expulsion of liquid, and reportedly and apparently to orgasm, on several occasions," they wrote. They named this erogenous zone the Gräfenberg spot, later called the G spot, in Gräfenberg's honor. (Gräfenberg, apparently a modest man, didn't call it anything in particular.) "When I informed a colleague about our discovery, he suggested we name the spot 'The Whipple Tickle,'" Whipple recalls. "I thought, no way. Gräfenberg deserved the credit. And besides, I had children in school and just didn't think that would be appropriate."

Whipple and Perry then proceeded to conduct a wider-scale study. More than 400 women volunteered to be examined by a physician or nurse. Each and every woman was found to have a G spot, although its size, sensitivity, and location varied— if one were to imagine a small clock inside the vagina with 12 o'clock pointing toward the navel, the majority of women would find their G spot between 11 and 1 o'clock. After Whipple appeared on *The Phil Donahue Show* to announce their discovery, Whipple received over 5,000 letters from people thanking them for bringing the G spot and female ejaculation to their attention. To further get the word out, Perry, Whipple, and Alice Kahn Ladas co-authored a book titled *The G Spot and Other Discoveries about Human Sexuality*. Chalk it up to the sexually inquisitive times or these researchers' savvy publicity efforts, but this time, news of the G spot stuck. Suddenly, hoards of women set off in search of this erogenous zone.

But what is the G spot, exactly? Some say it's the female equivalent of the male prostate. Others say it's part of the urethral sponge, still others the Skene's gland. As for what constitutes the mystery fluid that erupts as a result, for a long time that was also up for debate. For many years, doctors assumed it was urine—a momentary trickle of incontinence. Edwin Belzer, a professor at Dalhousi University in Nova Scotia, argued otherwise. That's because an anonymous woman had informed Belzer of an at-home experiment she tried where she popped a few Urised tablets—which would dye her urine blue—then stimulated her G spot to orgasm. The resulting wet spots, the woman reported, weren't blue in the slightest, although the urine she expelled afterward was as blue as could be. During one set of experiments, Perry and Whipple collected a few drops of female ejaculate in a cup and had its chemical composition analyzed. They found glucose, enzymes, and—strangest of all—prostatic acid phosphatase, which is also found in semen. Female ejaculate isn't all that different from male ejaculate. In some women, ejaculate is not always expelled, but remains in the urethra to be passed with their next urination, and thus might be missed entirely.

Many G spot expeditions came back empty-handed, prompting yet another wave of skepticism. Why have certain women found their G spots with ease while others come up empty? In 2008, Italian research Emmanuele Jannini published a study in the *Journal of Sexual Medicine* pointing to one possible answer. Jannini used ultrasound to scan the urethrovaginal space, the area of tissue between the vagina and urethra where the G spot was rumored to be lurking. Jannini scanned nine women who said they could reach orgasm vaginally, and eleven who could not. Women who could orgasm vaginally, he found, had a thicker urethrovaginal space than women who couldn't orgasm in this manner. His conclusion: Certain women have G spots, while others don't.

"For the first time it is possible to determine by a simple, rapid and inexpensive method if a woman has a G spot or not," Jannini says, pointing out that his discovery could help clear up a lot of confusion. Women without G spots could put an end to their fruitless searching, while women who discover they do have G spots can redouble their efforts. "One of my study subjects said she'd never had a vaginal orgasm, and yet my test revealed that her urethrovaginal space was very big, which suggested she had a G spot," Jannini recalls. "After a couple of weeks, this woman called me to say that thanks to my study, she had found her G spot herself and can now achieve orgasm vaginally. She was very happy."

G Spot Shot?

In the same way plastic surgeons can inject collagen to enlarge lips, they can inject collagen into G spot territory so the area becomes larger and supposedly more sensitive. These G spot enhancement surgeries, which are known by nifty names such as the "G-shot" or "G-Delight," have been so successful that some women claim they've had orgasms simply by walking (which is fixable, since that's clearly more than they bargained for). Jannini is skeptical, arguing that unless you have a G spot to begin with, no amount of collagen is going to make the area more sensitive.

Since then, women from around the world have made the trek to Jannini's laboratory to see if they have a G spot. Some find they do, but most do not. "The absence of the G spot is actually normal," says Jannini. How can this be, given that Whipple and Perry's pelvic examinations of 400 women found evidence of a G spot in all study subjects? One possible explanation, says Whipple, may lie in a discrepancy in what they were measuring—and how. Whipple and Perry used pelvic examinations to determine that all 400 study subjects had an extrasensitive area within the vagina, but they did not explore whether stimulation of this spot could produce orgasm. Jannini, on the other hand, did ask his study subjects whether they could reach orgasm vaginally, and concluded that women who could had a G spot, while those who couldn't did not. Jannini's definition of the G spot may merely be different from Whipple's. "We do need a

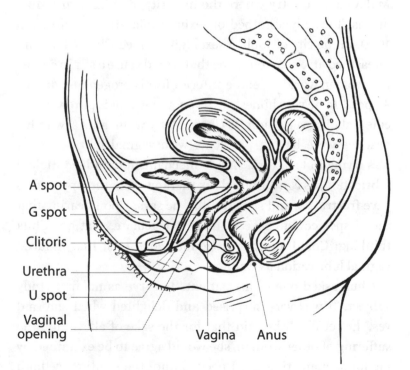

A woman's hidden hot spots

shared definition of the G spot that we do not have so far," says Jannini, adding that he hopes this issue will be resolved at a conference on the G spot in Florence next year. Whatever the definition ends up being, Jannini maintains that women shouldn't worry about their G spots so much. "Most women can still have an orgasm through the clitoris," he says. "It's like having a house with two doors. Some women have two doors into their house. Others have one. Who cares which door you use as long as you can get in?"

From Malaysia with Love: The A Spot

Malaysia, a country where the majority of citizens are Muslim, isn't exactly a hotbed of sexual exploration. And yet, in 1990, in the city of Ipoh, a sexologist named Chua Chee Ann unearthed an erogenous zone that would cause a stir in countless women worldwide: the anterior fornix erogenous zone, or A spot. "To be very honest with you, the A spot is purely an accidental discovery," admits Chua. Many women he saw in his practice were having problems with vaginal lubrication. "I was trying to look for a simple mechanism to induce vaginal lubrication, as conventional sex therapy—talk therapy—often gave frustrating and slow results," he says. Upon hearing that the G spot could cause women to ejaculate, that got Chua thinking: Could another erogenous zone exist that induced vaginal lubrication as well?

Chua asked one of his patients to serve as his first study subject. "I was very surprised and delighted when she said yes," he recalls. "She said that for the sake of alleviating the suffering of other women, she would agree to be examined by me for as many times as I needed until the solution we both were looking for was found." Chua also made sure his wife was comfortable with this arrangement. "When told that I had this idea of helping women with vaginal dryness and that I had a very brave volunteer standing by, my wife readily agreed that I carry on with my research program," he says. "I'm very lucky that she happens to be a very broad-minded person." For three months, Chua probed the vaginal environs of his volunteer and finally stumbled across an area on the front wall of the vagina two to three inches in, just past the rougher terrain of the urethral sponge, that seemed to do the trick. After learning from Chua how to stimulate the A spot herself, the woman brought her discovery home, "much to the surprise and delight of her husband," Chua recalls.

In 1997, Chua published the results of a more wide-scale study in the journal *Sexual and Relationship Therapy*. A total of 271 women from China, Malaysia, and India volunteered to have their A spots stimulated, which could cause some women to become lubricated in five to ten seconds and orgasmic in one to two minutes. "I remembered one particular case, a Chinese lady of 43 years, with complaints of chronic vaginal dryness," Chua recalls. "She literally blew her top the moment my finger touched her A spot. Within a few seconds she was having multiple orgasms." To date, no one has done any anatomical/physiological studies to show why the A spot is so sensitive. "Anatomically there does not appear to be a special bunch of nerves in that area," says Dr. Chua. "In essence, it appears to behave more like an acupuncture point."

Chua, who is currently semiretired and living in Ipoh, hasn't conducted any new studies on the A spot since then. Nonetheless, the questions his friends and neighbors ask him about his work belie that, traditional values or not, his culture is as curious about sex as any other. "Whenever people ask me whether I have used this technique in my personal life, I just flash them a very cheeky smile," Chua says. "My wife will give a rather coy smile when similarly asked. We both like to keep people guessing."

The Tiniest Erogenous Zone of All: The U Spot

One final spot on a woman's below-the-belt anatomy worth checking out lies just outside the vagina above its opening. This is the U spot, a half-inch-in-diameter donut of extra-sensitive tissue surrounding the urethral opening. Though tiny, the U spot has something special going for it: erectile tissue. With the right stimulation—light swipes of the fingers or tongue, for example—the U spot will inflate like a life preserver to salute these efforts.

No one has conducted a wide-scale study on the U spot yet, although Roy Levin at the University of Sheffield in the United Kingdom did perform his own preliminary investigation on the area (which he calls the periurethral glans) in a rather unusual way. Levin bought a bunch of porn, kept an eagle eye on the U spot during freeze-frame images of the tapes' closest close-ups, and found that the area gets pulled partway inside the vagina "on vaginal penile insertion and reappears on withdrawal, indicating that it is moved during coitus," according to his report in the journal *Experimental and Clinical Endocrinology*. Perhaps, Levin concluded, women who have orgasms during intercourse do so because their U spots are getting stimulated.

The Vagina: An Inside View

If you were a penis inside a vagina, what would you see? It's an odd question, but plenty of researchers have pondered it, and devised some pretty ingenious ways to get a peek. In 1890, Brooklyn gynecologist Robert Latou Dickinson inserted a glass test tube inside his female patients, peered into its depths, and sketched with crayons what he saw (patients "posed" for anywhere from five to sixty-two drawings apiece). In the 1960s, research team William Masters and Virginia Johnson took vaginal viewing high tech by inventing the "penis camera," a dildo-shaped device that could snap photos. In 1994, filmmakers for The Learning Channel documentary *The Human Animal* upgraded to video, attaching a fiber-optic endoscope to a man's penis. Altogether, what this footage reveals is that during sexual arousal, a woman's genitals undergo a complicated series of contortions.

For starters, the penis isn't the only organ that grows a few inches. The vagina also lengthens up to three to four inches. As circulation starts swirling through the pelvic region, capillaries on the surface of the vaginal walls start "sweating" small droplets that act to neutralize the vagina's normally acidic pH, thus making it more sperm-friendly. Soon, this chemical cocktail covers the vaginal sluiceway in a thin sheen. As excitement continues to build, the vagina continues its adjustments. The outer third constricts, which, in turn, puts even more of a squeeze on veins in the penis, helping trap blood there and keeping things firm. Meanwhile, the inner third of the vagina does the opposite and expands into a triangular, tentlike shape. It's setting up a base camp where sperm can convene before continuing on their journey.

Vaginal tenting may provide the lodging, but sperm have their methods of hunkering down and staying put. For one, seminal fluid has a jellylike consistency that doesn't easily budge after it's been dropped off. Right after sex, women can stand up, walk around, and even jump up and down without getting rid of it (this is also why jumping up and down after sex won't keep you from getting pregnant). And yet while seminal fluid's viscous consistency is great for staying power, it's also terrible for swimming—think of doing the backstroke through molasses. In anywhere from five to forty minutes, seminal fluid becomes more liquid, which allows sperm to move more easily. It also means some sperm will get washed out due to gravity or a sneeze. This forced mass exodus of sperm is called "flowback," but most people know it by another name that better explains the end results on your sheets: the wet spot. Not all sperm, of course, get kicked out. In general, flowback contains about half the number of sperm that went in. The other half are wiggling their way toward a tightly guarded, dimplelike entrance at the end of the vagina called the cervix.

As far as reproductive responsibilities go, the cervix has a tough job. Most times, the cervix spends its time barring bacteria and other foreign invaders from the uterus. Sperm, however, are welcome guests, which leads to a quandary: How do you usher sperm in while keeping unwanted materials out? The cervix has its methods. Let's say, for example, that you're a sperm cell treading seminal fluid in the vaginal tent, wondering how you're going to get into the uterus. You see the cervix in the distance and make a break for it, but still, it's a ways off and swimming is hard work. Not surprisingly, sperm get exhausted during their journey (those tiny sperm tails may be cute, but aren't really built for speed or distance). If left to their own devices, sperm would never make it.

This is where the cervix lends a helping hand. According to footage retrieved from penis videocameras during sexual intercourse, the cervix doesn't just wait for sperm to reach its entrance. Instead, the cervix begins to stretch, then dip down

How to Handle a Woman's Hot Spots

Treat the clitoris to some TLC. This nub is orgasm central for most women. In fact, in some cases the clitoris may be so sensitive, it's best to start with indirect stimulation around the outskirts. Try cupping your hand over the entire area and massaging or jiggling your hand back and forth. If that elicits a positive response, try stroking the clitoris with the flat of one finger. According to some experts, the clitoris even has a "sweet spot" at two o'clock.

Find the G spot. Insert one or two fingers into the vagina with your palm facing the same direction as her stomach. Anywhere from one to three inches in, push into the front wall of the vagina where you feel a dime-sized spongy area. That's the urethral sponge, under which is the G spot. To stimulate the area, a straight in-and-out thrusting motion of fingers generally won't do the trick, since the G spot requires firmer pressure. To deliver, press the pad of your finger into the G spot and crook your finger in a come-hither motion.

Turn on the A spot. With the woman lying on her back, insert your index finger palm up. Around two to three inches in, just past the rougher terrain of the urethral sponge, you should feel a smooth, flat surface on the roof of the vagina. That's the A spot. Once you've found it, gently crook your finger in a come-hither motion like you would for the G spot, but keep the pad of your finger flat as possible so you're stroking rather than pressing into the area. Once aroused, the A spot should prompt some noticeable lubrication, at which point you can lengthen your strokes to include the urethral sponge as well (you can get a full video tutorial for $97 on Chua's Web site, Aspot-pioneer.com).

Visit the U spot. The U spot is a fingernail-sized patch of sensitive tissue surrounding the urethra, just above the vaginal opening. Try a few light finger or tongue swipes over the area. The U spot also contains erectile tissue, so if you feel a tiny bump rise, that's a good sign.

Don't fret if she's not wet. While many people use wetness as the barometer of a woman's arousal levels, a woman's lubrication levels ebb and flow for all sorts of reasons beyond what's happening in bed. Certain stages of her menstrual cycle, medication she's on (such as antihistamines, antidepressants, and birth control pills), alcohol, and nicotine can affect the amount of lubrication down below. So if your efforts aren't producing much moisture, don't take it personally. Just grab a bottle of store-bought lubricant like K-Y Jelly to keep things going smoothly.

into the seminal pool like an elephant's trunk taking a sip of water. Knowing a free ride when they see one, sperm eagerly climb on board to take this escalator up into the uterus. After a few minutes, the cervix retracts and returns to its dimplelike state, at which point, game over. Whatever sperm are still left in the vagina will eventually get kicked out.

So what's keeping bacteria from climbing onto this stairway as well? That's where a woman's second line of defense comes in: cervical mucus. This mucus flows at a glacial pace out the cervix and down the vagina, carrying anything in its path from sperm to bacteria along with it. Sperm, however, can do something bacteria cannot—swim. And while sperm swim slowly, they do move faster than cervical mucus, which allows them to outpace the backsliding morass they're in and make it through the cervix's doorway.

Now that you've gotten a tour of your body on sex, let's take an elevator up to the top and see what's going on in mission control, your brain.

CHAPTER 6

This Is Your Brain on Sex

After their first impulsive night together, John and Jane continued seeing each other. Over time, their sex life went from good to great as they got in tune with each other's bodies. Reading each other's minds, though, was another matter.

During sex, John couldn't help wondering: What was Jane thinking? If he could spy on her private thoughts, what would he see—ego-inflating reveries about his sexual prowess, or much less steamy musings about whether his bedspread matched his curtains? Were those orgasms she seemed to be having for real, or were they just really convincing fakes? Jane was trying to read John's mind, too, although on an entirely different matter: Were she and John falling in love, or was this just garden-variety lust? She couldn't tell, and no matter how many times she read through John's e-mails, analyzing small turns of phrase and even typos with her friends, the answer didn't emerge.

Further complicating matters was that now that they were clocking serious amounts of time together, the couple had begun butting heads over certain issues that didn't seem to bode well for their relationship. Jane felt she could talk to John for hours on end, but John rarely called, which made Jane wonder if he truly cared about her. John had noticed that Jane wasn't initiating sex as often as she used to, which made John wonder if she truly cared about him. Unless they cleared up the cloud of confusion that had descended on their relationship, odds were high their budding romance would crash and burn. If only John and Jane could take a peek inside each other's minds, they'd have the answers they were looking for. But would they like what they saw?

I N THE 1980s, neuroscientists began sliding people into MRI machines. Their mission: to take X-ray-style pictures of the brain called fMRI scans to identify which portions get activated during various activities. If, for example, someone were to ask you what you ate for breakfast this morning, a seahorse-shaped area near the base of the brain would light up—that's the hippocampus, which is in charge of memory collection. Wiggle your toes, and an arc of gray matter spanning the top of your head would sparkle like a tiara—that's the primary motor cortex, which holds sway over the body's movements. Brain scans can even tell if you're lying, as was proved in one experiment at Temple University in Philadelphia where study subjects were told to fib about something they'd recently done (in this case, firing a toy gun). Fabrications set a whole rash of areas on the frontal, temporal, and limbic lobes of the brain ablaze. Thus the creation of No Lie MRI, a company that offers cops an alternative to old-fashioned polygraphs. According to one study, fMRIs can divine fact from fib with a 93 percent accuracy rate, while typically polygraphs are accurate only 60 to 70 percent of the time.

It was inevitable, of course, that scientists would try to see

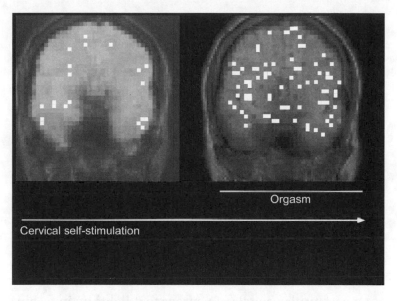

Orgasm

Cervical self-stimulation

fMRI of the brain at rest (left) and having an orgasm (right)

Adapted from Komisaruk, B. R., B. Whipple, A. Crawford, S. Grimes, W. C. Liu, A. Kalnin, and K. Mosier, 2004. "Brain activation during vaginocervical self-stimulation and orgasm in women with complete spinal cord injury: fMRI evidence of mediation by the vagus nerves." *Brain Research* 1024 (1–2): 77–88. Reprinted with permission from Elsevier.

what the brain looks like on sex. And as luck would have it, most MRI machines come with a TV screen inside, on which researchers could pipe in porn like a high-tech peep-show booth. As volunteer after volunteer climbed inside to enjoy some X-rated entertainment, researchers examined which gears were turning between their ears. What they saw helps explain questions we've all pondered at some point: Why does sex feel so good? Why do we do and say things during sex that we regret later? Is there a way to tell if someone's in love with you or just in lust, or faking an orgasm rather than having a real one? The answers to all these questions became clear with a brain scan, since you can't hide from an MRI. To shore up your own mind-reading skills, let's take a trip down the brain's 60,000 miles of wiring and make some pit stops at a few highlights.

A Map of Your Mind

Chances are, when you picture the brain, you envision something that looks like a big pile of macaroni—they don't call it your "noodle" for nothing. An fMRI scan looks similar, only in color. There's a burst of yellow here, a dash of blue there, all of which signal that particular bundles of neurons are activated. While most of our daily activities fire up only small portions, sex is different: It ignites many areas all at once.

One particular bundle of neurons that lights up in technicolor is the nucleus accumbens. Stashed deep within the brain, the nucleus accumbens is no bigger than a peanut, and yet it packs a huge wallop in the pleasure department. In experiments on rats where metal electrodes were implanted in this area of the brain, the rodents pressed a lever to stimulate this spot hundreds of times per hour, foregoing food and water until they eventually died of exhaustion. Thankfully, this same experiment hasn't been done on humans (although what a way to go), but brain scans do show that this area glows when you're having a good time—and not just in bed. Studies also show that the nucleus accumbens gets revved up during the rush induced by nicotine or cocaine. No wonder we say sex feels like a drug, because as far as our brain is concerned, it has the same effect.

Another area that goes berserk during sex is the anterior cingulate cortex, which is located on the sides of the brain and, strangely, is also activated when you're in pain. How such polar opposites as pain and pleasure can occupy the same neurological real estate still puzzles researchers, although some surmise that the anterior cingulate cortex isn't involved in the *sensation* of pain and pleasure, but its *expression*. Ever notice that how people's faces look when they orgasm bears a

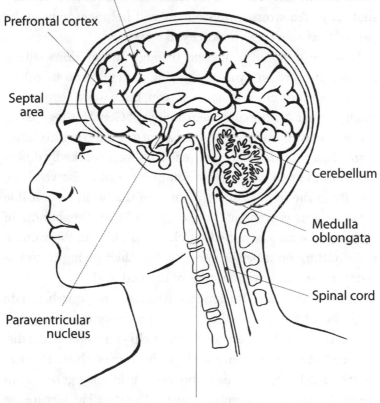

Areas of the brain that get activated during sexual arousal

striking resemblance to how they would look if they had just stubbed their toe, are suffering a bad case of gas, or are otherwise in some sort of physical distress? In all instances, that's the anterior cingulate cortex scrunching their face in those interesting shapes.

While sex gets certain portions of the brain buzzing, other parts shut down completely. One such spot is the amygdala, an almond-shaped nugget of neurons near the base of the brain that triggers emotions such as fear and anxiety. The upshot: If you're stressed, having sex will help you unplug the part of the brain that's making you worry.

If you're tempted to just go through the motions with a partner and pretend you're enjoying yourself, you might be able to fool the person in bed with you, but a brain scan would catch your lie. Netherlands neuroscientist Gert Holstege asked his female study subjects to fake an orgasm during his brain scans. Images of fakes, Holstege found, were markedly different from the real ones. While genuine orgasms showed little activity in the motor cortex, an area of the brain responsible for conscious movement, fake orgasms lit up this bundle of neurons like an alarm bell—a clear tip-off that the women were putting on a performance rather than giving in to the spontaneous shakes and rattles of the real deal.

Brain scans can also ferret out other lies your bedmate might be feeding you. Arthur Aron, a professor at Stony Brook University New York, claims he can help you suss out the difference between true love and garden-variety lust. He performed MRI scans on men and women as they gazed upon photos of people they were in love with as well as pictures of attractive acquaintances. Results showed that the two sets of photos affected the brain in different ways. Photos of loved ones generated more activity in the right side of the brain, namely, the ventral tegmental area, dorsal caudate body, and caudate tail, areas that are associated with romantic feelings. Photos of attractive people, on the other hand, stirred up more activity within similar areas on the *left* side of the brain—the seat of sexual urges. If someone you were dating were to succumb to such an experiment, activity on the right side of the brain would mean his or her romantic feelings for you were real, while activity on the left would mean it was just sexual attraction. We might be able to fool others or even ourselves on this point, but our brains know better.

Even if you and your partner have been together for years, an fMRI scan can tell if you're *still* in love in that fluttery, infatuated, can't-keep-my-hands-off-you way—a tall order given this initial rush tends to fade over time. To find out how certain duos kept those sparks flying, Aron scanned brains of couples who claimed to be as crazy about each other today as they were decades earlier when they'd first met. Deep within their brains, he discovered a specific collection of neurons that burned bright in these couples called the ventral pallidum. This area of the brain has one mission only: It gets couples to remain in a relationship, a phenomenon scientists call pair bonding.

Consider all the romantic quandaries a quick trip to your local MRI clinic could solve. Players who vow up and down they're devoted to you could be ratted out in the space of one doctor's appointment. Confused couples who swear they're in love but are actually just having hot sex will hold off on those impromptu wedding plans. At No Lie MRI, couples can pay $5,000 to get a scan revealing the answers to these questions (currently there are offices in Los Angeles and San Diego). "We've gotten calls from around the world from jealous husbands willing to fly their wives in," says the company's founder, Joel Huizenga. Occasionally if someone gets dragged in, they'll balk at getting scanned at the last minute. Those who do follow through, though, are usually certain their scans will soothe a partner's suspicions. "It's a self-selective process," Huizenga explains. "People willing to get a scan are most likely telling the truth." As a result, so far, most couples leave No Lie MRI feeling happier and more confident about their relationship than they did going in.

Brain scans can also reveal whether you and your partner are compatible. For that answer, you can book an appointment at Daniel Amen's lab.

When Good Brains Go Bad

In 2002, when a twenty-nine-year-old British bicycle warehouse worker named Stephen Tame hit his head falling from scaffolding, Tame's sexual tastes turned from mild to wild overnight. After accosting his new wife to the point that she moved out to escape his amorous advances, Tame turned to a steady diet of porn, prostitutes, and sexual affairs, including a fling with a fifty-seven-year-old woman from his church. In 2006, Tame was awarded £3.2 million in damages from his former employer. Just months later, a twenty-eight-year-old Australian delivery driver named Kunal Karl Lindsay suffered a similar head injury that erased his sexual inhibitions, leading him to pester his wife daily for sex and talk dirty at inappropriate moments. Eventually, she moved out, taking their infant son with her. Lindsay was awarded £1.2 million in damages.

Are We a Match? Check the MRI

For neuroscientist Daniel Amen, the idea of offering brain scans to couples came to him one day when he was getting ready to head to the office for an appointment with Betsy and Bob. Amen, who is also a marital therapist, was the fifth couples counselor they had seen, and in nine months of treatment, their relationship had gone from bad to worse. "My stomach hurt at the thought of seeing them," he recalls. "So I said to myself, 'Today I'm going to tell them to get a divorce.'"

As a last resort, though, Amen decided to request brain scans of the couple. He'd never done this before, but the minute he received the images and analyzed the results with a specialist, everything clicked. Betsy's scan showed increased activity in an area of the brain called the anterior cingular gyrus—the brain's "gear shifter" that allows people to move fluidly from one task to the next. When overactive, the anterior cingular gyrus can cause people to get stuck on negative thoughts, which could easily explain why Betsy couldn't let go of a grudge. Meanwhile, Bob's scan showed low activity in the prefrontal cortex, a common symptom of attention-deficit/ hyperactivity disorder (ADHD), which shed light on why he'd become inattentive to his wife's needs. So far, their conditions were low-level enough that they had gone undiagnosed. Had Betsy and Bob been married to other people, perhaps their mental quirks would have never become a problem. Paired together, though, Betsy's and Bob's brains were destined to clash. No matter how much they loved each other, their minds weren't a match.

Luckily, both disorders were easily treatable (with Prozac for Betsy and Ritalin for Bob), and the couple's relationship quickly improved. Since then, Amen has performed brain scans on more than three hundred couples with compatibility issues, often revealing in an instant what decades of therapy might have never been able to solve. Perhaps that's why Amen has had his own brain scanned numerous times, has scanned the brains of all the women he's dated, and has also extended an offer to scan the brains of his daughters and any guys they are dating. Amen stresses that these are offers, not mandates. So far, everyone has taken him up on it—not that they weren't occasionally nervous. "It's like taking off your clothes in front of someone," explains Amen, who's the author of *Sex on the Brain* and other books. "People worry whether I'll like what I see."

MRIs have revealed other differences between men's and women's brains which helps explain why couples often butt heads over certain issues, in bed and out of it. For one, scans show that women's brains contain 11 percent more neurons in the language region than men's do. No wonder, then, that women use an average of 20,000 words per day and men use a mere 7,000—and that women crave more communication while men are content to just sit there and watch ESPN in the evenings. MRI scans also show that the hippocampus, the main hub for memory formation, is larger in women, which could account for their amazing (or, men might say, annoying) ability to recount in vivid detail something their mates did three days, three months, or even thirty years earlier.

So what's all that extra real estate in men's minds devoted to? You guessed it: A significant portion is programmed for sex, which occupies two and a half times the space in men's brains than women's. As a result, men not only think about sex more often, they also read sex into situations where none may exist. Researchers scanned the brains of men and women while they watched a silent video of a couple engaged in a conversation. Brain scans of men showed that the sexual regions of their brains were lit up, while the same areas of women's brains remained dormant. Men were assuming the conversation between the man and woman was a prelude to sex—that, if they were to fast-forward the video, the couple would soon strip down and swing from the chandeliers. Women, on the other hand, assumed that the conversation in the video was just that: a conversation. Nothing more.

Go Ahead, Push My Button

Long before MRI machines gave us a peek at the brain on sex, scientists were poking around in our noggins via even more direct means—by implanting electrodes in our gray matter and turning on the juice. As early as the 1960s, these procedures helped treat various neurological disorders from epilepsy to Parkinson's. The sexual side effects were purely accidental—not that the patients seemed to mind. One beneficiary, referred to as B-7, who was given a control panel with buttons he could press for a jolt, reported that the button connected to the septal area of the brain deep near its core "made him feel as if he were building up to a sexual orgasm," his doctor Robert Heath wrote in his notes. Unfortunately, the stimulation wasn't quite enough to send B-7 overboard, which led to frantic button-pushing and tons of frustration.

The great divide between men and women doesn't end there. Studies suggest that when women are depressed or stressed, they become less interested in sex. Men in these emotional downturns, however, become even *more* interested in sex in an attempt to improve their mood. While women might incredulously think *How can he be copping a feel the very day he's laid off from work?*, for men, sex is the ultimate cure-all. They reach for sex like they'd reach for a beer.

How to Prep Your Brain for Better Sex

Keep the blood pumping. Your brain, like your genitals, thrives on healthy blood flow. As a result, it's best to avoid things that stem the flow of blood to your head, such as caffeine, nicotine, and lack of sleep. People who regularly sleep less than seven hours a night showed lower levels of brain activity than those who slept more. Get plenty of shut-eye, then, and you'll be much more inspired to get those bedsprings singing.

Put your brain on a healthy diet. Certain foods have also been shown to improve brain function, including lean protein, complex carbohydrates, and those rich in omega-3 fatty acids such as tuna, salmon, walnuts, olive oil, and canola oil. Low levels of omega-3 fatty acids have been linked to depression, ADD, dementia, and even suicide, all of which can clearly put a major crimp in the carnal activities.

Give your brain some exercise. In brain terms, "exercise" means taking on new challenges. Try keeping your wits sharp with a weekly crossword puzzle or bridge game. The better conditioned your brain, the steamier sex can get once it starts.

What Your Brain and Car Have in Common

Understanding the brain on sex isn't all about MRI scans. They might give us the lay of the land, but that's like looking at a map of Disney World instead of taking a spin on all the rides. So, now that you've been introduced to how the brain works when it's whipped into a frenzy, it's time to get to know what your brain's actually thinking. Because whether you realize it or not, you *are* thinking plenty.

Try tuning in to your thoughts during your next bedroom romp, and it may sound a lot like a sportscaster delivering plays on the field—fast, furious, and flying in a million directions at once. Maybe, for example, you're thinking *Hey, this feels great!*, which instantly flip-flops to *Wait, are we ready to take this step?* Or maybe you're thinking *Dang, we don't have a condom so we should stop*, which quickly caves into *Well, maybe having sex without one is okay just this once.* On sex, your brain doesn't just act like any old sportscaster. It acts like a sportscaster with a split personality. One second, our brains are ranting that we should throw caution to the wind. The next, they're preaching we should play it safe. Caught in the crosshairs of these conflicting emotions, no wonder we sometimes have trouble letting loose—or, conversely, we overshoot the mark, doing and saying things we regret later. This mental patter may appear to lack all rhyme and reason. And yet, one researcher named Erick Janssen at the Kinsey Institute has come up with an elegant explanation based on a model we can all understand: driving a car.

Whether you're the proud owner of a Prius or a gas-guzzling SUV, pretty much all cars come with an accelerator and brakes. Our brains on sex, says Janssen, are wired in a similar manner. There's a nerve pathway for excitability (the accelerator) and a pathway for inhibition (the brakes). In any given "car" (or individual), each pedal may be easier or harder to press. People with strong accelerators and strong brakes, for example, will be easy to excite sexually, and yet might just as quickly stifle that response—think hot 'n' heavy make-out session followed by a "We really shouldn't be doing this; maybe we should call it a night" type. People with weak accelerators and weak brakes, on the other hand, might be tough to get going, but once they're rolling, won't stop unless the ceiling collapses on top of them—think stuffy librarian type who turns into a hellcat in bed. Still others might be cursed with weak accelerators and strong brakes, which means they'll likely stall before they make it out of the starting gates, going on dates but never closing the deal. Meanwhile, someone with a strong accelerator and weak brakes will hurtle headlong into just about anyone's bed and do just about anything, regardless of the consequences.

Curious to road test his car-pedal model on people, Janssen developed a questionnaire that would measure the strength of people's excitability and inhibition. The questionnaire asks respondents to agree or disagree on a scale from one to five with forty-five statements such as the following:

- When a sexually attractive stranger looks me in the eye, I become aroused.

- When I'm taking a shower or a bath, I easily become sexually aroused.

- Sometimes I become sexually aroused just by lying in the sun.

- If I am distracted by hearing music, the television, or conversation, I am unlikely to stay sexually aroused.

- If I am masturbating on my own and I realize someone is likely to come into the room at any moment, I will lose my erection.

- If there is a risk of unwanted pregnancy, I am unlikely to get sexually aroused.

As you've probably guessed, the first three questions test the strength of your accelerator (excitability), the last three test the brake (inhibition). After administering the test to over four hundred men, Janssen moved on to testing whether their reproductive systems were in agreement. He ushered them into a quiet, low-lit room with a comfy recliner where they could kick back, relax, and watch a variety of erotic film clips. Meanwhile, Janssen attached an aptly named "RigiScan" to the men's genitals to measure blood flow down below. Results showed that, indeed, men's minds and bodies were largely in alignment. Easily excitable men quickly developed erections when viewing porn. And yet, if they were also highly inhibited, they quickly lost altitude when viewing films depicting dangerous or brutal sexual scenarios such as rape. Meanwhile, men with low inhibition maintained their erections like SCUD missiles while watching clips depicting all kinds of sex—violent, dangerous, distasteful, or otherwise.

Getting turned on *watching* sexual violence is different from actually *doing* it, although with further questioning, Janssen's study did find that men with low inhibition take more sexual risks in real life, such as intercourse without condoms and sex with strangers. Could Janssen's questionnaire be a handy tool for people looking for Mr. (or Mrs.) Right? "I could see this being beneficial to a matchmaking site like eHarmony," he says. "And yet, that doesn't mean that people who score low for sexual inhibition will necessarily cheat, have unsafe sex, or rape. They might have a higher propensity to do so, but that doesn't mean they will. So if you say 'I'm out of here' because of someone's score, you might be making a big mistake. Still, that doesn't mean this couldn't be educational."

One thing Janssen's study doesn't answer about sexual risk-taking is why, once sex enters the picture, does the sense of reason that rules the rest of our lives bail when we need it most? Another researcher named Dan Ariely knows the answer . . . and it's not pretty.

Why Sex Makes Us Stupid

Would you have unprotected sex with a stranger? Or force sex on someone who's said "no"? Or have sex with a horse? Chances are, your answer to the above questions would be no, no, and hell, no. And yet, no matter how certain you are about your responses, Dan Ariely says he knows how to get your resolution wavering: by asking you those same questions once you're *already* aroused. In a riled up state, he argues, people are open to all kinds of sexual activities they'd never contemplate otherwise. Plus, Ariely's got proof of how quickly our standards start crumbling, based on an experiment involving thirty-five male college students and a bunch of Saran-Wrapped iBooks.

To conduct this unique experiment, Ariely kicked things off by handing out iBooks (sans Saran Wrap) to his volunteers, who were asked to find a time when they'd be alone in their dorm rooms to open the laptop and take a questionnaire that had been programmed to pop up on screen. On a scale from one to a hundred, students were asked how much they agreed with nineteen statements depicting a variety of disturbing scenarios. Here's a sampling:

Can you imagine being attracted to a twelve-year-old girl?

Can you imagine having sex with a sixty-year-old woman?

Could it be fun to have sex with someone who was extremely fat?

Can you imagine getting sexually excited by contact with an animal?

Would you keep trying to have sex after your date says "no"?

As you might have guessed, most of the undergrads vehemently disagreed with the above statements. Upon returning the iBook, however, volunteers were handed another iBook—this one Saran-Wrapped—and asked to take it home, carve out some alone time, and turn it on. This time, the men watched as porn popped up on screen, to which they were instructed to masturbate but not ejaculate (the Saran Wrap was there just in case they went overboard). Then, men were yet again asked to answer the same questionnaire they took before.

During the initial rounds of this study with the non-Saran-Wrapped set of iBooks, these men had expressed little interest in having sex with twelve-year-old girls, sixty-year-old women, fat people, farm animals, and the other prospects. And yet when they were asked to consider these same activities a second time—and in an aroused state—their answers changed. Their willingness to have unprotected sex, for example, rose by 25 percent. Their openness to having sex with animals doubled. Their willingness to engage in immoral activities like rape *more* than doubled. Across the board, just about everything they once deemed immoral, dangerous, or downright disgusting seemed kind of hot.

If one were to meet Ariely's study subjects at a dinner party

How to Avoid Dumb Mistakes During Sex

Given sexual arousal is such a slippery slope, what can we do to avoid sliding our way toward some regrettable snafus? The solution is to take a few precautions.

Keep condoms handy. People might *say* they'd never have sex without one, but clearly, that resolve weakens once clothes are flying and passions flaring. So no matter how presumptuous it looks, keep condoms well within reach.

Steer clear of temptation. If you're on a date and are certain you don't want to have sex, stick to a kiss on the cheek at your date's doorstep and split. You might think you know just how far you'll go before you put on the brakes, but sexual arousal has a way of blurring those boundaries. So it's best to draw the line before our bodies get turned on, and our minds turn to mush.

Don't judge others. Suppose a friend or lover admits they've engaged in sexual behavior that you find dangerous (sex without condoms) or offensive (sex with cousins, animals, or otherwise). While your first reaction might be to say "How awful—I'd never do that," don't be so sure. That might be your reaction in a non-aroused, rational state. If you were in their shoes and in the heat of the moment, though, it might surprise you what you'd do.

or on a date, they would come across as polite, upstanding chaps who respect women, use condoms, and would never even think of fornicating with a goat. And yet, sexual arousal had a way of temporarily weakening their resolve. Ariely, who's the author of *Predictably Irrational*, a book that explores just how illogical people can be, puts it this way: "The old Robin Williams joke might be true: God gave men a penis and a brain, and only enough blood to run one at a time."

What Bonobos Reveal About How Women's Minds Work

One good thing about male sexual circuitry is that it's amazingly straightforward. Body and mind are perfectly aligned. If the brain sees something sexy, the below-the-belt hardware agrees and inflates. If the brain is turned off, the hardware goes soft. Simple. Women, however, are wired differently. Consider, for example, women's reaction to Bonobo porn.

At the Center for Addiction and Mental Health in Toronto, Meredith Chivers has been showing female study subjects videos of men and women and two women having sex. She has also been showing them videos of Bonobos having sex. "One thing that I think some women were taken aback by was how humanlike Bonobo sex can be," Chivers recalls. "In the film I used, there is a sequence where the Bonobos are mating missionary-style, and the female gives a huge, toothy smile. More than one participant chuckled knowingly."

To measure women's physiological responses to their viewing material, Chivers had women insert a vaginal photoplethysmograph, a tamponlike device that measures lubrication levels. Surprisingly, these readings showed that *all* film clips—guy on girl, girl on girl, Bonobo on Bonobo—sparked lubrication down below. Women's genitals got turned on by everything. Their minds, though, were another matter. When Chivers asked her study subjects what they thought of the videos they had viewed, the women confidently declared that they found certain scenes arousing, others less so, and still others (like those Bonobos) interesting, but definitely not arousing. So then why were their genitals getting riled up by all of the above? Chivers theorizes that the vagina's nondiscriminating tastes are a protective mechanism. By lubricating to all sexual scenarios, the vagina is prepared for sex even when a woman might not even want it, which can be an asset since it cuts down on friction and could keep her reproductive tract from tearing or incurring injuries.

"After hearing about my research, one woman wrote to express her gratitude: She had been perplexed by her sexual response to women and was questioning her sexual orientation, since she was heterosexual," Chivers recalls. "She was happy to learn that, for women, getting turned on by other women is probably not uncommon and that her sexual response may not have much bearing on her sexual orientation."

Chivers's work may shed some light on one small part of women's sexual circuitry, but a bigger question remains: Why don't women seem to want sex as much as men?

A New View of the "I Have a Headache" Excuse

For Danielle, a day care supervisor in Hamden, Connecticut, getting dressed in the morning for work can be a challenge. That's because if her husband spots her naked, he begs her to stay naked—the sight of Danielle stepping out of the shower is all it takes to get his sexual motor running. For the most part, Danielle is flattered that, even after eight years of marriage, her husband can't keep his hands off her. Still, this does create problems, and not just in terms of getting to work on time.

"I always enjoy sex once it gets going," Danielle says. And yet, rarely is she struck with sudden, spontaneous urges to grab her husband herself. This has him worried. Back in the first few years of their relationship, Danielle used to initiate sex. Was her lack of initiative now a sign her attraction levels were waning? Danielle swears that's not the case. She's wondered if she has a libido problem, and has considered getting her hormone levels checked. She's asked her married friends how often they made the moves on their husbands, and was somewhat relieved to find that she had plenty of company.

"Please," one friend said. "Even if my husband looked like George Clooney, I don't think I'd be attacking him every time he stepped out of the shower. Women just aren't like that." Since Danielle's lack of initiative was far from uncommon, did she really have a problem, or was it possible women just aren't designed to spring into action the way men are?

For men, sex is simple: They see. They want. They make a play for it. For a long time, this model was thought to be the way all people ended up having sex. Back in the 1960s, sex researchers William Masters and Virginia Johnson developed a model that encompassed this mental process. First, there's a stage called desire (a spontaneous, overwhelming urge to reach out and touch someone), followed by arousal (the body and mind start heating up), culminating in sex and all the satisfaction that ensues. This pretty much describes what unfolds in men's minds to a tee.

Women's minds may occasionally adhere to the same model, but many, like Danielle, stall in the starting gates. They wait and wait for that lightning bolt of desire to strike, but it never

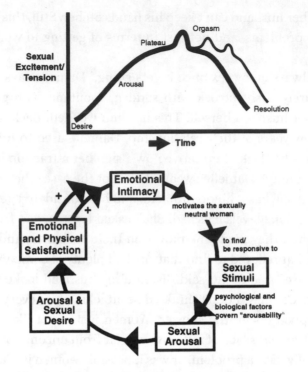

How women's minds work. In the 1960s, sex researchers Masters and Johnson theorized that sexual arousal builds in a linear fashion, from desire to arousal to orgasm (shown top). Men may adhere to this model, but in 2001, Rosemary Basson argued that women's sexual arousal tends to follow a circular pattern, and need not begin with feelings of sexual desire (Basson's model shown bottom).

From Basson, Rosemary (2001). "Female sexual response: The role of drugs in the management of sexual dysfunction." *Obstetrics & Gynecology* 98 (2): 350–53. Reprinted with permission.

hits. Currently, the *Diagnostic and Statistical Manual of Mental Disorders (DSM IV)* deems that women like Danielle suffer from Hypoactive Sexual Desire Disorder, which is estimated to affect one in five women nationwide. Drug companies have spent millions trying to create a pill that would solve this problem. And yet Rosemary Basson, a physician at the Center for Sexual Medicine at Vancouver, argues that many of these women don't have a problem. The problem is that current definitions of sexual arousal don't take the inner workings of women's minds into account.

"As a family doctor, women would speak to me of their sexual response," she says. She found that many women initiated sex even when they felt *no* desire at all. Instead, they initiated sex out of a wish for intimacy, or to make their partners happy. Then, once the clothes were off, the physical stimulation of sex could trigger arousal and desire, which could then further fan a woman's wish for intimacy, triggering *more* arousal and desire, perpetuating a feedback loop. Women's sexual arousal, rather than occurring in a linear fashion, was more circular, with one stage leading to another. The key, then, isn't to "fix" women's arousal, but to understand that men and women can experience a range of motivations for having sex—and that for women, being "in the mood" might not always do the trick. Women, rather than *wait* for the mood to strike, can *make* the mood strike merely by getting sex rolling. Once the body's warmed up, the mind will follow.

Next, let's head even deeper into the mind's dark corridors and explore a few secrets it doesn't give up so easily. An MRI can't detect them. And chances are, you'd be mortified to share them with your partner. What am I talking about? Your sexual fantasies, of course. In our next chapter, we'll lift the lid on this topic and see what lies within.

Whipped Cream, High Heels, and a Dog (and You Thought *Your* Fantasies Were Weird!)

John and Jane were in bed together, indulging in some lazy Sunday afternoon lovemaking. Their minds, however, were light years away from the action unfolding in front of them. John was fantasizing about having a threesome with Jane and a friend of hers he'd recently met. Jane had mentally jetted off to indulge in some equally illicit visions of a lunch date with her ex-boyfriend, who was looking deep into her eyes, saying he'd missed her, his hand on her thigh under the tablecloth, slowly inching upward . . .

"What are you thinking?" John asked, interrupting Jane's reverie.

"Nothing," Jane said. "What are you thinking?"

"Nothing," John said. They both knew this was hogwash. But then again, could either of them handle the truth?

Both John and Jane found fantasizing during sex an incredible turn-on. And yet, they also felt kind of guilty about it. Did it mean their real-life sex life wasn't up to snuff? John was

curious to hear about Jane's sexual fantasies, and Jane his.
And yet, swapping these thoughts was a frightening prospect.
If John revealed he thought about a threesome with one of her
friends, wouldn't Jane flip? If Jane mentioned she was still
mooning over her ex, would John suspect she was cheating?
Deep down, did they wish their fantasies would come true?
Neither of them knew the answers, which was all the more rea-
son to keep their fantasies under wraps—a dirty secret they'd
rather die than reveal to each other.

FANTASIES ARE LIKE that closet in our homes where we stash things we hold dear but would be embarrassed to reveal to others. Even our partners—the very people who know and love everything about us, from our insanely ticklish kneecaps to our late-night Häagen Dazs habit—are rarely privy to the visions that unfold in our heads during sex. Airing your secret desires can be a dangerous business. What if your partner freaks when you confess you've been mooning over your yoga instructor? Or what if your fantasies involve stranger stuff, from post-dinner-party orgies to prison guards? As titillating as these reveries can be, it's hard not to see fantasies as trouble. Let's crack the door, see what's inside, and shed some light on what it all means.

A Tour Through the Land of Make-Believe

Back in the 1970s, University of Minnesota psychologist Eric Klinger handed out pagers to men and women and asked them to jot down what they were thinking every time it went off. Talk about a nuisance—what if you're speeding down a freeway? Or, worse yet, having sex?—but Klinger's study subjects gamely gave it a go. After collecting his data, he discovered something interesting: that people spend very little of their lives thinking about, well, their real lives. Rather, we daydream nonstop—while sitting in conference rooms, while cooking pork chops, no matter where we are, our minds are elsewhere. On average, between 40 and 50 percent of our waking hours are spent on idle reveries, some as mundane as *Man, I wish I had A-1 Sauce for these pork chops* to wilder what-if scenarios like *Boy I'd love to tell my boss where to stick his stupid mission statement*. A rare 4 percent, called somnambules, spend up to 90 percent of their waking hours in the land of make-believe. Some people's fantasies are so vivid they can count the number of coconuts on the palm trees, others are mere fragments of conversations or hazy images. Even people who claim they don't fantasize much do so vicariously by watching movies, reading books, or participating in fantasy baseball leagues. They're like Rent-a-Fantasies. Sometimes, it's easier to borrow than come up with your own mental material.

While envisioning running the Red Sox or living on a *Gone With the Wind*–style Southern plantation are certainly pleasurable flights of fancy, fantasies about sex also enter the picture, and pretty often. To determine how frequently we dwell on carnal encounters, Jennifer Jones and David Barlow at New York State University in Albany asked a hundred male and female college students to jot down every sexual thought that flitted through their minds for seven days straight. All told, they found that men indulge in 7.2 sexual fantasies per day, women 4.5. To a certain extent, the stereotype is true: Men really do think about sex more than women, although the old maxim that men think about sex every seven seconds is an overstatement.

The difference between men's and women's fantasy lives don't end there. Jones and Barlow's study showed that men's fantasies are sparked more often by their surroundings—i.e., that hot blonde who just breezed by—while women's spring from internal sources, such as memories of things they've already done or made-up scenarios they imagine might be fun. Other studies suggest that men's fantasies are also more graphic, less emotional, and often involve harems of babes at their beck and call. One particularly imaginative male study subject interviewed in the journal *Medical Aspects of Human Sexuality* fancied himself "mayor of a small town filled with nude girls from 20 to 24," where he'd take walks, pick out the best-looking one that day, and indulge to his heart's content. Meanwhile, women dwell on more romantic aspects such as ambience (Fireplace? Bear rug? Check, check) and emotion (longing glances, I love you's), but remain hazy on the graphic details of sex itself.

That doesn't mean that women's fantasies are all romance and rose petals. The first researcher to show that nice girls can concoct some pretty crass tales, of course, was Nancy Friday, who was inspired to write her 1973 bestseller *My Secret Garden* after confessing a fantasy of her own to a lover. In Friday's fantasy, she gets ravished by a stranger in the bleachers at a football game. Sports and sex: What's not to love as far as a guy is concerned? Nonetheless, Friday's lover promptly got out of bed, put on his pants, and fled. Baffled by his reaction and curious whether her musings were all that unusual, Friday placed ads in newspapers asking women to send in their fantasies. What rolled in was much wilder than Friday's football fiasco. Some envisioned getting tied up and gangbanged by fraternities, others imagined being forced to fellate policemen after being stopped for a ticket. One woman imagined a scenario involving Betty Crocker cake batter, Bovril beef extract, and the neighborhood dog.

More recent studies suggest that men's and women's fantasy lives aren't as different as we might think. In 1994, Bing Hsu at the University of California in Los Angeles published the results of a study which presented a list of fifty-five different fantasy scenarios, from mild to wild, to a group of 166 men and women and asked them which ones they had entertained. Surprisingly, men's and women's most popular picks were fairly G-rated. "Touching/kissing sensuously," "being seduced," and even "walking hand in hand" all made it into the top ten. Half of men and three-quarters of women didn't just daydream about getting married, but found these fantasies highly arousing while having sex. One in four men and one in two women also harbored sexual fantasies of being rescued from danger by a lover—talk about romantic. Fantasies involving racier scenarios, though, were also very common among both men and women. Half of men and one-third of women had fantasized about participating in an orgy. One in three women and one in five men had dreamt of a homosexual encounter if they were heterosexual, or a heterosexual encounter if they were homosexual. One in ten women and twice as many men fantasized about having sex with a close relative.

What Cheating in Your Mind Really Means

In eighteen years of marriage, Mr. Franciosi has never cheated on his wife, and claims he never would. And yet, during sex with his spouse, his thoughts constantly turn to a female office assistant at work . . . doing her from behind . . . over the photocopier. "It's classic, I know," Mr. Franciosi confessed to psychotherapist Brett Kahr. Then Mr. Franciosi promptly burst into tears.

Kahr, who's heard people spill more than 22,000 sexual fantasies over the years as part of his International Sexual Fantasy Research Project, says crying is common when people reveal their fantasies. Clearly, Mr. Franciosi was worried: Did his recurrent fantasies about his office assistant mean there was something wrong with his marriage? If Sigmund Freud were around to put in his two cents, he'd say people like Mr. Franciosi are right to be concerned. "A happy person never fantasizes," Freud was fond of saying, "only an unsatisfied one." This is called the "deficiency theory," which states that for whatever's lacking in our lives that we want—more sex, more orgasms, or a partner that could appear in a Victoria's Secret fashion show—we'll conjure up a virtual stand-in. The more conjuring we do, the less satisfying our real-life sex lives must be.

But is this true? On the contrary, Kahr has found that fantasies, even about people other than our partner, can be beneficial to the health of long-term relationships. After all, without fantasies, Mr. Franciosi wouldn't be inspired to have sex with his wife as often, which would probably be more detrimental to his relationship in the long run. As further evidence that frequent fantasizers aren't in trouble, Harold Leitenberg at the University of Vermont compared data about how often people fantasized with other aspects of their relationship. What he found was that frequent fantasizers don't feel sexually deprived in the slightest. On the contrary, they have more sex, more orgasms, enjoy a wider variety of sexual activities, and all in all have more fun in bed than those who don't daydream that often. Fantasy isn't a substitute for reality that's less than ideal; it's a *double* dose of stimulation that makes good sex even better.

Whether people who "mentally cheat" are more likely to cheat in real life is unknown. For women, at least, there seems to be a correlation between the two. In Leitenberg's study, female respondents who claimed they were faithful fantasized about men outside their relationship only 30 percent of the time. Women who had cheated fantasized about other men 55 percent of the time. Does this mean women who fantasize about other men are more likely to have an affair? Not necessarily. Since Leitenberg's study didn't separate what came first—fantasy or affair—it's also possible the affair triggered more thoughts of the affair partner. Men, on the other hand, fantasize about other women 53 percent of the time regardless of whether they're faithful or not, which suggests that they're even more hardwired than women to crave variety in their fantasy lives, regardless of what they do in real life.

Michael Bader, a psychologist in San Francisco and author of *Arousal: The Secret Logic of Sexual Fantasies,* has encountered many men and women in his practice who worry their fantasies might lead to action. To allay their concerns, Bader often tells his patients to consider *other* fantasies they enjoy with complete confidence that they would never follow through. "If you longed to own a Lamborghini, would you sink yourself into thousands of dollars of debt to own one? Probably not," Bader points out. "It's like the story of Odysseus sailing through the seas where he could hear the sirens' song. He tied himself to the mast so he could hear them and experience that longing, but not steer his ship toward certain death. People and their fantasies are similar. We want to experience the novelty of a new lover, but without the risk. You might even argue that fantasies keep relationships together, where otherwise boredom might lead people to stray. Fantasies offer the freedom of variety without hurting the ones we love."

Sometimes we tune in to fantasies so we can tune out some unsavory aspect of sex—not because the sex is bad, but because even in the best of circumstances, strange sounds, funky smells, and answering machine messages from your mother may intrude at some point. Given these distractions are bound to kill the mood, calling in the fantasy reinforcements can serve as a bulwark to keep the negative thoughts at bay. Sexy visions can even ward off pain, a fact that anesthesiologist Peter Staats at Johns Hopkins University discovered by forcing forty college students to plunge their hand into a tank of ice water and keep it there as long as possible. Those who were instructed to think about kissing and flirting with someone could keep their hand in the ice bucket twice as long as those who'd been asked to think about mundane things (such as walking to class) or to think about nothing in particular. The reason steamy visions make us so stalwart, Staats says, is because sexy thoughts and emotions are thought to be processed in the thalamus, a region of the brain also involved in pain response. The thalamus has a hard time doing two things at once, so by homing in on fantasies, we essentially divert the number of brain cells available to scream *Ouch, that hurts*—which is bound to come in handy in bed where back-contorting sexual positions, sore muscles, and general fatigue can creep in at any moment.

We also turn to fantasies to feel better about ourselves. In one study of over a hundred men and women by Michael Becker at Pennsylvania State University in Harrisburg, men tended to fantasize that their penises were larger, women that their breasts were bigger and their butts smaller. Both genders also imagined themselves as more easily aroused and orgasmic than in real life. Fantasies don't just serve to jazz up our surroundings, they can also serve to give ourselves a makeover and a jolt of self-confidence.

In addition to all the benefits fantasies can bring us, there's the sheer fact that those who try to repress their fantasies are fighting a losing battle, since by trying to *not* think about something, you end up thinking about it more than ever. This paradox was illustrated in the "white bear" experiment, in which Daniel Wegner at Trinity University asked volunteers to try to not think about a white bear for five minutes, but to ring a bell if they did. Try as they might to push that bear out of their minds, the bear and bell kept on chiming in. And once the experiment was over and volunteers could let their minds wander freely, the bear reared its furry head even *more* often, which suggests that attempts to repress thoughts will bring them back later in spades.

Oh, Fabio . . .

Women who keep their fantasy fires stoked by reading romance novels may be more inclined to heat up their real-life love lives as well. According to a study by Claire Coles at Emory Medical School, women who read bodice rippers have sex twice as often as those who abstain from this form of entertainment.

Do We Want Our Fantasies to Come True?

Kirk, a hotel manager in Boulder, Colorado, would soon be celebrating his thirtieth birthday. His girlfriend, Karen, asked him if there was something in particular he wanted as a gift.

"How about a threesome?" he joked. Having sex with two women had been a fantasy of his as long as he could remember. It never occurred to him that Karen would consider following through.

Days later, the couple was out at a bar when Karen started flirting with a woman they'd never met. At some point, Karen gave Kirk a knowing glance that suggested that his birthday wish might soon be granted. Suddenly, Kirk got a huge case of cold feet. "It's not that the girl Karen was flirting with wasn't hot—in fact, she was exactly the kind of girl I'd imagine Karen with," he admits. But now that the possibility of a threesome was upon him, all kinds of logistical questions cropped up. Could he satisfy two girls at once? What if Karen liked the other woman more than him?

Karen's efforts at landing a threesome that night didn't pan out. Kirk was simultaneously disappointed, relieved, and unsettled how quickly his fantasy lost its appeal once it became apparent it could become real. "I feel like a wimp," he says. "I could swear I'd wanted it to happen, but apparently, that was not the case."

Some men, of course, might have killed to be in Kirk's shoes. And yet, Bader points out that many men feel exactly like Kirk, and prefer to keep their fantasies just that—fantasies. According to one study, fewer than one in five fantasies are ever acted upon. As Friday once put it, "I think that for every person who has written to me about the joys of performing their sex dreams in reality, there have been three or four who knew in advance that it wouldn't work or who tried it and were disappointed." Why? A lot of it comes down to logistics. "In our minds, our fantasies are carefully crafted to our tastes," explains Bader. "Replicating this mirage in real life would be all but impossible, and all too quickly those asynchronous moments could ruin the mood." As a result, even in situations where people can safely realize a fantasy, it would be wise to weigh how the fantasy would really play out.

Even if we're certain we don't want our fantasies to come true, don't they embody something we want on *some* level? Because if not, then why do we fantasize about certain scenarios at all? Tamara, a musician living in Sacramento, California, has often been troubled by this question. Her songs are all about female empowerment; she's married to a wonderful man who treats her like a queen. "In my fantasies, though, I dream about men who are his polar opposite. They're brutes," she admits. One scenario involves a man who gets her drunk at a bar, drags her home, and forces himself on her. "The fact that I fantasize about this has always bothered me," she says. "Does it mean that deep down, I just want men to be jerks and boss me around?"

Rape fantasies mystify women and scientists alike, who've developed many theories to explain their existence. One thing they're sure of is that most women with rape fantasies don't find the prospect of actual rape arousing in the slightest. In one study by Susan Bond at Manchester Community College published in *The Journal of Sex Research*, 104 women volunteered to participate in a guided imagery exercise where they were led to imagine one of two scenarios: an "erotic" rape scenario and a "real" rape scenario. In the "erotic" scenario, an attractive man is overwhelmed with desire for the woman, who puts up a token resistance but clearly enjoys what's happening. In the "real" scenario, a cruel man violently forces himself on his victim. When asked how they felt about the scenarios, the results were clear. Envisioning "erotic" rape was hot. Envisioning "real" rape was repugnant. In another study of 137 women in the *Archives of Sexual Behavior*, women with

"So What *Do* You Think About During Sex?"

How to Share Your Fantasies with Your Mate

Make a pact. Many couples find talking about their fantasies together a turn on. But it can also be scary or embarrassing, so here's how to do damage control. For starters, promise each other that you won't get mad, laugh, or recoil if your partner reveals a whim that's not your cup of tea. Easier said than done, right? Move on to our next tip.

Start small. When you first start discussing your fantasies, steer clear of open-ended questions like "What are your fantasies?" Instead, opt for safer versions like "What are your fantasies about *us*? What are we doing?" That way, you can avoid blurting out that you fantasize about your partner's boss or having a threesome with your partner's best friend, which might be too much to handle at first. Once you're comfortable discussing fantasies that involve the two of you, you can branch out and try bringing a third (or fourth, or fifth) person into the mix, although it's still best not to name names until you're certain your mate won't mind.

Manage expectations. Agree that just because you're talking about fantasies doesn't mean you're going to follow through (unless you both want to, of course). Discussing your fantasies is a pleasurable end in itself.

rape fantasies were no more likely to have been raped than women who didn't harbor these fantasies, further supporting the idea that these fantasies bore no relation to women's actual experiences.

The reigning explanation why women have rape fantasies is a phenomenon known as "sexual blame avoidance." Women with rape fantasies aren't driven by a self-destructive streak, but by the feeling that they have *too* much control and would rather let someone else take the reins for a while in the one place it's safe to do so: in their minds. "Women with rape fantasies often feel guilty or uncomfortable expressing the full force of their sexuality," says Bader. "Rape fantasies are a simple solution to that problem. Since in her fantasy she's being forced to have sex, the discomfort she feels being an active sexual agent is lifted, so she's free to enjoy herself." Or, as Friday once put it in her 1991 book *Women on Top*, "The most popular guilt-avoiding device was the so-called rape fantasy. Saying that she was 'raped' was the most expedient way of getting past the big 'No' to sex that had been imprinted on her mind since childhood."

Fantasies are reflections of who we are, but not always in the ways we might think. So, don't fret about them so much. And if someone you're sleeping with does pop that question during sex—"What are you thinking?"—maybe you should open up. Fantasies may be musings we'd be mortified to reveal to others, but you might be surprised how much you'll learn about someone you swore you knew so well already.

CHAPTER 8

The Wild World of Kinky Sex

John and Jane were moving their make-out session from the couch to the bedroom when John asked, "Want to try something a little different tonight?"

Jane knew exactly what those words meant—and they made her feel curious, excited, and scared all at once. They'd been dating for three months, and while the sex they were having was great, it was also fairly vanilla. Time to kick things up a notch.

"I'm game," Jane said. "But what should we try?"

John started peeling off Jane's stocking. "How about I use these to tie you up?"

Within minutes, Jane was lying flat on her back on the bed, her wrists tied to the bedposts. And even though Jane knew she could break loose if she wanted to, the mere suggestion that John could have his way with her was enough to get her squirming in anticipation.

John started out by teasing her, caressing her body from head to toe but avoiding her most obvious hot spots. This got Jane so riled up she found herself asking—and, eventually, begging—for more. John was happy to deliver. That night,

Jane discovered that while she preferred having a say in typical date-night duties such as dinner plans, handing over the reins in bed felt oddly freeing: She could turn off her brain, tune in to her body, and really let loose. John also found that he enjoyed taking charge. And seeing Jane beg for sex . . . well, that was downright fantastic.

Afterward, as they lay in each other's arms, the couple pondered what their first foray into kinky sex meant. Clearly, they had found it enjoyable, but why? And now that they had, where could their kinks take them next?

KINKY SEX is a jungle of unknowns. Where do kinks come from, and what do they mean? How common is it for couples to dabble beyond the usual "vanilla" activities, anyway? Researchers estimate that as many as 60 percent of adults harbor fantasies with unconventional themes, and that 14 percent of men and 11 percent of women will follow through with them at some point. Scientists call kinks paraphilias, a combination of the Greek works for "around" and "love." It's an apt expression, since kinks *do* seem like a pretty roundabout way to love just about anything. Why, when we could kiss someone on the lips, would we stoop and lick some smelly old shoe? Why would anyone choose pain over the straightforward payoff of pleasure?

Kinks are riddled with contradictions, but scientists who've examined them say they do have their own strange logic. Whether you're interested in experimenting, are a kink veteran who's curious what science has to say about your proclivities, or are just here to see just how wild and crazy sex can get, you've come to the right place.

That's Sick! Or Is It?

In the mid-1800s, Dr. Richard von Krafft-Ebing, an Austro-German psychiatrist, began seeing patients with a variety of baffling afflictions.

Case 111. Z. began to masturbate at the age of twelve. From that time he could not see a woman's handkerchief without having orgasm and ejaculation . . . but he chose only such handkerchiefs as had black and white borders or violet stripes running through them.

Case 48. A married man presented himself with numerous scars of cuts on his arms. He told their origin as follows: When he wished to approach his wife, who was young and somewhat "nervous," he first had to make a cut in his arm. Then she would suck the wound and during the act become violently excited sexually.

Case 123. B., thirty years of age . . . he incessantly bought roses; kissing them would produce erection. He took them to bed with him.

Krafft-Ebing was intrigued. Hoping his case studies could serve as a useful reference for other doctors, he began gathering them into a book. Wary that the public would also be tempted to peek in its pages and have a laugh at his patients' expense, Krafft-Ebing did his best to discourage lay readers by writing the juiciest portions in Latin. It didn't help. Published in 1886, *Psychopathia Sexualis* became an instant hit. Krafft-Ebing had coined new terms to describe what he saw in his practice:

Agalmatophilia: attraction to statues or mannequins

Autagonistophilia: arousal from being on stage, camera, or a reality show

Body inflation fans: people who get aroused at the idea of their body or certain body parts inflating to balloon-like proportions

Chremastistophilia: arousal from being robbed

Crush freaks: people who become aroused watching bugs and other small animals get crushed underfoot, which has spawned "animal snuff films"

Formicophilia: attraction to small animals or insects crawling on parts of the body

Furverts: people who get aroused by furry animal costumes

Gerontophilia: attraction to significantly older partners

Giantessophilia: arousal from the idea of being at the mercy of a giant

Hybristophilia: attraction to criminals

Kleptophilia: arousal from stealing

Lactaphilia: arousal from breast milk

Looners: people who become aroused inflating or popping balloons

Menophilia: arousal from menstruation

Mucophilia: arousal from human mucus

Mysophilia: attraction to dirty or decaying materials

Nasophilia: arousal from noses

Olfactophilia: arousal from smells or odors

Omorashi: arousal from having a full bladder or witnessing a partner with one

Ponyplay: arousal from dressing up and acting like a horse

Scatophilia: arousal from involving feces

Somnophilia: arousal from sleeping or unconscious people

Sploshers: people who get aroused sitting on pies, wallowing in spaghetti, and otherwise creating a mess

Symphorophilia: arousal from disasters

Tamakeri: arousal from being kicked in the groin

Telephonicophilia: arousal from making obscene phone calls to strangers

Trichophilia: arousal from hair

Vampirism: arousal from drinking blood

Vomerophilia: attraction to vomit

Voraphilia: arousal to the idea of being eaten or swallowed alive

Wakamezake: arousal by drinking alcohol from a woman's body

Fetishism. Sadism. Masochism. Nymphomania. Necrophilia. Pedophilia. Kinks swept through the public consciousness.

Today, scientists estimate there are more than fifty kinds of kinks total. Some are culturally based. In Great Britain in the wake of World War II, hundreds of people developed a fetish for wearing gas masks. After the 1950s, when balloons became popular party favors, "looners" appeared, claiming they got off on inflating and popping them. There are kinks based on certain sci-fi novels such as *Chronicles of Gor*, and on religions ("Christian kink," for example, operates on the premise that men should be heads of the household). Meanwhile, in Japan, the niche pursuit of "nose torture" is booming. Still other kinks have become less popular over the years, such as braid cutting, most likely due to changing hairstyles.

By bringing kink out of the closet, Krafft-Ebing didn't merely turn it into a curiosity. He also turned what was long considered a moral problem into a medical one. Before Krafft-Ebing's time, people with atypical sexual tastes were often denounced as sinners and stuck in jail. On the contrary, Krafft-Ebing argued, these people weren't evil, they were just sick and in need of a cure. Which might seem like *some* improvement, except that Krafft-Ebing's definition of "kinky" included just about every sexual activity under the sun. Homosexuality? Masturbation? Both mental illnesses in his book. Not surprisingly, his treatments weren't all that effective. Krafft-Ebing's cure for homosexuality was marriage. For masturbation, it was electroshock, or metal-spiked penis rings that would make erections extremely painful (and could be hooked up to an electric bell as an added deterrent), and leeches on the genitals. If that didn't work, castration was always an option.

While homosexuality and masturbation are no longer considered mental illnesses, attitudes didn't change overnight. The medical establishment saw masturbation as a malady up until the 1940s, when Alfred Kinsey posited that on the contrary, a little self-love was actually good for your health. Homosexuality was deemed a mental illness up until 1973, when the American Psychiatric Association finally removed it from the *Diagnostic and Statistical Manual of Mental Disorders (DSM)*. This deletion was a major milestone for gays, since it meant they could apply for high-security jobs or child custody without being branded psychologically unfit. Which is certainly a step in the right direction, although other groups on the *DSM*'s hit list haven't been so lucky.

Currently, the *DSM* still includes sexual sadism, sexual masochism, fetishism, and transvestic fetishism (cross-dressing) among its list of mental illnesses, which means people who engage in these activities can—and do—suffer some serious consequences if they're exposed. According to a 2008 survey of 3,000 people in the BDSM-fetish and cross-dressing communities by Susan Wright, founder of the National Coalition for Sexual Freedom, 20 percent of respondents had been fired or denied work and 6 percent had lost custody of a child as a result of their sexual tastes, which are often outed by vengeful ex-spouses or coworkers. Occasionally, kinky people have run-ins with the law. In 2000, Stefany Reed, a thirty-eight-year-old businesswoman in Attleboro, Massachusetts, attending a private SM party, was accused by police of assault and battery with a dangerous weapon—a wooden spoon.

As further proof that most kinky people are no more psychologically unstable than the rest of us, Patricia Cross at the University of Ottawa posted a call for study subjects on SM-themed Internet newsgroups such as alt.personals .spanking and alt.sex.bondage. Ninety-seven men and women responded and participated in her study, which involved taking a battery of thirty tests measuring psychological health, including the Rosenberg Self-Esteem Scale, the Symptom Checklist-90 (which provides measures of anxiety, hostility, and psychoticism), and the Feminist Attitudes Scale (to measure specifically whether men who identified as sadists were closet misogynists). To serve as a comparison, Cross also recruited "normal" volunteers from mainstream dating sites to take the same tests. After comparing their results, Cross found that kinky people were as psychologically healthy as her "normal" sample—and often healthier. For example, Cross found that men and women in her SM group considered themselves feminists and saw women as equals to a greater degree than those in her regular control group.

Kink: The Extreme Sports of Sex

Hannah has run three marathons. On most weekends, you'll find her racking up more mileage running through the streets and along the bike paths of Portland, Maine. A personal trainer by trade, she's a staunch believer in the "no pain, no gain" mantra when it comes to sports. It took Hank, however, to introduce her to how this principle could apply in bed.

Hank and Hannah had been dating for two months when he informed her that he was into SM and "topping" women. He had even taken classes. Intrigued, Hannah proposed he try topping her one night, at which point Hank procured a suitcase from his closet containing ropes, paddles, and riding crops. Hank explained that if things got too intense, she could utter a "safe word"—a word of Hannah's choosing that would stop their scene in an instant. "So what do you want your safe word to be?" Hank asked.

Hannah thought for a moment. "Chihuahua."

"Chihuahua it is," Hank said. "Now, bend over the bed."

At first, Hannah couldn't help giggling. This felt silly, not sexy. The first few smacks she received on her backside were light, almost pleasant. Then, they got harder. Hannah considered saying "Chihuahua," but a voice inside her head stopped her. *This is nothing,* the voice said. *You can handle it.* Once Hank and Hannah started having sex, the blows on her butt became even more intense. Hannah, however, found that the pain wasn't all that unpleasant. In fact, she liked it, a lot. It was like pushing through that twenty-sixth mile in a marathon. Even though she knew she was "on bottom," she felt powerful, unstoppable. To her surprise, it was a sexual high.

Hannah's story is a testament to what is perhaps the most puzzling aspect of kinky sex: How can pain be pleasurable?

Part of the answer may be stashed in a basement laboratory at Rutgers University, in an instrument known as the Ugo Basile Analgesia Meter. Its sole purpose is to induce pain. Subjects place their finger on the tiny platform, then wait as a steel point slowly presses down on their finger pad—first lightly, then with heavier pressure until the subject cries uncle. A variety of volunteers have subjected themselves to this mild form of torture while, with their other hand, they stimulated themselves sexually. Why? Because the masterminds behind this experiment, Barry Komisaruk and Beverly Whipple, were measuring whether sexual arousal increases our pain thresholds. In the previous chapter, you might remember that sexual fantasies can also curb our perceptions of pain, but fantasies don't hold a candle to the pain-dampening effects of physical arousal. In women, vaginal stimulation increases pain tolerance by approximately 50 percent. Orgasm increases pain tolerance by over 100 percent. Strangely, these changes are not accompanied by a dip in sensitivity to non-painful stimuli, which meant that the effects of sexual arousal and orgasm were truly analgesic rather than distracting.

Scientists haven't only proved that sexual pleasure can reduce pain, they've even pinpointed the chemical that could be producing this effect: oxytocin. Released into the bloodstream during sex, oxytocin dulls our sensitivity to pain much like a runner's adrenaline high helps him sally onward in spite of discomforts. Kinky scenarios that might *look* painful to outside observers actually aren't from the perspective of the person getting pierced, paddled, or whipped. Ask a kink veteran why pain can be pleasurable, and he might genuinely reply with *What pain?* Or, perhaps she'd cite Hannah's mantra: No pain, no gain. Fine, so kinky sex might be a little uncomfortable or scary, but that's half the fun. It's like completing an Ironman, or skydiving. Pushing your limits is a rush.

Too Kinky for Their Own Good?

While most kinky people stay well within the bounds of the safe, sane, and consensual credo, there are a few desperados out there whose activities push the envelope. These activities, known as "edgeplay," aren't conventionally condoned by SM communities, and it's not hard to figure out why. They include things like breathplay (choking), bloodplay (anything that draws blood through the use of knives, biting, or otherwise), and even gunplay (the use of a gun, fake or real, empty or even loaded). Edgeplay also includes forms of extreme body mutilation, such as voluntary castration, clitorectomies, and even limb amputation, a paraphilia known as apotemnophilia.

While most people in the SM community would never dream of dabbling in anything this dangerous, fans of edgeplay argue that with training and by taking some necessary precautions, these activities can remain fairly safe—and that the rush is worth the risk. What's considered edgeplay also changes over the years. In the mid-1990s, "ageplay" (where couples assume an adult/child sexual relationship) and scat (arousal by feces) were considered too edgy to merit a panel at the Living in Leather convention. In 2000, however, both activities became part of Living in Leather's usual programming.

Hannah's love of extreme sports and extreme sex isn't just a coincidence. Her story also illustrates that certain people are particularly drawn to kinky sex. SM fans tend to score high in a personality trait called "sensation seeking," a measure of one's need for new and varied experiences. In a pilot study, Richard Sprott at the Community-Academic Consortium for Research on Alternative Sexualities (CARAS) asked seventy members of the SM community to complete the Sensation Seeking Scale questionnaire, which asks subjects to agree or disagree with statements like "I'll try anything once" and "I like to have new and exciting experiences and sensations even if they are a little frightening." While the average score for men and women hangs in the high teens and low twenties, scores for SM scensters were significantly higher, in the mid to high twenties— right up there with firefighters, mountain climbers, and other risky professions. Sensation seeking is also considered to be a highly heritable trait, says Sprott, adding that nearly 60 percent of these thrill-seeking impulses are based on genetics. In some people, these genes will express themselves in a trek to the top of Mount Kilimanjaro. In others, these genes will express themselves in a desire to push their boundaries in bed.

The Mysterious Link Between Kinks and STDs

James Giannini, an addiction psychiatrist living in Georgia, has a preoccupation with feet. "I see them everywhere," he confesses. Just the other day, he saw a couple sitting in a park where the woman was rubbing her bare feet against the back of her boyfriend's jeans. He saw another couple where the woman was running one foot up her boyfriend's leg. On TV, he recently saw a bourbon commercial intoning *Never put anything in bourbon . . . well, except maybe one thing.* On-screen, a woman's big toe was dipped in the glass.

Is Giannini a foot fetishist? "You'd have to date me for a while before I'd even consider answering that question," he jokes. And yet, this question is one Giannini fields all too often, since in 1998 he published a paper putting forward a unique theory about where this fetish comes from.

Published in *Psychological Reports,* the study is titled "Sexualization of the Female Foot as a Response to Sexually Transmitted Epidemics." Giannini, who is also an art historian, had noticed in his research that during the gonorrhea epidemic of the thirteenth century, bare feet began popping up as a sexual focal point in paintings and troubadour poetry, only to vanish as soon as the epidemic was over. During an outbreak of syphilis in the sixteenth century, the foot reappeared in art (certain painters specialized in depicting the foot) and fashion (this is when "toe cleavage" became all the rage). During the nineteenth century, another outbreak of syphilis was accompanied by a surge in foot fetishism in neo-Mannerist, pre-Raphaelite, and Romantic paintings, which died down soon after the introduction of an effective treatment for syphilis in 1909. During periods when STDs weren't of epidemic proportions, the erotic focus in art and literature shifted to other areas of the body, including breasts, buttocks, and thighs.

That got Giannini thinking: Did foot fetishism rise in the wake of STD epidemics because it served as a safe-sex alternative that could keep practitioners disease-free? To find out if his hunch held water, he decided to take a closer look at the latest epidemic: AIDS. He and a team of researchers poured through the pages of the eight top-circulating porn magazines—including *Playboy, Penthouse,* and *High Society*—from a period spanning from 1965 to 1994. Page by page, issue by issue, they tallied each appearance of a bared female foot in a sexually suggestive context then plotted the results on a timeline. From 1965 to 1994, the number of images depicting feet as a turn-on quadrupled.

In Giannini's opinion, this rise in foot admiration is no accident. It's the direct result of our collective subconscious thinking *This is not a good time to be exchanging bodily fluids—let's develop a foot fetish instead.* Many academics find Giannini's theory a bit far-fetched, and Giannini is quick to say that his study doesn't contain hard proof. "Still, the evidence I've found is strong," he says. "Penicillin was prescribed on less evidence." Given the AIDS crisis has subsided somewhat, perhaps additional proof of Giannini's theory isn't too far off. "Kids today are growing up without much fear of AIDS," he points out. So maybe by the time they reach adulthood, foot fetishism will again be on the outs.

Do We Learn to be Kinky or Are Some People Just Born That Way?

Back in the mid-1800s, a boy named Havelock Ellis was being pushed around the park in a baby carriage when the nurse doing the perambulating stopped in her tracks. At this point, Ellis recounts in his autobiography, *My Life*, he "heard a mysterious sound as if a stream of water descending to the earth." Ellis's nurse was taking a bathroom break—a common occurrence back then because of the lack of public restrooms (women often skipped the underwear so they could relieve themselves when necessary). However par for the course the nurse's call to nature appeared to nearby onlookers, it made quite an impression on young Ellis. Ellis grew up to become a prominent sexologist, and a remarkably tolerant one at that. Everything from sex with goats to men dressing in ball gowns was sexually healthy in his opinion. Maybe that's because he had his own fascination: urolagnia. Ellis loved watching women pee.

Ellis's kink might seem unusual, but the way he acquired it is commonplace. Ever convinced a four-year-old that the Easter Bunny is real? Or that eating bread crusts will put hair on his chest? Then you're already well aware of the fact that kids are highly impressionable. This process, which is known as "imprinting," has long been observed in animals. Newly hatched ducklings, for example, will imprint onto any object that crosses their path—mother duck, human, or even a roller skate—and waddle after it. A related phenomenon known as "sexual imprinting" helps determine whom we find attractive; in chapter 2 we explored how it prompts us to pursue people who look like our parents. But that's not where the effects of sexual imprinting end. It can also affect our attraction to certain sexual activities. For some, a memorable childhood game of cowboys and Indians might lead to a love of bondage. For others, being spanked as a toddler might morph into a penchant for corporal punishment. These experiences might not seem sexual when they initially happen; at first they might merely seem interesting, or embarrassing, or even traumatic. For any of an assortment of reasons, it sticks.

Not all kinks are caused by one pivotal, life-altering moment. More often, kinks form gradually, creating what psychoanalysts call a "lovemap." This term, coined by John Money at Johns Hopkins University in the 1980s, is pretty much what it sounds like. It's a map delineating how, and with whom, we prefer to pursue sexual pleasure. Lovemaps are a great way to trace how conventional sexual tastes turn kinky. In essence, when we hop into bed, we're all trying to get from point A (our humdrum, everyday existence) to point B (sweat-soaked, sheet-ripping orgasmic finale). People with conventional lovemaps tend to take the straightforward path with vanilla sex. People with kinky lovemaps, however, may not have this avenue open to them. That's because as children, they may have experienced feelings of guilt, fear, or shame—fostered by a parent or other important figure—that caused rifts in their lovemap to develop. In adulthood, these rifts make it more difficult to forge a conventional sexual connection with others. The human mind has discovered an ingenious way to circumnavigate the pitfalls and problem areas in our lovemaps—namely, taking a more roundabout route by developing kinky tastes.

Case histories of kinky patients abound in psychoanalytic literature, and in 1998, Joseph Weiss, a prominent San Francisco psychoanalyst, published a paper in *Psychoanalytic Quarterly* analyzing Robert, a forty-two-year-old businessman. Robert had had a fairly normal childhood. His mother, however, was often depressed. If Robert got too rambunctious during playtime, his mom would claim she had a headache and retire to her bedroom. As a result, Robert grew up fearing that his exuberance might hurt women if he wasn't careful, and this fear ended up manifesting itself later in his romantic relationships with women. During sex, Robert confessed, he often felt that he couldn't really let loose. There was, however, one sexual activity that worked like a charm: bondage. Which makes sense: If one were to view Robert's lovemap, his guilt and fear of hurting women was standing in the way of his pursuit for sexual pleasure. Bondage was his way of doing a psychological end run around this problem. If he was tied up, his exuberance couldn't hurt anyone. By indulging in his kink, Robert could jettison the worries that were putting a damper on his sexuality and have fun.

In 2003, psychologist Michael Bader published a book delineating all the ways kinks develop, *Arousal: The Secret Logic Behind Sexual Fantasies*. He revealed that people who want to be overpowered during sex—through bondage or beating, for example—may have grown up feeling that they had *too* much power, over the happiness of a parent or otherwise. By handing over the controls to their partner, these people can abandon this libido-sapping sense of responsibility and enjoy the ride. Sadists or "tops," on the other hand, may have felt helpless as children. By dominating their lover, they can feel safe and in control, and thus allow their sexuality to flourish. Exhibitionists may have struggled as children with feelings of neglect or shame, which can be instantly overcome by being ogled by an appreciative lover.

While many people assume that all cross-dressers are gay, studies show that 95 percent of them are actually straight— and many, Bader argues, may merely be struggling with feelings of alienation toward their mothers. By donning a dress and fishnets, they're essentially saying, "See? Men and women aren't that different!" which can help them forge a connection with a wife or girlfriend. Even the most baffling kinks—like those involving urine or feces—have a logic to them. Being defecated on and thus degraded may help eliminate feelings of contempt and hostility they might have felt toward a parent while growing up. Maybe, as kids, they acted "shitty" toward their father or mother and now, as adults, they feel guilty for it.

"This does not mean that people with kinks come from un-happy homes," cautions Bader. "These childhood problems are fairly common." While some people choose to act out their fantasies in real life in a role-play scenario, fantasizing alone can serve the same purpose. It depends largely on what you're more comfortable with. "The advantages of role-play are that it's happening in front of you, which can feel more intense," says Bader. "But the downside is that certain variables might not exactly match the vision in your mind. So it's a trade-off. Some are prone to act out their fantasies, while others might be fine to visualize them or discuss them with a partner."

Kink: An Acquired Taste?

As far as slide shows go, it was a memorable one to say the least. First, an image of black, knee-high women's boots flashed on-screen for fifteen seconds. Then, a second later, an image of an attractive naked woman followed, remaining on-screen for thirty seconds. Then the screen went dark for one to three minutes, then repeated the above boots-then-babes combo again. And again. The audience members—three young, unmarried male psychologists—had their genitals hooked up to penile plethysmographs to measure their levels of blood flow below the belt.

This experiment, conducted by Stanley Rachman, a psychiatrist at Maudsley Hospital in London, set out to prove that people with normal "vanilla" sexual tastes could be trained to be kinky through simple conditioning. At first, as Rachman had expected, the men's genitals remained unmoved by the boots, but quickly rose to attention once the women appeared on-screen. But as men continued viewing the procession of boots and nude women twenty, thirty, and forty times, something interesting happened: They began getting erections when viewing boots alone. In the same way that Pavlov's dogs learned to associate the sound of a bell with food, men could be trained to subconsciously associate shoes with sex.

Rachman's makeshift shoe fetishists, however, didn't be-

How to Join Club Kink

Find your kink. If you're unsure how to start experimenting, try tuning in to what you find a turn-on already and take it from there. If, for example, you get aroused when your partner pins your wrists or keeps you teetering on the brink of orgasm (or if you enjoy doing those things), then bondage may be a logical next step. Or if you really get into rough sex, complete with back scratching and nips on the neck, upping the pain quotient with some light spanking, a paddle, or a riding crop might do the trick. And while people typically think of fetishes in terms of feet, a preoccupation with any body part or article of clothing also counts. If underwear turns you or your partner on, embark on a lingerie shopping spree together or take your sweet time peeling them off.

Draw up a plan. Let's say you've decided to dabble in some sort of top/bottom, master/slave sort of arrangement one evening. It's not wise to pick up a whip and just wing it. Instead, sit down with your partner beforehand and hash out what you hope will happen in your scene like movie directors. This will ensure you're both on the same page and reduce the possibility that your evening will veer off in a direction that's not comfortable.

Establish a safe word. This is a random word like "elephant," "uncle" or plain old "safe word" that, if uttered during sex, will put the action instantly on hold. That way, if you're submitting to some pain or humiliation, you can scream "No!" or "Stop, that hurts!" to your heart's content without your partner wondering *Does he mean it or is it just part of the act?*

Get some guidance. Cooking classes, surfing lessons, and triathlon trainers exist for a reason: Sometimes, it's easier to learn the ropes from the masters. The same is true with kink. Search online or in your local paper for classes in your area, or buy a book for beginners like *SM 101: A Realistic Introduction* or *How to Be a Dominant Diva*.

Know the lingo. If you decide to hit an SM party or club and want to blend in with the scene, here's a travel tip: It's not called "S&M." The correct term is just "SM," without the "&" in the middle. SM veterans joke that "S&M" actually stands for "Stand and Model," a derisive reference to people who just enjoy wearing the elaborate get-ups.

come *permanent* shoe fetishists. A week after the experiment was over, the three men were relieved to report that their affinity for boots had faded.

There's even evidence that our sexual interests are designed to evolve over time. In another experiment conducted by Dolf Zillmann at Indiana University, men and women volunteered to come into his office once per week, be ushered into a private viewing booth, and watch pornographic videos for an hour. At first, study subjects reported thoroughly enjoying the viewing material, which included the fairly standard X-rated fare of heterosexual couples engaged in intercourse and oral sex. As the weeks wore on, though, their enjoyment levels waned. Zillman chalked this up to "excitatory habituation," which, in plain English, means his study subjects got bored.

At week eight, Zillman spiced up the selection to include some triple-X alternatives, including videos featuring spankings, whippings, bondage, and discipline. While few people would have voluntarily chosen to watch these risqué videos at the outset of the experiment, by week eight many were so tired of conventional porn that they made a beeline for the triple-X movies when they became available.

Sooner or later, many of us may be curious enough to head into the uncharted territory of kinky sex. Some of us may already be kinky and not know it yet. Just ask Ian, a Chicago stockbroker who, one night while surfing the Internet, stumbled across a Web site where he could pay to play strip poker. Ian, a gambling man by nature, prided himself on his poker skills. Plus, the recent college grad had been in a dry spell with dating, and was craving a little eye candy. Why not give it a try?

After signing up, Ian was told to turn on his computer's own video camera so the women could watch him strip, too. Ian didn't have a problem with that—after all, he doubted these women's abilities were on a par with his own. For the most part, he was right. Round after round, the women's clothes came off. Occasionally, Ian lost and had to take off something himself. As he continued dabbling in strip poker sites over the next few months, something odd occurred to him: He liked losing more than winning. "I realized I'd rather *be* naked than see naked women," he says. "Before this point, I'd always considered strip poker to be as normal a turn-on as a guy could have. Now, though, it dawned on me that I was a bit of an exhibitionist."

And not any old exhibitionist. Ian discovered that he was into a specific type of exhibitionism known as CFNM, which stands for Clothed Female Naked Male. There were tons of Web sites and clubs devoted to this one activity. Ian was shocked—not only to find that his particular penchant had a name, but that there were plenty of guys just like him. "I guess it was also comforting," Ian says. "I wasn't alone. I wasn't weird. I had plenty of company."

CHAPTER 9

The Cheat Sheet

John and Jane had been dating for six months when she started noticing he was acting a little . . . strange. In the past, he'd always answer his cell phone when she called, but these days, he'd often be hard to reach for hours. For the first time in their relationship, he'd started saying he was "too tired" for sex, although that didn't stop him from surfing the Web well into the night. What was going on? Suspecting that his computer might hold the answers, Jane started sifting through his e-mails one evening when he was out. That's when she spotted something that made her stomach turn—an online transcript he'd saved that kicked off with John asking someone: So what do u look like?*

Jane was livid. "Who is this woman?" she asked John as soon as he got home, presenting him with the evidence.

"What are you doing on my computer?" John huffed, but his anger quickly devolved into defensiveness. "She's no one. I've never met her," John said, explaining that his online dalliance had begun while cruising an online chat room. "I know it looks bad, but I swear, I'm not cheating on you."

"Yes, you are!" Jane snarled, as she stormed out of John's

apartment, flipped over her cell phone, and called the perfect person to deal with this crisis: Tom.

Tom was "just a friend"—or so Jane had been insisting ever since John had started airing suspicions that she and Tom seemed to be close. Maybe too close. And perhaps John was right. As Jane ranted on the phone about what a jerk John was, Tom agreed. "You deserve better," Tom said. "You deserve a guy who loves you and only you."

Tom said it in a way that Jane instantly knew what he was really saying: that his feelings for her had grown beyond friendship. And deep down, Jane was pretty sure she'd fallen for Tom, too. Did that mean she was cheating? If John had tapped her phone and listened in on this conversation, would he feel equally betrayed? Did this mean Jane's relationship with John was over?

IT HAPPENS TO the best of us: There you are, cruising along in a wonderful relationship when, out of the corner of your eye, you spot some road signs that make you worry. Suddenly, his Saturday nights always seem booked, or a "big work project" has her clocking some late nights at the office. His enthusiasm in bed begins to wane—or, one night, she whips out some wild new technique that makes you wonder *Whoa, where'd she learn that?*

As the signs turn from hairy to hazardous, you start wondering: Is your partner cheating? According to a 2006 survey of over 10,000 married Americans by the National Opinion Research Center (NORC), 22 percent of men and 13 percent of women will cheat on their spouse at some point. Some researchers argue that these statistics are only the tip of the iceberg, since they fail to take into account the vast array of ways couples can two-time each other today. After all, what *is* cheating? That depends on who you ask. According to a 2007 msnbc/ivillage.com poll of more than 70,000 adults by sociologist Janet Lever, nearly everyone said sexual intercourse or oral sex with someone else fit the bill. Other dalliances, though, fell into more of a gray area. Seventy-seven percent of men and 89 percent of women considered kissing cheating. Two-thirds of men and women chalked up sexually explicit online chat as cheating. Even 6 percent of men and 16 percent of women pegged watching porn as cheating. Given these differences, tallying the total number of cheaters is tricky. Then, of course, there's the fact that cheaters lie—not only to their partners, but to pollsters and other professionals. In another study examining 750 individuals who entered therapy, 30 percent initially admitted to infidelity. As therapists continued to probe, an additional 30 percent spilled the beans, bringing the total count up to 60 percent.

Some people suspect when infidelity is afoot; others are completely blindsided right when they could swear their relationship couldn't be better. Angie, a fashion consultant in Poughkeepsie, New York, knows this fact all too well. She and her husband Adam were married for six years, had just bought their first home, and were trying to have a baby. Angie couldn't have been happier. Then one day while cleaning the guest bedroom, she came across evidence that would instantly derail all her plans: a used condom. That's when her heart lurched.

"What is *this*?!" Angie asked, throwing the condom in Adam's face when he arrived home. Adam infuriated Angie by denying the obvious, but Angie wasn't buying it. Soon, Adam moved into the guest bedroom, then out of the house completely. Through the grapevine, when Angie heard that Adam had moved in with the woman he'd been seeing behind her back, she filed for divorce. Angie has no regrets about ending her marriage, but is still haunted by questions. Why hadn't she noticed the warning signs sooner? Had she done something to drive Adam away? And now that she was back out there and dating, would she ever be able to trust someone new?

Whatever role you're playing in your own private soap opera—victim, perpetrator, paranoid lover in pursuit of some answers—this chapter will guide you through this treacherous terrain. Infidelity is bound to break hearts and bruise a few egos, but knowing the facts can cushion the blow.

Cheaters by Design?

Three dildos, one silicone vagina. That's what was on Gordon Gallup's shopping list that day. After browsing his options at a local sex-toy store, he brought his selections up to the cashier, made his purchase, and carted them back to his laboratory at the University of New York in Albany. Gallup's next order of business was to mix up a batch of artificial semen. "At first we tried water and corn starch, but that tended to congeal quickly," Gallup says. "So I called a colleague in Florida and asked for his recipe. He said flour and water works best."

After mixing up a few batches of simulated semen with different flour-to-water ratios, Gallup brought these mixtures to a boil, let them simmer for fifteen minutes while being stirred, then set them aside to cool. Gallup presented these mixtures to a panel of three male judges, who dipped a finger in each and voted which one felt most like the real thing. Too much flour resulted in a gluey consistency; too little was too runny. (The winning formula ended up being 18.8 grams of flour mixed with 250 milliliters of water.) Once the simulated semen recipe had been perfected, Gallup took a paring knife to the dildos, carving them into various shapes. Gallup then filled the vagina with the semen and inserted each dildo, one after the other.

Gallup was exploring how penis shape affected sperm displacement. On pigs, Gallup had noticed, the penis is shaped like a corkscrew to prevent the female from disengaging. On kangaroos, it's forked at the end—all the better to fit his mate's two vaginas. Dolphins can swivel the end of their penis like a submarine telescope, which can come in handy keeping two dolphin bodies together given they lack arms, legs, and gravity to remain entwined. The blueprint for the human penis, Gallup found, also serves a purpose, starting with its bulbous, mushroom-shaped head (or the glans).

What Gallup's experiment revealed was that during intercourse, the glans acts as a semen displacement device which, during thrusting, helps scoop out any semen that's already in the vagina. In his study, dildos with a glans displaced 91 percent of the semen, while modified dildos with no glans removed only 35 percent. Even the frenulum—that vertical notch on the front side of the glans—is designed to help shuttle old semen back and make room for a new batch. Why is this important? Because cheating puts a man at risk of raising another man's child. The glans is his first line of defense to prevent that from happening. Of course, there's also the possibility that a guy will displace his *own* semen, but that's not likely for three reasons. "After a man ejaculates, he loses his erection, which makes further thrusting and semen displacement difficult," Gallup points out. "Men also have a refractory period, which prevents them from getting a new erection anytime soon. Finally, even once a guy is physically capable of getting a second erection, he might not be all that inspired to have sex, given he's so recently been sated." What this means is that if a guy is displacing anyone's semen, most likely it's another man's.

As further evidence that infidelity is a fact of life, let's take another look at a guy's testicles. Here, size, not shape, is the crucial factor. The bigger the testicles, the more sperm they unload during sex, which stands in a man's favor if he's trying to outnumber a rival's sperm and get his partner pregnant. David Buss, a professor at the University of Texas in Austin, compared human testicles to those of other primates. Gorillas have miniscule testicles for their body weight. Meanwhile, tiny chimpanzees have huge testes. Men's testicles fall in the middle of these extremes size-wise. What do scientists conclude from this? Well, when you consider the fact that gorillas with small testicles are incredibly faithful, chimps with large testicles are rampantly promiscuous, and human males with medium-size testicles fall in the middle on the sleeping-around scale, it suggests testicle size may be a sign we're biologically designed to stray occasionally.

Even sperm itself is designed for the possibility that people cheat. Robin Baker, author of *Sperm Wars*, has examined more seminal fluid under a microscope than you'd dare or care to imagine. He found that only around 1 percent of sperm looks like your classic "egg getters" with a cute oval head and sleek whippet of a tail. Another type of sperm, called "blockers," have two heads, three heads, or four heads with short, long, or coiled tails. Yet another type of sperm called "killers" have pear-shaped heads, thanks to a poison reservoir perched on the front. So what exactly are these sperm "blocking" and "killing?" Other men's sperm.

At any one point, sperm from more than one guy could be competing to fertilize a woman's egg. Whether either man actually *wants* to father this woman's child is irrelevant. To win, sperm fight dirty. Blocker sperm act like football linebackers, standing in the way of any sperm that might try to get past (sometimes they block sperm from the same source, but that's not a problem when at least some of their own egg getters are already en route to the egg). Meanwhile, killer sperm cruise around and, if they encounter an egg getter that's not on their team, they impale this intruder with their pear-shaped poison heads. If killers and blockers do their job well, that leaves their own egg getters clear for landing.

Men's sperm count may automatically adjust to compensate for the possibility that their partner might cheat. Baker recruited men willing to submit ejaculate samples from condoms every time they had sex with their partners. Then, they

Egg getters   Killers

Blockers

The different types of sperm

counted the number of sperm in each ejaculate and compared that to the amount of time the couple had spent together since last having sex (and by "time together," Baker and Bellis counted any moments a man could keep tabs on a woman's whereabouts, so being in separate rooms in the same house or at opposite ends of a department store sufficed). They calculated that over a three-day period, men who spent 100 percent of their time with their partners since last having sex would inseminate their partners with 389 million sperm per ejaculate. Men who spent only 5 percent of their time with their partner since last having sex would inseminate their partner with 712 million sperm per ejaculate. The greater the risk that a man's partner could have had sex with somebody else, the more sperm he inseminates into her to compensate.

Women's bodies are equally prepared for the possibility that men will have sex behind their backs. Their first line of defense is a phenomenon called concealed estrus. Estrus, you may recall from chapter 2, is the time when females are ovulating and most fertile (which is typically day fourteen of a twenty-eight-day menstrual cycle). Many animals announce their estrus loud and clear—cats wail, baboons' behinds turn red. Women also advertise when they're in estrus by dressing in skimpier clothing and acting more sexually aggressive, while men appear to pick up on these cues (which is why men in strip clubs give ovulating strippers bigger tips). Still, relative to the clear-as-day signs of a wailing cat or a baboon's red behind, the signs in human estrus are subtle. Even if their actions suggest that they're subconsciously tuned in to ovulation, most men—and women, for that matter—have no idea it's happening.

Women keep their estrus largely under wraps for good reason: It keeps a guy by her side *all* month rather than just once a month. "If women showed clear signs of estrus the way some animals do, their male partners would only stay by their side when they were ovulating, then wander off the rest of the time," says Martie Haselton, a professor at the University of California in Los Angeles. "Concealed estrus, however, is more like a poker game. Women aren't showing their cards. So men err on the side of caution and continue to spend time with their mates all month."

While ovulation might not prompt any over-the-top alterations in a woman's appearance, inside her mind, some potentially disturbing changes are afoot. In one study by Haselton, thirty-eight women were asked to keep a daily diary describing how often they fantasized about their partner as well as other men. She found that women's sexual thoughts about their primary partner remained steady throughout the month—but that their steamy musings about other men spiked right around ovulation. There's also some evidence that women don't just *think* about other men when they ovulate, but are prone to act on those impulses. In one survey of 1,152 women, Robin Baker and Mark Bellis at the School of Biological Sciences in Manchester, England, found that women tend to have affairs right when they're ovulating. Women's bodies aren't designed to have flings just for fun. They're programmed to fool around right when the odds are best they'll end up conceiving another man's child. According to a study analyzing the DNA of parents and their children in the *Journal of Epidemiology and Community Health*, one in twenty-five dads could be unknowingly raising a child who is not his own.

Men might not be consciously aware of when women are ovulating and likely to stray, but they might be able to sense it on a subconscious level. Haselton's diarists were also asked to keep tabs on their mate's behavior toward them throughout

the month. Near ovulation, women reported that their partners acted more amorous, attentive, jealous, and possessive
than at other times. "Most likely men aren't aware they're
doing this," Haselton points out. "I've never heard a man say
'my partner's ovulating and I'm so jealous.' Still, it does seem
like they're picking up on something."

Inside the Mind of a Cheater

Mark, a New York stockbroker in his late twenties, is every
woman's worst nightmare. "I am a ninja of infidelity," he says.
"I've cheated on many of my girlfriends, but never once been
caught or even suspected of cheating. I really am that good."
To cover his tracks, Mark lives by a few easy rules. Rule #1:
Clear the cache and cookies from your computer so your girlfriend can't snoop for evidence. Rule #2: Keep your cell phone
on you at all times, rather than lying on a kitchen counter
where someone can pick it up and sift through your call history. Rule #3: Treat your girlfriend like a queen. "Random
calls and texts saying 'thinking of u' give her a sense that the
relationship is going great. And it is," Mark says. "I really am
happy in my relationship. But I'm human. Someday I will stop
cheating, but I'm young, and figure this is par for the course.
Everyone cheats. The trick is just not getting caught. I tend to
think that men who get caught want to get caught."

Many assume that cheaters must be unhappy with their
current relationship. And yet, when researcher Shirley Glass
polled more than three hundred men and women on this
question, she found that 56 percent of men and 34 percent of
women who had had affairs rated their marriage as "happy" or
even "very happy." Keeping someone satisfied on the home

front is no guarantee your relationship will remain infidelity-free. The real problem may lie within the cheating mind itself.

To pinpoint which personality traits prompt people to cheat, Todd Shackelford at Florida Atlantic University and David Buss at the University of Texas in Austin gave 107 newlywed couples a battery of personality tests. In addition to self-reports, they questioned spouses about the other's behavior. Over a hundred characteristics were measured, from "adventurousness" to "zaniness," but only three were reliable tip-offs that someone might become a two-timer down the line. The first trait was narcissism. Narcissists have an over-developed sense of self-importance, which often gives itself away with the tiniest actions, like grabbing the best piece of food off a plate for themselves. The second trait that portends infidelity is low conscientiousness, an inability to see how their own actions impact others. These people tend to be late, forgetful, and are probably constantly apologizing for their slip-ups. The third trait was psychoticism, or a lack of impulse control that can manifest itself by sudden disappearances or breaking off friendships without explanation. Taken together, this triumvirate of personality traits spells trouble.

Someone's sexual past can also offer a glimpse into the future. According to a study of over 2,500 men and women published in the *Journal of Marriage and the Family*, every person you sleep with until marriage increases your likelihood to cheat by 1 percent. So if you've slept with seven people before settling down, that increases your likelihood to cheat by 7 percent. This also means that those who "sow their wild oats before settling down" are actually *more* likely to cheat than sexually conservative sorts. People are more likely to stray if their parents or friends have, and if they believe infidelity can be justified—by, say, a partner's lack of interest in sex. When asked if they felt guilty about their actions, two-thirds of cheaters said they don't regret it. Just over 10 percent were actually *glad* they cheated.

All that said, cheaters don't act in a vacuum. The relationship they're in can also tip the scales, especially when one party is much more of a catch than the other. We've all seen mismatched pairs like this and wondered, "What is she doing with him?" or "What does he see in her?" According to one study titled "Equity and Extramarital Sexuality" in the *Archives of Sexual Behavior*, these relationships are indeed at high risk for affairs. The poll asked men and women two questions: Do you consider yourself more, less, or equally as desirable as your partner? And since dating your current partner, have you had sex with someone else, or would you be open to it? Fifty-eight percent of respondents considered themselves evenly matched. Of those who weren't, the partner who judged him- or herself to be the more attractive of the pair was more likely to have an affair, and earlier in their marriage (six to eight years) than those who considered themselves on par with their partner, who tended to wait an average of twelve to fifteen years to cheat, and that's if they cheated at all. People who think they can do better are more likely to fool around behind their partner's back, either in a one-time fling or a more serious affair that could provide them with an escape hatch from their current relationship.

The Truth About the Philandering French (and Why Russians Cheat at the Beach)

When *Wall Street Journal* writer Pamela Druckerman was posted to Latin America, she was at first shocked by all the propositions she received from married men. "Even when these 'suitors' were otherwise appealing, I found their offers repugnant. What about their obligations to their wives?" she recalls. Once, when she confronted one man about his casual invitation to have an affair, he was equally perplexed that she found his offer so insulting.

Curious how much culture influences people's attitudes toward infidelity, Druckerman traveled to two dozen cities in ten countries—interviewing psychologists, marriage counselors, and adulterers—and published her findings in a book titled *Lust in Translation*. After amassing her data, Druckerman discovered that Americans were a relatively faithful lot: On average, only 3.9 percent of men and 3.1 percent of women had cheated on their spouse in the past year. We out-cheat supposedly sexually libertine France (where only 3.8 percent of men and 2 percent of women commit adultery annually) and those lotharios in Italy (3.5 percent of men and 0.9 percent of women cheat per year). And yet, in Great Britain, 7.3 percent of men and 3.5 percent of women cheat on their spouse every year. The numbers rise even higher in Latin American countries, at least for men (in Brazil, 12 percent of men cheat annually; in Mexico City 15 percent of men do the same). In Africa, infidelity is rampant, in part due to polygamous practices. Druckerman found that the most extreme adulterers are in Togo, where 37 percent of married or cohabiting men have slept with more than one partner in the past year.

Even when cultures generally frown on infidelity, Druckerman found that this rule was riddled with exceptions. In Brazil, cheating is overlooked during Mardi Gras. In Russia, you're in the clear if the fling occurs at a beach resort. In South Africa, being drunk is a legitimate excuse for stumbling into a stranger's bed. In Japan, it's not considered cheating if you pay for it.

Location matters on a smaller scale as well. City dwellers will out-cheat country dwellers by 47 percent. And if you live together before marriage, your grandparents' disapproving stares might be justified, since it will up the odds of adultery during your marriage by 39 percent.

The Tangled World Wide Web We Weave

In real life, Sara was your typical married mom with two daughters living in Toronto. Online, Sara was a sex goddess, and her chat buddy, Edward from Australia, was smitten.

> **Edward:** *You are my world.*

> **Sara:** *I feel so close to you. I feel as though we have reached an intimacy that can only increase as time goes by. This relationship has made me feel more alive than I ever thought possible. When we're together, we are alone, safe, and excited! I love it!*

> **Edward:** *Let's do it again, right now. I picture you lying down. I am running my hand down your smooth back . . .*

Sara, who shared her story with Marlene Maheu, a psychologist and author of *Infidelity on the Internet*, is typical of how a growing number of people cheat today. In sociologist Janet Lever's infidelity poll, 15 percent of men and 7 percent of women admitted that they have engaged in an online affair. Rather than hazard the potential mess of an affair in the flesh, these people log on, get off, and log off without divulging their name or knowing anything about their online lover. It's no-strings-attached infidelity at its finest.

Long before online chat rooms existed, scientists explored whether anonymity paves the way to questionable behavior. In the 1970s, Kenneth Gergen at Swarthmore College rigged up a real-life version of an anonymous chat by placing a group of strangers in a pitch-black room for an hour, promising all involved that they'd never see each other's faces or meet again (at least not knowingly). Unbeknownst to the students, their actions were being picked up by infrared camera and audio recording devices. At first, the men and women in the room were silent, uncertain what to do. Then they started talking to the nameless, faceless people around them. Given the room was only ten by twelve feet, it was inevitable that they'd accidentally touch each other. Soon, though, the touching became deliberate. Nearly half exchanged hugs. A few even kissed. When students were asked to write about their experience afterwards, one male participant wrote, "As I was sitting Beth came up and we started to play touchy face and touchy body." Then, "we decided to pass our 'love' on, to share it with other people. So we split up and Laurie took her place. We had just started touchy face and touchy body and kissed a few times before I was tapped to leave."

Gergen's conclusion: People, when granted anonymity, tend to get intimate awfully fast. According to his recollection of this study published in *Psychology Today*, "With the simple subtraction of light, a group of perfect strangers moved within approximately thirty minutes to a stage of intimacy often not attained in years of normal acquaintanceship." When this experiment was repeated in a lit room, none of the aforementioned touchy-feely stuff occurred.

In 2007, Beatriz Mileham, a graduate student at the University of Gainesville in Florida, published a study on her travails through Yahoo.com's "Married and Flirting" and msn.com's

"Married but Flirting" chat rooms looking for interview subjects. She quickly found that flirting wasn't all that was happening on these sites. Some men tried to barter with Mileham: cybersex first, interview later. As one thirty-two-year-old male Mileham interviewed put it, "I will help [with the research] but I am stressed and need to let go of steam. So I need your help too then, you sound nice." Mileham declined those invitations. Of the eighty-six married men and women Mileham did interview, nearly all admitted that anonymity was a large part of the allure. "Anonymity is fun and liberating. You can let your usual guard down," wrote one forty-year-old male. "We can show those emotions that we usually hide because it's so easy not to have to face the person."

In spite of the intimate, X-rated content Mileham's interview subjects claimed they exchanged, 83 percent didn't consider themselves to be cheating. In their opinion, they were in the clear because no physical contact occurred. Some compared their experiences to watching a porn video, or participating in an interactive steamy novel. The remaining 17 percent deemed cybercheating a "weak" form of infidelity nowhere near as bad as a face-to-face affair.

And yet, however blameless they claimed to be, all but two of Mileham's study subjects hid their online activities from their spouses. And while most swore up and down they'd never meet an online liaison in person, their actions indicated otherwise. Twenty-six of the eighty-six study participants went on to meet at least one online liaison in person. Of these, twenty-four ended up having in-the-flesh affairs. One sixty-six-year-old married man admitted that by meeting people online, he'd had thirteen real-life affairs. Cybercheating, whether it's seen as "real" cheating or not, is a slippery slope.

Philanderers who know from the get-go they're interested

in cheating can log on to AshleyMadison.com—which might sound like an upscale clothing boutique, but Capri pants and A-line skirts aren't what they're selling. Log on and browse, and you'll quickly see it's an online dating site, only with an interesting twist. It's primarily for married folks interested in having affairs with other married folks. As one thirty-four-year-old member in Alberta, Canada, explained in his profile:

> *I'm married, happy in my relationship, not looking to get out of my marriage but just need a change every now and then . . . I'm not looking to run away with someone nor am I looking to spend every stolen moment possible away from my family. For one my wife would be too suspicious, two my life is way too busy. I'm looking for someone that would like to escape for an occasional clandestine rendezvous, whether it be once a week or once a month. To escape from the thousands of invisible ties that bind us to our every day lives, jobs, families, households.*

In an era when you can find anything from real estate to a sperm donor online, it makes sense you can find affairs there, too. AshleyMadison.com, the most popular site of its kind with two million members, was founded in 2001 by Darren Morgenstern, a Toronto-based entrepreneur. After reading a newspaper article estimating that 20 to 30 percent of people on traditional dating Web sites were married and merely masquerading as single, Morgenstern figured these affair seekers would flock to a site where they could be upfront about their marital status, and he was right. The site's slogan is: "When monogamy becomes monotony."

Technology has made it easier than ever to cheat. And yet scientific advances have made getting caught easier as well.

How to Catch a Cheater

Martha, who's in her seventies and living in Tallahassee, Florida, is hardly the most technologically savvy woman on the block. But the day she received her Tru-test infidelity detection kit in the mail, she snuck into her husband's office when he wasn't there and got to work. First, she plugged in the ultraviolet light, which had been calibrated to pick up trace amounts of vaginal and seminal fluids. Shining the light on his desk, Martha was shocked to see its surface light up like a Christmas tree. As she'd suspected, Martha's husband of fifty years was having an affair, and his desk was the scene of the crime. "I'd been wondering why he had that prescription for Viagra," she told David Vitalli, a private investigator who had first come up with the idea of marketing Tru-test in 2006. "Because he certainly wasn't using it with me!"

These days, to track down a cheater, there's an array of high-tech equipment at your disposal. In addition to Tru-test (available at Trutestinc.com), there's CheckMate, an eyedropper of enzymes that turn purple in the presence of semen. If you suspect your partner's computer contains the incriminating evidence, software such as OverSpy will allow you to monitor any Web sites, chat rooms, and e-mails sent or received, even if they're judiciously deleted. To keep tabs on someone's cell phone, install FlexiSpy, which allows you to listen in on calls and read texts. Or, if you want to see if your honey's really working late or shacked up at the Ramada Inn, TrackStick, a pocketknife-sized GPS device, can easily be slipped into a car, coat, or briefcase and allow you to plot where it roams on Google Earth.

Sure, these *CSI*-style tactics may seem a little extreme. They also violate some states' privacy laws, which makes the evidence inadmissible during divorce proceedings and occasionally worthy of a short prison sentence. Still, in Lever's study, only one in five people said they'd confront their partner with the suspicions of infidelity directly. As a result, many turn immediately toward covert operations. More than half of survey respondents said they'd have no qualms taking a peek at their partner's e-mail, rifling through phone records, or even going the old fashioned route and hiring a private investigator.

Cheaters aren't taking this lying down. Instead, they've fought back with technology that helps them cover their tracks. A service called the Alibi Network, for example, furnishes philanderers with fake plane tickets and forged documents to make any "business trip" they take seem real. Plus, if their spouses want to call their "hotel in Chicago" while they're actually working their way through the *Kama Sutra* with a bartender in St. Barths, this company will provide a phony phone number with the right area code and even a fake hotel receptionist so cheaters can receive the call. Last but not least, all questionable credit card purchases, including the services of the Alibi Network, get funneled through a series of dummy companies that keep this elaborate fib airtight to the end.

Further complicating matters is that while we might pride ourselves on our ability to read our partners like a book, people are pretty good at keeping their wandering eye under wraps. Eric Anderson and Bella DePaulo at the University of Virginia set up an experiment where they flashed slides of glamorous and average-looking people at volunteers and asked "Do you think that person is attractive?" Half were instructed to lie, the other half to tell the truth. Meanwhile, study subjects' significant others sat nearby unable to see the slides, and were asked to deduce from their partners' facial expressions whether they were answering honestly. Their accuracy rate was awful—just 52 percent, when they could have gotten 50 percent right simply by guessing. Meanwhile, when total strangers were brought in and asked to blow the horn on people's fibs, they got it right 58 percent of the time. Love tends to muddle our lie detectors.

What Cheating Means for Your Relationship

In 1643, Mary Latham, who had just celebrated her eighteenth birthday, was hanged in Massachusetts along with her lover, James Britton. Their crime? Adultery. How far we've come since then. In the past, female philanderers were usually forced to forfeit their home, savings, and even their children in divorce court. That started changing in the 1970s when states began adopting "no-fault divorce" laws allowing couples to split simply because they were unhappy, as well as providing for equitable distribution clauses so wives wouldn't be left high and dry, even if they were the ones who'd cheated. While women statistically cheat less often than men, they're quickly closing the gap. In one study of 16,000 individuals in fifty-three countries by David Schmitt as part of the International Sexuality Description Project, the greater the equality between the sexes in a given culture, the more women's infidelity rates rival men's.

Oddly, though, as the penalties for adultery have loosened, we've grown more judgmental about it. In 1973, 70 percent of Americans surveyed said adultery was wrong under any circumstances; by 2004, that number had risen to 82 percent. In a 2006 Gallup poll, more Americans deemed adultery immoral than polygamy or human cloning. In other words, it's not *great* when husbands have harems or scientists try creating carbon copies of humans, but cheaters are the true villains. Support Web sites for victims of infidelity feed this dire, post-apocalyptic view, dubbing the initial discovery of the betrayal "D-day," and suggesting that cheating can lead to symptoms of Post Traumatic Stress Disorder.

Busted for *What?!*

Even today, adultery is illegal in about half of the states in America, although these laws are rarely enforced. Still, in case you're concerned, here's a rundown of some of the fines and penalties you might face from least to most severe:

Maryland: maximum fine of $10

Virginia: maximum fine of $250

Rhode Island: maximum fine of $500

Alabama: minimum fine of $100 and maximum of six months prison or hard labor

Utah: maximum six months imprisonment

Illinois: maximum one year in prison

Michigan: Given adultery is a felony, in 2007, a Michigan judge interpreted state laws as indicating that this crime could carry the penalty of life in prison.

And yet, what couples actually *do* in the aftermath of an affair tells a different story. Laura, a florist living in Philadelphia, always assumed that if she ever found out her husband was cheating, she would get a divorce. And yet, when her husband confessed to having an affair five years into their marriage, her resolve to end the relationship wasn't as strong as she thought it would be. "At first, I was livid," she recalls. She ordered her husband to move out, and he did. As the weeks went by, though, she found herself missing him.

"I started thinking long and hard about how nobody's perfect, and that everyone makes mistakes," she says. Plus, at least her husband had told her about the affair—a one-time fling, fueled by too much booze during a business trip. Clearly, her husband felt awful about it, and swore he'd never do it again. Compounding Laura's confusion was the fact that now, in her forties, she was dreading the thought of dipping back into the dating pool. Who was to say she'd find someone else who made her as happy as her husband did, or that this new guy would remain true? In the end, Laura concluded that the devil she knew was a better bet than the devil she didn't. She invited her husband to move back in, saying she was willing to give him a second chance. "And here we are, celebrating our tenth wedding anniversary," she says. "I'm not saying our relationship has completely healed, but I'd say we're happy, and I truly believe that my husband has remained faithful since then. Still, my friends think I'm crazy for staying. Sometimes *I* think I'm crazy. Was I just afraid of being single again? I don't know. But I'm glad I stuck it out."

In one study of 164 recovering sex addicts by Jennifer Schneider, 60 percent of partners threaten to leave initially, but only 24 percent end up actually packing their bags. According to divorce statistics nationwide, approximately one in four couples who file for divorce never sign on the dotted line. To a certain extent, a couple's ability to weather the storm depends on the type of infidelity they're hit with. When Buss polled 107 couples about how they'd react if they found out their partner had been unfaithful, a one-night stand would convince only half of men and women to pull the plug. About two-thirds of men and women would bail if their partner had a serious, long-term affair. Still, that leaves one third of men and women who *wouldn't* seek a divorce even in this extreme circumstance.

Most couples who attempt to tough it out cite a reason along these lines: *I've already put so much into this relationship, I can't bail now.* It's such a common sentiment that economists have a word for it: the Concorde Fallacy, named after a supersonic plane that British and French governments continued to build even after it became painfully clear it would never be profitable. These past investments or "sunk costs," however, are rarely a good reason to continue muddling onward. Instead, researchers who've studied infidelity say it's wiser to look to "future yield." Look not to your past, but how profitable your endeavor—plane, relationship, or otherwise—is likely to be down the line. If you feel your partner is truly repentant and will change, then perhaps it's worth sticking around. If you have a hunch your future holds more of the same shenanigans, then perhaps it's time to cut your losses, no matter how much time and energy you've invested in the relationship already.

Gender can also affect our reactions to cheating, as Buss found out when he asked men and women which type of infidelity was worse: (a) finding out your partner had had sex with someone, or (b) finding out your partner had fallen in love. Neither sounds like fun, but when forced to choose, most men picked "a" and women "b." Generally, the study suggested, men can have sex without being in love. Meanwhile, women can be in love without bringing sex into the picture.

Men and women also differ in how they cope with rivals. When Joyce Shettel-Neuber at San Diego State University asked men and women how they'd react if they were at a party and walked in on their partner talking a little too intimately with an ex, men said they'd deal in one of two ways: by getting angry, or getting drunk. Women said they'd embark on a self-improvement rampage—that in the ensuing days and weeks, they'd hit the gym, pay more attention to their appearance, and go all out to outshine the interloper. Both men and women also said they'd find ways to casually point out their rival's flaws, focusing on the very areas where they felt that they themselves excelled. For example, if a woman was slim, she might say, "That girl was cute, but man, her thighs were enormous!" Men who made a decent salary might say, "Did Jerry mention he's still working at that video rental store near campus?" Often, jealous lovers target things that would be hard to confirm directly, like someone's intentions (*he's only out to get laid*) or rumors that a rival has an STD (since after all, who would want to verify info like that?).

Are any of the aforementioned tactics actually effective? No one knows—testing them out in a real-life relationship would be tricky, if not impossible, although Schmitt points out that derogating a competitor can be a risky strategy since it may not reflect so well on you. "You're giving away the fact that you need to derogate and that you might not be of sufficient value to retain your mate," he points out. People concerned about their mate's wandering eye might benefit from focusing on their partner instead. After examining a total of 104 mate-retention tactics, Buss determined these five to be the most effective, according to his book, *The Dangerous Passion*: Telling your mate you love him/her; going out of your way to be kind, nice, and caring; complimenting him/her on her appearance; being helpful when he/she really needs it; and displaying greater affection.

How to Stop Yourself from Straying

Those who are afraid of cheating can take steps to immunize themselves when temptation strikes. The trick is to take a second to focus on the moment you first fell in love with your current partner. In an experiment by Martie Haselton at the University of California in Los Angeles, 120 undergraduates in relationships were asked to pore over photographs of attractive strangers and pick out a dozen or so they liked the most. Then, they were asked to compose an essay on one of three subjects: the time they felt most in love with their current partner, the time they felt most attracted to their current partner, or an essay on anything they wanted.

While writing, the undergrads were instructed to put a check mark to the side of their essay at every point the attractive strangers from those photos popped into their heads. Undergrads who had written essays about their love for their partner averaged only about a check mark every two pages. Meanwhile, those writing about being attracted to their partner averaged more than two check marks per page, and people writing about anything averaged almost four check marks per page. Afterward, the undergrads were asked to write down any alluring attributes they recalled from those photos, from bulging biceps to a low-cut blouse. Undergrads from the love group recalled only about two-thirds as many attractive details as the others. Merely appreciating what you've got can rig you with blinders.

Tips to Cheat-proof Your Relationship

Define what cheating is. Everyone's definition is a little bit different, which can lead to misunderstandings down the road when one partner insists the other has violated their marriage vows while the other swears he's innocent ("It was just cybersex/a kiss/a lap dance. . . !"). To avoid this scenario, sit down and discuss what, exactly, you consider cheating—and which actions are so dire you'd leave the relationship. Here are some possible scenarios to discuss:

- watching pornography
- getting a lap dance
- exchanging flirtatious e-mails with someone
- cybersex
- kissing someone
- developing an emotional attachment to someone

Beware the slippery slope. These days, temptation is rarely as obvious as a vamp in a hotel bar. Instead, things start out innocently with someone we know and interact with already. According to a study by sociologist Janet Lever, 40 percent of philanderers end up falling for friends, another 35 percent for coworkers. While it's normal and healthy to bond with friends and coworkers outside your relationship, if you find yourself sharing more of your life with them than your partner, that could be a sign your alignment is shifting. Online, intimacy can also develop much faster than in face-to-face encounters, so don't assume a few flirtatious e-mails are harmless fun. Keep an eye out for small white lies you tell your partner. Omitting the fact that you met your ex for lunch might not seem so bad, but small secrets tend to become bigger secrets.

Snooping won't give you all the answers. Checking your partner's e-mail or cell phone records might seem like the easy way to confirm your hunch. It can also become time-consuming, and the evidence can be inconclusive. Plus, "one of the main tenets of a marriage is trust, and you've just broken it," says Marlene Maheu, author of *Infidelity and the Internet.* Instead, ask your partner outright, saying you'd rather know the truth, even if it hurts. At first, your partner might deny it. In one study, 84 percent of cheaters denied all wrongdoing when first confronted. Over time, though, 96 percent believed disclosure was the best course.

Redouble your displays of affection. Offer a helping hand unloading the dishwasher. Say "I love you" right before bed-time. While it's a myth that people only cheat when they're unhappy in their relationship, showering your partner with love and affection was deemed to be the most effective way to keep a partner from wandering off.

Remember what a great mate you've got. When the temptation of infidelity strikes, it can help to think back to those moments when you and your partner first fell in love. By dwelling on the good times, you can keep thoughts of straying at bay and strengthen your resolve to remain true.

A Cheating Screen . . . and Vaccine?

The future may hold more promise for those of us who hope to hold onto our mates. The secret may lie in rodents called voles—in particular, a vole named Clinton.

"Voles look like rats, but with a fatter tail," explains Larry Young, a professor at Emory University, who has performed experiments on hundreds of voles in an effort to understand their mating behavior. How voles act depends on which type of vole you're talking about. Prairie voles stick with one mate for life. Meadow voles are wildly promiscuous. Clinton, if you hadn't guessed, belonged to the latter group. What prompted Clinton to jump from nest to nest while his cousins the prairie voles remained content with one partner?

The key, says Young, was related to the number of vasopressin receptors in an area of the brain known as the ventral pallidum. Monogamous prairie voles had copious vasopressin receptors in this area, which helped them link the smell of a certain mate to sexual pleasure and encouraged them to settle down. Promiscuous meadow voles sorely lacked vasopressin receptors in this area, which could easily explain why they'd wander off from a female soon after mating. Young decided to try tinkering with this response by injecting the ventral pallidum in Clinton with a genetic virus that would boost the number of vasopressin receptors in this area of the brain. After receiving his injection, Clinton morphed overnight from a freewheeling player into a total monogamist. This experiment was repeated on hundreds of other promiscuous voles, all of whom followed in Clinton's footsteps and settled down.

So did this mean a "cheating vaccine" might one day be available for humans? "Could we use a virus to transform human behavior? I wouldn't really want to speculate too much toward that," says Young. A more likely scenario, though, is that people might one day be able to test someone's likelihood of straying by analyzing their genes.

In 2008, Swedish researcher Hasse Walum published the results of a study of 552 couples who had been together for at least five years. Confidentially, couples were asked a variety of questions to gauge their commitment levels, such as whether they had ever regretted getting married or discussed their desire to get divorced with a friend. Scientists also analyzed their genes, homing in on one particular variation on gene *AVPR1A*, called the 334 allele, which is responsible for coding for vasopressin receptors. In men carrying no copies or just one copy of the 334 allele, 15 to 16 percent reported a marital crisis in the past year. In men carrying two copies of the allele, 34 percent reported marital discord.

Other studies also support the idea that cheating may boil down to genetics. According to a survey of 1,600 female twins by Timothy Spector at the Twin Research Unit at St. Thomas' Hospital in London, if one twin commits adultery, the other twin has twice the normal chance of straying. Spector has even pinpointed regions on chromosomes 3, 7, and 20 that might harbor these cheating genes.

A genetic screening test for infidelity isn't available to the public yet, and even if it were, Young isn't so sure he'd recommend that couples rush to sign up. "I've got three girls who are eventually going to get married," says Young. "Do I want to buy a kit and test all their potential partners to see if they have a good genotype? That's a completely reasonable thing to think about, although I'd probably say no. It's dangerous. We're not dictated by our genes." For better or for worse, divining a relationship's staying power will remain up to us.

CHAPTER 10

Prescription for Perfect Sex?

In spite of some rocky moments, John and Jane continued dating and made it to the one-year mark. It was time to celebrate. Only how? Sure, meeting up for a fancy dinner was a good start. They had something else planned for afterward, though, that they hoped would make the occasion especially memorable: Orgasma, the ultimate pleasure pill.

Jane and John had stumbled across Orgasma while surfing the Internet. According to the manufacturer's Web site, this pill brought on orgasms galore for both men and women.

"That can't work," John scoffed.

Jane agreed. "Still," she pointed out, "how can we say for sure unless we give it a try?"

On a whim, they ordered a bottle. After their anniversary dinner, they each popped a pill, hopped into bed, then waited to see what would happen. Fifteen minutes passed. Then a half hour. "I don't feel anything," John said. "So much for that."

Jane, however, swore she could feel something—a slight tingling perhaps. John, upon hearing this, suddenly felt a little tingly, too, which was as much of an excuse that they needed to hop in the saddle and ride their way toward some pretty anniversary-worthy finales. Still, was the pill responsible, or was it just the placebo effect? Did any of those pills, potions, or patches John and Jane had heard about online or otherwise possess aphrodisiacal powers?

A S LONG AS we've been having sex, people have been experimenting with elixirs that supposedly make sex better. Had John and Jane been living in ancient Persia, they might have rubbed boiled alligator testes on their feet. Egyptians took a more direct approach and smeared crocodile hearts right on the penis. Today, pills are all the rage, although there are also patches, ointments, and plenty of other panaceas being sold online or in TV infomercials that promise to catapult your sex life to new levels. Only do any of them work?

Scientists have scrutinized many of the quick fixes currently on the market, and have found a few that actually do deliver on their claims (as well as many that don't). In this chapter, you'll learn how to separate the good from the bad so you can stock your medicine cabinet with the right stuff, and get a look at what might be coming down the pike.

Penis Pumps, Testicle Implants, and Injections, Oh My! A History of Sexual Healing

Sexual performance panaceas didn't morph overnight from crocodile hearts into pills. Along the way, scientists have tried other ideas, some more palatable than others. In 1889, seventy-two-year-old French endocrinologist Charles Édouard Brown-Séquard announced he'd fully regained his youthful virility by injecting crushed testicles from guinea pigs and dogs into his body. Soon enough, doctors struck upon an even better idea:

Why inject just the extract of testicles when you could use the whole thing? Physicians began implanting entire testicles from goats and monkeys inside men's scrotums, which easily expanded to make room for their new guest. In 1918, things went from weird to really macabre when Leo Stanley, resident physician at San Quentin prison in California, began transplanting human testicles from executed prisoners into other inmates. In most cases, men who received such treatments claimed they *felt* more virile, but reliable erections rarely resulted from these experiments. The race was still on to build a better hard-on. In 1982, the first leg of this relay was won thanks to a tire shop owner.

Geddings Osbon, who struggled with impotence, was determined to find a way to make love to his wife. And so, tinkering around in his tire shop one day, he built a contraption that did the trick. Osbon's vacuum pump fit over the penis and literally Hoovered more blood into the area. To keep the blood from flowing back out, Osbon placed an elastic ring around the base of his penis. This contraption, no matter how excruciating it sounds, certainly worked better than testicle implants. It went on to win FDA approval and is still prescribed to this day. For the ladies, there's even an FDA-approved clitoral pump. Still, while devices often fixed the problem, it made having sex about as suave as unclogging a drainpipe. There had to be a better way.

In 1983, Professor Giles Brindley stepped on stage at a urology conference in Las Vegas. His specialty? Erectile dysfunction, a field in which he had recently made notable progress. Rather than put his audience to sleep with a PowerPoint presentation, though, the British physiologist had more memorable evidence. Brindley announced that just prior to his presentation, he'd injected himself with a drug called papaverine, which helped get more blood flowing due south. To prove it, he pulled down his pants and displayed exhibit A: his erection.

The audience sat stunned. A few women in the front row squealed as Brindley hopped off stage to allow them a closer inspection. Erectile dysfunction, his presentation made abundantly clear, could be treated with medication. Papaverine injections were one possibility, but perhaps there were even easier methods on the horizon. Like pills.

In 1998, the U.S. Food and Drug Administration approved Viagra for the treatment of male erectile dysfunction. In its first year on the market, Pfizer sold $788 million worth of Viagra prescriptions. Even men who couldn't afford Viagra were getting handouts, thanks to Alan Greenberg, head of investment firm Bear Stearns, who reportedly donated $1 million to New York City's Hospital for Special Surgery to give it away to men in need. The invention of Viagra changed not only the lives of millions of men, but the very way scientists view sexual problems and come to solutions. If there's a pill to help guys get it up, then maybe there's also a pill to rev our libidos, reach orgasm more easily, and improve every facet of sex as we know it. The next step, of course, would be to invent a little pink pill for women so all those blue ones don't go to waste. Easy, right?

Women's Viagra: What's the Holdup?

More than a decade has passed since the arrival of Viagra, and scientists in search of a women's version are still scratching their heads. In trials by Pfizer, the effects of Viagra on Female Sexual Arousal Disorder remained inconclusive. The problem, say some scientists, may be that while blood flow plays a role in women's arousal, a far bigger hold-up is that women lack desire—the drive to strip down and hop into bed in the first place. Without desire, arousal is a moot point. It's like fixing the cart when the horse isn't inspired to pull the load. What women need, then, is something that would give the horse more get up and go, which led scientists to start tinkering with testosterone.

Testosterone serves as the jet fuel for both men's and women's libidos. Boost testosterone, and it stands to reason that women's sex drives will rise as well. This treatment seemed especially promising for women who have undergone menopause, since this can cause a significant drop in testosterone levels. From June 2002 to October 2003, Procter & Gamble tested a testosterone patch called Intrinsa on 549 women who had undergone menopause. Women on Intrinsa reported a 73 percent increase in satisfying sexual activity, compared to 19 percent for placebo users. And yet, Intrinsa was not recommended for approval by the FDA Advisory Committee, who cited the need for additional long-term safety studies. Since then, Procter & Gamble has conducted several larger studies on Intrinsa. That said, testosterone may not be the answer for everyone, since most pre-menopausal women don't have low testosterone levels. As we discussed a bit in chapter 6, these women's libido problems may lie within the brain.

During sex, most guys are thinking about one thing: sex. Women's minds, however, tend to wander—to the undone laundry, to the size of their thighs, to an earlier snide comment from a coworker, the possibilities are endless. Women can become too distracted to relish the sensations sex is designed to deliver, which could potentially be solved with a drug that helps them stay focused. To that end, some doctors have started prescribing low doses of Ritalin to increase

3 Viagra Facts You Didn't Know

It may cure jet lag. A team of Argentinean researchers led by Patricia Agostino administered Viagra to hamsters, then induced jet lag by turning the lights on and off at odd hours. Hamsters on Viagra recovered 50 percent faster, as was evidenced by their performance on exercise wheels. According to the study, Viagra affects enzymes in the body that regulate circadian rhythms. It only helped, though, when the hamster experiments simulated eastbound flights. Viagra is not approved by the FDA for the treatment of jet lag, so Pfizer does not recommend the drug for this condition.

Some may see the world through blue-tinted goggles. A small percentage of Viagra takers experience temporary changes in color vision where they see objects with a blue tinge or have trouble distinguishing blue and green objects. For this reason, Donato Borillo, Commander of Flight Medicine at Wright-Patterson Air Force Base, wrote a report in the *Federal Air Surgeon's Medical Bulletin* recommending that pilots wait a minimum of six hours from taking Viagra to hopping in a cockpit, since color vision is often crucial for flights, particularly at night.

It may reduce male fertility. One 2008 study in the journal *Fertility and Sterility* found that mice given Viagra produce 40 percent fewer embryos than other mice. According to study authors David Glenn and Sheena Lewis at the University of Belfast, this may occur because Viagra damages the acrosome, a caplike structure on the sperm head containing enzymes that help sperm break down the egg's outer layer. When the acrosome is damaged, these enzymes are released too early, rendering sperm infertile. That said, Pfizer points out that this research was not performed on human subjects, which suggests that more tests should be conducted before drawing any conclusions.

women's ability to concentrate in bed, although the FDA hasn't approved the drug for this purpose. Other medications that affect women's brain chemistry are also in the works. Scientists were surprised when a drug named flibanserin, originally tested as an antidepressant, was found to trigger a surge in women's sex drives, most likely due to its effect on neurotransmitters in the brain such as serotonin. Currently, the drug's maker, Boehringer Ingelheim, is conducting clinical trials evaluating the drug's libido-enhancing effects on 5,000 women. Still, in spite of a few contenders, if years of false starts and failed experiments prove anything, it's this: Women are complicated, and it might take more than a magic pill to solve any sexual problems they may have.

Crushed Beatles, Toad Sweat, and Other Quack Cures

What rhymes with Viagra, comes in a blue bottle, and supposedly sends women's sex drives into orbit? Niagara—an energy drink whose name was later changed to Nexcite after Pfizer sued the manufacturer for trademark infringement in 2001. Still, even without the catchy name, everyone was buzzing for a while about whether the beverage's patented formula of so-called "love herbs from Sweden"—damiana, ginseng, guarana, maté, and schizandra among others—could deliver on its sex-craze-inducing claims. A full 1,400 bottles were shipped to the Playboy mansion. At one point, Julia Roberts and Adam Sandler discussed making a movie about it. And yet does the drink live up to the hype, or is it just clever marketing wrapped in cute packaging?

Some libido-enhancing products might look legit, but be warned, the FDA's rules governing herbal and dietary supplements treat them as foods rather than drugs, which means that their safety and effectiveness aren't held to the same high standards as prescription and over-the-counter medications. As a result, many of these so-called panaceas can pose serious health risks, and yet they are easy to buy online or even in your local health food store without your being aware of the consequences. In 2004, Albert Sabucedo at the International Forensic Research Institute published a report in *JAMA* stating he'd bought bottles of the sexual enhancement herbal supplement Actra-Rx, also known as Yilishen, at a local alternative health food store. After analyzing its ingredients, he found that Actra-Rx contained prescription-strength levels of sildenafil—the active ingredient in Viagra. In the United States, Viagra is only available by prescription from a physician, and there's a good reason for this. The use of Viagra along with organic nitrates (often prescribed for chest pain) may cause a sudden, unsafe drop in blood pressure. Actra-Rx, however, had snuck through the cracks as an herbal supplement until Sabucedo's team sounded the alarm. The FDA promptly issued a warning that people shouldn't buy the supplement.

Next, let's take a closer look at the most legendary aphrodisiac of them all: Spanish fly. This powder is made from crushed beetles containing cantharidin, a compound that causes inflammation in the urethra after urination and produces an itchy sensation in the genitals that you'll feel compelled to scratch. Its status as a sexual stimulant is legendary. In ancient Rome, it was slipped into drinks to inspire indiscretions that could be later cashed in as blackmail. In 1772, the Marquis de Sade got an orgy going with the help of Spanish fly–laced candy. But this love drug has serious side effects. It can lead to painful urination, bloody discharge, and permanent damage to the kidneys and genitals. The FDA has banned the use of Spanish fly in the United States, although few have heard about its dangers and can easily buy it online. Most likely, the only reason more people aren't suffering is that most Spanish fly is fake (i.e., pills of cayenne pepper).

As yet another cautionary tale, consider the "Love Stone," a lump of ointment made of toad secretions containing a hallucinogen called bufotenine. Also called Piedra, Jamaica Stone, Black Stone, and Chinese Rock, this "street aphrodisiac" was sold in New York smoke shops. While it's usually rubbed on the genitals, in the mid-1990s, five men decided to eat it instead. Four died of heart failure. And that's just the tip of the iceberg. Another popular aphrodisiac, horny goat weed—so named because a Chinese goat herder observed that his flocks of goats got frisky after eating the plant—has been found to have adverse effects on pregnant women if they eat it. Yohimbe, stripped from the bark of a West African tree, can cause a dangerous rise in blood pressure if taken in the wrong quantities.

Even in cases where sexual enhancement products aren't life threatening, most are still ineffective. The FDA maintains that no aphrodisiac works. And yet, not all scientists were willing to write off every quick fix without taking a closer look. And what they found may surprise you.

Roots, Weeds, and Other Worthy Contenders

Ginseng is Chinese for "man root," and describes the root's pale, humanoid appearance—like a turnip with arms and legs. In spite of its troll-like looks, ginseng has a lot going for it, according to some scientists. For one, it enhances the activity of neurotransmitters in the brain and increases blood flow to the pelvic region, making it helpful for all sorts of bedroom-related problems. In one double-blind, placebo-controlled study published in the *Journal of Urology*, Korean researchers administered 900 milligrams of red ginseng three times daily to patients with erectile dysfunction for sixteen weeks. Over that time period, men's progress was monitored in the lab via penile duplex ultrasonography, which uses sound waves to provide detailed images of veins and arteries. Men also answered a questionnaire called the International Index of Erectile Function, which tabulated how often they were able to achieve erection and sexual intercourse at home. By the end of the experiment, men on ginseng had improved significantly on all parameters—frequency of erection, penetration, libido, and sexual satisfaction, showing more improvement than those who took a placebo.

Another product that shows promise for women is Zestra, an ointment rubbed on the genitals containing dozens of herbs, each with its own arousal-enhancing effects. Borage and evening primrose oils are high in gamma-linolinic acid, which helps increase blood flow and nerve conductivity. Coleus forskohlii extract acts as a stimulant. Angelica root extract contains the chemical osthole, which may boost hormone production. In 2007, 256 women struggling with issues of libido, arousal, or orgasm participated in a double-blind, placebo-controlled study in which they used Zestra and kept running tabs on their love life via a questionnaire called the Female Sexual Function Index (FSFI). The FSFI calibrates nineteen different variables, including the frequency and the strength of sexual desire, the ease of reaching orgasm, and how satisfied women felt when they reached their peaks. For women on Zestra, their FSFI scores shot up significantly compared to those on placebo, which suggests that this unassuming salve with a rubber stopper has more going for it than clever marketing and a cute name.

Still other contenders may merely require some tinkering before they do the trick. Take horny goat weed. This herb contains icariin, a compound that acts like a PDE-5 inhibitor, a chemical found in the body that dilates blood vessels throughout the body, including the penis. Viagra's active ingredient, sildenafil, is also a PDE-5 inhibitor, although it's eighty times as effective as the icariin in horny goat weed, according to research by Italian researcher Mario Dell'Agli. When Dell'Agli extracted icarriin from the plant and produced a modified version, he hit upon a new formula that could inhibit PDE-5 as well as sildenafil, he says. So far, Dell'Agli's new concoction hasn't been tested on live subjects, so the effects on humans are unknown and more tests should be done before any conclusions are drawn. Still, Dell'Agli plans to keep tinkering and testing, hoping to hit upon a winning formula.

Another aphrodisiac where the jury's still out on its effectiveness is *Tribulus terrestris*, a star-shaped fruit that first gained notoriety in the United States after Bulgarian athletes touted it as their secret weapon to winning the Olympics. The active ingredient is most likely protodioscin, a chemical that's related to DHEA, a "prohormone" found in our bodies that serves as the precursor to testosterone, estrogen, and other substances that keep our sexual motors running. In studies on rats, *Tribulus* produced more mounting activity, although the impact of *Tribulus* on men's mounting activities remain inconclusive. In one Bulgarian study involving twenty-one men published in the *Journal of Ethnopharmacology*, men's testosterone levels remained the same whether they were taking *Tribulus* or not.

Aphrodisiacs in Your Home

But what about those aphrodisiacs rumored to be lying in the recesses of your fridge or your local restaurant? Chocolate. Oysters. Do any of these things work? If you were to simply look at a breakdown of the chemicals contained in chocolate, it might look promising. Chocolate contains phenylethylamine, which is also released in the brain when people fall in love—no wonder a box of Godiva is the gift of choice on Valentine's Day. Still, scientists, never ones to put much stock in mushy holidays, decided to put this confection to the test under laboratory conditions. In one study, they measured the levels of phenylethylamine in women who had eaten chocolate and those who hadn't. No difference was found between the two groups, leading researchers to conclude that the phenylethylamine in chocolate is metabolized in the stomach long before it can reach the brain and induce its amorous effects. In another study published in *The Journal of Sexual Medicine*, Italian researchers compared scores on the Female Sexual Function Index among 163 women, some of whom reported regularly eating one serving of chocolate a day, others more than three servings, and still others who didn't indulge much at all. Women in all three groups scored similarly. Chocolate may provide a sugar rush, but it isn't the gift that keeps on giving, so don't count on getting lucky if you treat your sweetheart to a box.

But what about oysters? At the very least, they *look* sexually suggestive, which may explain why Casanova reportedly downed dozens to prepare for his legendary lovemaking marathons. The logic cited by proponents of this aphrodisiac is that oysters are high in zinc, and deficiencies of this mineral can cause impotence. Pop a zinc supplement, and studies show that higher libido, testosterone levels, and more frequent sex will ensue. That said, the levels of zinc in a pill far outstrip the amount found in several dozen oysters. So, unless you eat oysters all day, every day, we doubt you'll feel much of a difference in bed—and that's assuming you've got a zinc deficiency, which is fairly uncommon today. Many aphrodisiacs, including oysters, in fact, might have worked back in the day when certain nutrients essential to sexual functioning were scarce. Rhinoceros horn, for example, is rich in calcium and phosphorus, which are essential to healthy energy levels. If some ancient people's levels were low to begin with, it's certainly plausible that a dose of Rhino horn could bring someone's libido back.

In one study titled "Coffee, Tea, and Me" published in the journal *Pharmacology, Biochemistry and Behaviour,* Fay Guarraci at Southwestern University administered a tiny jolt of caffeine to over a hundred female rats, then set them loose to mate with males. After mating once, the caffeinated rats quickly returned for another romp. Guarraci theorizes that caffeine stimulates neurotransmitters in the hypothalamus, which plays a leading role in sexual arousal. That said, these libido-enhancing effects would probably only occur in humans who don't drink coffee regularly.

How to Tell Which Aphrodisiacs Work

Don't believe everything you hear about herbal supplements. Herbal supplements aren't regulated by the FDA in the same way prescription and over-the-counter drugs are, and could therefore pose serious health risks. If a product's claim seems too good to be true (for example, *add two inches to your erection!*), it probably is. Make sure to check the FDA Web site for reliable information and updates about various substances.

Opt for safer alternatives. There is some evidence that certain products can improve sexual function, such as ginseng and the topical ointment Zestra. Even coffee and vitamin C supplements may have a positive effect, although you should always do your research and check with your doctor to make sure the risks don't outweigh the benefits.

Plain old vitamin C may also juice up your sex life when not battling colds and the flu on your body's behalf. In one study published in *Biological Psychiatry*, men and women who took 3,000 milligrams of sustained-release vitamin C supplements had penile/vaginal intercourse significantly more often than those popping a placebo. That's because vitamin C increases catecholaminergic activity, which boosts the levels of certain sexually arousing chemicals such as epinephrine, norepinephrine, and dopamine coursing through your body. Keep in mind, 3,000 milligrams of vitamin C is a pretty high dose. It's not dangerous, and reported adverse side effects (stomach upset, diarrhea) were no higher in those taking the supplement than in the placebo group, but Brody conditions that people with Iron Overload Disease or problems with Glucose-6-Phosphate Dehydrogenase (G6PD) deficiency, a common human enzyme deficiency, should consult their physician before taking such a high dose of vitamin C. And don't expect fruit alone to fast-track your sex life, given that the average orange contains only 70 milligrams of vitamin C. That means you'd be eating nearly fifty oranges a day to get your dose.

Pills may solve some sexual problems, but they'll never be the answer to everything. After all, aside from the occasional bug, our bodies are designed to deliver their own natural highs in bed—which is why in our next chapter, we'll turn to the very moment during sex that feels much like a drug itself. Orgasm.

All About Orgasms

"Are you close?" John asked.

"Not yet," Jane said.

During sex, this exchange was fairly typical for John and Jane as they made the trek toward their peaks. John conjured up baseball statistics, thoughts about funerals, and did anything else he could to keep his excitement levels in check, while Jane, the orgasm underdog, struggled to catch up. After more reaching, fiddling, and contorting, Jane often gave up hope. And yet, tonight, she was surprised to feel something stirring down below.

"Don't stop!" she whispered.

John, hearing those words, came perilously close to losing it. It was like walking a tight wire: One wrong move, and he was done for. After a brief pause, he resumed what he was doing. "That's it," Jane murmured. "Right there . . . god, that feels good . . . OhmygodohmygodyesyesYES!"

It was worth the wait. It was always worth the wait. But no matter how often John and Jane had sex, figuring out the secret formula to orgasms remained a work in progress. Jane wasn't always the one left in the dust. While her climaxes tended to arrive late, once they came, Jane could keep on com-

ing. John had tried to emulate this enviable feat, but still needed to rest up between rounds. They'd also heard rumors that some people could think their way to an orgasm, no below-the-belt rubbing required. Was this a hoax, or were certain people blessed with highly orgasmic bodies, or could anyone learn how to channel their sexual energy into a hands-free orgasm with the right training?

Probably the only thing John and Jane knew for sure about orgasms was their power to put everything about their relationship back in perspective. Arguments they'd been squabbling about for weeks didn't seem all that important. Whatever worries they had about their future together faded from view. Orgasms really were that good. So what could they do to make them longer, stronger, and easier to reach than ever?

ORGASMS MAY BE the most mind-boggling mystery of sex. Sometimes, they stampede through our body like a bull in a china shop. Other times, no matter how patiently we wait, the O-train never arrives. Some scientists have even induced orgasms in unwitting study subjects by accident. Consider the story of Stuart Meloy.

In 1998, Meloy, an anesthesiologist in Winston-Salem, North Carolina, invented a device that he hoped would cure back pain. After recruiting a female patient who was willing to give it a try, Meloy implanted an electrode in her lower spine, then pressed the remote control to power it up. Within seconds, the anesthesiologist heard "something between a shriek and a moan," he recalls. Alarmed, Meloy cut the power and asked the woman what was wrong. Nothing, however, was wrong. Quite the contrary. "You'll have to teach my husband how to do that!" the woman joked. Meloy's invention, it appears, did a whole lot more than he'd bargained for: It had given his patient an orgasm with the push of a button.

In the 1973 movie *Sleeper*, Woody Allen stumbles into a closet-sized contraption called the orgasmatron, where he happily sits having orgasm after orgasm until he's discovered. Now that Meloy had stumbled upon a *real* orgasmatron, what should he do? At first, the anesthesiologist chalked up this surprising twist of fate as nothing more than a funny story to tell his wife and friends. After regaling a few colleagues with his serendipitous discovery, though, a gynecologist pointed out the obvious. Wouldn't many people—millions of people, in fact—want to give Meloy's orgasmatron a try?

Artistic endeavors abound with odes to orgasm that try to pin down what it's all about. Some describe it as laughing between your legs. Still others say it feels like an exploding watermelon, electric flesh arrows, a little death, a ripple, a fluttering, a flash, or a glorious sneeze. These descriptions, however poetic, don't really help us understand the nature of the beast. How do orgasms happen? Is there a way to make the highs higher, those eye-rollingly amazing sensations last longer? Scientists have explored orgasms inside and out, and have made significant strides in pinpointing what makes them happen. They've even identified different types of orgasms to shoot for—multiple orgasms, serial orgasms, blended orgasms, brain orgasms, the list goes on and on. Let's get to know the Big O a little better.

The Big Bang Explained

What, exactly, happens when we reach our peak? Back in the 1960s, William Masters and Virginia Johnson attempted to answer this question by inviting 694 men and women into their labs in St. Louis, Missouri. Once their volunteers had stripped down, Masters and Johnson attached electrodes, blood pressure cuffs, heart monitors, and other medical paraphernalia to various parts of their bodies. Then, they politely asked their study subjects to have an orgasm—through sex, masturbation, vibrator, cucumber, or however else struck their fancy. All told, Masters and Johnson estimate that they observed "10,000 complete cycles of sexual response."

What Masters and Johnson discovered was that orgasm triggers a tsunami of physiological changes that helps explain why we feel so breathless and shell-shocked once it's over. Hearts race anywhere from 110 to 180 beats per minute. Blood pressure skyrockets. The muscles in our pelvic region start contracting at 0.8-second intervals. Measuring these contractions with a machine called an automatic recording drum, Masters and Johnson determined that a mild orgasm was generally accompanied by three to five contractions, an intense orgasm by eight to twelve, and their longest-recorded orgasm on record involved twenty-five contractions over forty-three seconds.

A few evolutionary theorists believe that the whole purpose of orgasm is to tucker us out so that we have no choice but to remain horizontal for a while, which helps sperm inside the vagina stay put and increases the odds of conception. This theory is called the knockout hypothesis or the poleax hypothesis, named after a medieval sledgehammer used to kill cows with a blow to the head. Most scientists no longer put much stock in this theory, since conception occurs regardless of whether women climax or not, or hop out of bed or stay put. Still, given all the body parts that shake, rattle, and roll during orgasm, it's no wonder that afterward people often laugh, cry, become uncommonly ticklish, fall asleep, or even temporarily lose consciousness, according to observations by Kinsey and other researchers.

And that's just what happens on a muscular level. Beneath that, there's more. In the same way the appliances in your home won't run unless they're plugged in, your muscles, heart rate, and blood pressure levels won't budge an inch until your nervous system gives them the signal. Barry Komisaruk, co-author of *The Science of Orgasm* and a professor at Rutgers University, has studied how this electrical storm builds in our bodies, and how it spreads. The first neurons within the brain to react are "low threshold" neurons, which ignite easily like kindling in a fire. Get enough kindling going, and this activates nearby "high threshold" neurons, resulting in a domino effect that turns mild sensations into full-blown magnificent ones. Neurons also have a refractory period where, after they've fired, they won't fire again until they have a moment to rest up. As a result, the timing of the sensory input they receive is important. "It's like pushing a swing," explains Komisaruk. "Push too fast or too hard, and the swing will wobble or stall in its tracks. Push at the right time with an appropriate amount of force, and the swing will rise higher and higher." This is why an orgasm takes time, finesse, and, yes, rhythm to build properly.

Neurons communicate with each other via neurotransmitters, chemicals that get released by one neuron, and detected by the next, which triggers the signal to continue down the line like a torch from one relay runner to the next. Free-flowing neurotransmitter traffic is key to reaching status orgasmus, although as anyone who's never gotten there knows, there are plenty of roadblocks you can encounter along the way. If, during sex, your mind wanders toward that new crack in the ceiling or worries you'll wake the kids, this can divert the neurotransmitter brigade, which is why it's so important to stay focused during sex. Medications like antidepressants called SSRIs (selective serotonin reuptake inhibitors) can also stall neurotransmitters in their tracks by blocking the space between neurons so signals can't sail through. As a result, up to 70 percent of people on SSRIs like Prozac experience sexual side effects, where they're slow to rouse or unable to reach orgasm at all. Luckily, by tinkering with the type of SSRIs people are on or by adding other medications like Wellbutrin, these problems can often be circumvented so orgasms arrive more easily.

Neurotransmitters come in all kinds and varieties, and each produces its own special effects. Many work in tandem, and two worth noting are "excitatory neurotransmitters" (such as glutamate and substance T) and "inhibitory neurotransmitters" (including gamma aminobutyric acid and glycine). Excitatory neurotransmitters do just what their name suggests: Their sole purpose is to stir us into a frenzy, which is why they're released in droves the instant an orgasm hits. Hot on their tails, though, comes a wave of inhibitory neurotransmitters, which relax you and calm things down. Excitatory neurotransmitters may sound a whole lot more exciting than inhibitory ones, but during an orgasm, both are equally necessary. Why? Because without this one-two punch, orgasms would just get bigger and bigger and last forever, which might sound dreamy until you had to go to work.

Another neurotransmitter that's released during orgasm is oxytocin. This hormone's pain-reducing effects were discussed in chapter 8, but oxytocin can do a lot more than just that. In a study of nearly two hundred men in Zurich, Switzerland, the oxytocin spray gave people a "trust high" that made them more willing to contribute their money to dubious investments. Oxytocin also improves people's mind-reading skills, as was proved in another study where men snorting the spray were asked to gauge strangers' moods based on their eye movements. It may even help couples remain calm during arguments. When Beate Ditzen at Emory University asked fifty couples to engage in mock fights by discussing an unresolved aspect of their relationship, those who'd gotten a whiff of oxytocin showed lower levels of the stress hormone cortisol in their bloodstream afterward, which suggests they weren't as ruffled and might have more luck smoothing things over. Ditzen isn't about to brand oxytocin the solution to every marital spat, although she does believe it merits further research. In the meantime, the rest of us can reap the benefits of oxytocin with good old-fashioned orgasms.

For those who assume an orgasm feels different in men verses women, one study suggests that the sensations each gender feels are *so* similar, it's impossible to tell them apart. Ellen Vance and Nathaniel Wagner at the University of Washington recruited 246 men and women to write essays describing what orgasm felt like. These descriptions were then submitted anonymously to a panel of seventy "orgasm experts" (namely, gynecologists and psychologists) to see if they could guess whether a man or woman had written them. Here's a sampling of the entries:

Tension building up until you think it can't build up anymore, then release . . . feeling contractions in the genitals. Tingling all over.

I often see spots in front of my eyes during orgasm . . . I suppose the words "fluttering sensation" describe the physical feeling I get. All nerve endings sort of burst and quiver.

It's like jumping into a cool swimming pool after hours of sweating turmoil.

A building up of tensions—like getting ready for takeoff from a launching pad, then a sudden blossoming relief that extends all over the body.

It's like shooting junk on a sunny day in a big, green, open field.

None of the panelists could reliably distinguish whether a man or woman had written each description. Male and female orgasms "have long been considered to be qualitatively different," the study authors write. But their findings suggest that "the experience of orgasm for males and females is subjectively the same."

The Orgasm Gap Between Men and Women

For men, an orgasm can be as easy as sticking item A in slot B. But for many women, the solution is hardly so simple. Studies show that two thirds of women don't regularly reach orgasm during sexual intercourse, while a full 15 to 20 percent of cases seen in sex therapy involve women who've never had an orgasm at all, alone or with a partner. Is the Orgasm Gap just a fact of life in the same way that men are generally taller and stronger and can pee standing up, or is something else at work?

Scientists have examined the Orgasm Gap thoroughly, and have come up with plenty of theories about what causes the rift. One obvious challenge lies in the layout of a woman's genitals, which places her main orgasm trigger—her clitoris—fairly far from where all the action is usually going on down below. In 1924, one enterprising woman named Princess Marie Bonaparte, great grandniece to King Napolean I of France, delineated this problem further in a paper published in the surgical journal *Bruxelle-Médical*. In her study, she measured the genitals of 243 female volunteers and found that women whose clitorises and vaginas were closer together had more orgasms during intercourse than those cursed with wider gaps. Of Bonaparte's sample, 69 percent had clitorises located less than an inch from their vaginas, which highly increased the odds of having an orgasm during intercourse. Meanwhile, 10 percent of her sample had clitorises located exactly an inch from their vaginas, and 21 percent of her sample had clitorises located more than an inch from their vaginas, which all but doomed their odds of orgasm to failure. Bonaparte called the first lucky group *paraclitoridiennes* (*para* meaning "alongside"), the second group *mesoclitoridiennes* (*meso* meaning "in the middle"), and the third group *téléclitoridiennes* (*télé* meaning "far"). Bonaparte was a *téléclitoridienne*, which helped explain why she couldn't have orgasms during sexual intercourse. But she wasn't about to accept her fate.

In 1927, Bonaparte met with Viennese surgeon Josef Halban, who proceeded to surgically detach her clitoris and reattach it further down. After writing about her operation in another journal article (which showed before-and-after photos no less), Bonaparte inspired at least two other women to undergo the procedure. Based on their positive reviews, Bonaparte declared the experiment a success. Bonaparte, however, wasn't so lucky. Still unable to reach orgasm vaginally, Bonaparte accepted Halban's offer to redo her surgery, which proved no better than the first try.

Granted, Bonaparte's decision to move her clitoris closer to her vagina might seem nuts. Still, scientists who've analyzed her findings since then say that overall, her theory is right. There's even a pithy phrase to help women figure out whether their clitorises and vaginas are close enough together: If the distance is less than the width of your thumb, you are likely to come. Measure the dimensions on your own privates, ladies, and it may answer all kinds of questions (and even if you find you fall in the *téléclitoridienne* camp, there are plenty of ways to improve your chances for orgasm that we'll explore in the next section).

Today, there's even evidence that a woman's ability to reach orgasm may boil down to her genes. In 2005, Timothy Spector, director of the Twin Research Unit at St. Thomas' Hospital in London, published the results of a survey where he had asked more than 6,000 female twins—both identical and fraternal—to fill out a questionnaire about how often they achieved orgasm during intercourse. Given these twins had been raised in the same household with similar religious and sexual beliefs, Spector theorized that both identical and fraternal twins should have similar success rates on the orgasm front. And yet, by comparing one group to the other, Spector found that nonidentical twins were all over the map, while identical twins showed striking similarities. Spector concluded that 34 percent of a woman's abilities to reach orgasm are genetic.

Still other scientists suggest a far stranger theory for the

Orgasm Gap: that women who claim they aren't having orgasms actually *are* having them and just don't know it. William Hartman and Marilyn Fithian at the Center for Marital and Sexual Studies in Long Beach, California, invited twenty women into their offices who had all claimed they had never had an orgasm. And yet, when Hartman and Fithian asked them to masturbate while hooked up to equipment measuring their physiological responses, the women were informed that even though they didn't think they were having orgasms, their bodies showed clear-as-day signs that they were. Pelvic muscle contractions, the most classic indicator of climax, were rippling through these women's nether regions as usual. Once they were clued in to these cues, the women did a double take: Oh, so *that's* what an orgasm feels like? Many of these women, it turns out, had read or heard overblown accounts of how orgasms should feel and felt that their own experiences fell short of the hype and therefore weren't the real deal. All they needed was an attitude adjustment.

On the flip side, Joseph Bohlen, a urologist at the University of Minnesota in Minneapolis, invited eleven self-professed orgasmic women into his office to masturbate while hooked up to a similar battery of equipment. Upon reaching their peaks, nine displayed those tell-tale pelvic muscle contractions. Two, however, did not. Were they faking it? The women insisted they weren't, leading Bohlen to believe that they were having a *new* kind of orgasm. Bohlen called these ultra-quiet orgasms "Type IV." (Types I, II, and III all include pelvic muscle contractions varying in strength, duration, and rhythm).

Regardless of what type of orgasm women have, Indiana University biologist Elizabeth Lloyd has another theory why they're so hard to reach. It's called the "Fantastic Bonus" theory, although it's hardly what women would call fantastic. The general premise is, most men can orgasm easily because if they couldn't, they wouldn't be able to impregnate women, and would quickly get weeded out of the gene pool as a result. A woman, however, can conceive without climaxing. That makes her own orgasm nothing more than a pleasant perk— nice, but not necessary, evolutionarily speaking.

Some scientists argue that a woman's orgasm does serve a purpose in that it aids in conception by increasing the number of sperm she retains after sex. In one experiment, Robin Baker collected sperm discharged from women after intercourse and counted under a microscope the number of sperm expelled. Baker found that women who reach orgasm anywhere from one minute before a man to forty-five minutes afterwards retain more sperm than those who climax outside this time frame.

"So Did You Come?" Why Women Should Be Glad He Asked

Jessica, a graphic designer in Columbia, Missouri, was dating a guy named Gary who, no matter what, made sure she had an orgasm every time they had sex. She should be in heaven, right? Not exactly.

"I'm sure many women would thank their lucky stars to date a guy like this, but I wasn't into it," Jessica admits. Sometimes, when they were in bed together, if Jessica sensed a climax wasn't in the cards for her, she would say, *It's okay, I don't want to come, sex feels good to me anyway.* Gary, however, would insist. At first, his stubbornness seemed sweet. But over time, his efforts got a little annoying. "I know it sounds like a great thing that he was willing to do the work, but what I don't think he realized was that it can be a lot of work on *my* end to have an orgasm," Jessica explains. "There are just so many thoughts in my head sometimes, and distractions, and hiccups in my thinking, all of which can hold me back." By setting the bar too high, Gary had made sex so stressful Jessica couldn't enjoy herself.

Modern-day women may roll their eyes when a guy asks "So . . . did you come?," but it can help to remember that throughout most of history, bringing a woman to orgasm was considered "the job nobody wanted," according to Rachel Maines, a historian and author of *The Technology of Orgasm*. While it's impossible to say how often women in the past were hitting a high note with their husbands or lovers, some circumstantial evidence suggests it wasn't happening all that often. From the time of Hippocrates, around 450 BC, to Freud in the 1930s, scores of women were diagnosed with "hysteria"—a condition thought to result from lack of sexual gratification characterized by symptoms such as nervousness, insomnia, irritability, and the tendency to cause trouble, according to diagnostic manuals. The best treatment, physicians found, was "vulvular massage" to "paroxysm"—in other words, doctors began manually stimulating these sexually frustrated women to orgasm right in their offices. No one knows exactly how common this treatment was, although some historical literature suggests it was a cash cow to the medical profession, and that affluent women who could afford regular appointments were going (or rather, coming) as often as women today might head to a spa. One Parisian doctor even took photos of women during these paroxysms and published them in a three-volume medical work along with written descriptions: "Her body curves into an arc and holds this position for several seconds. One then observes some slight movements of the pelvis . . . she raises herself, lies flat again, utters cries of pleasure, laughs, makes several lubricious movements and sinks down on to the vulva and right hip."

Oddly, there's no evidence on record that doctors found this work as rewarding as you might think. For many patients, the procedure took up to an hour; in 1660 one physician named Nathanial Highmore noted in his book *De Passione Hysterica* that the technique was so challenging that it was "not unlike that game of boys in which they try to rub their stomachs with one hand and pat their heads with the other." Often, doctors would try to convince husbands to help, but were rarely successful in passing the buck. In 1886, the invention of the vibrator helped cut down considerably on the time these sessions took, and it wasn't long before vibrators were being marketed directly to women, cutting doctors out of the equation. By Kinsey's arrival in the 1950s, a growing number of men were realizing that they could (and should) pitch in to help their wives and girlfriends reach their peaks. Perhaps the pendulum has swung too far and men are too obsessed with whether women have orgasms, but it sure beats booking a doctor's appointment.

To Fake, or Not to Fake?

Thank god Jim smokes.

Marcy often had this thought after having sex with Jim, although she'd rather die than tell him why. During sex, Marcy faked her orgasms. While Jim headed outside for a post-coital cigarette, Marcy would masturbate. It wasn't ideal, but it seemed easier than the alternative. "I'm pretty shy about speaking up in bed," she says, adding that she'd faked with most of her ex-boyfriends as well. In her mind, the prospect of giving guys explicit directions was embarrassing, not to mention unromantic. And besides, it was bound to make Jim worry that his skills weren't up to snuff. Why rock the boat, since everything else about their five-month-long relationship was going so well?

Marcy's reluctance to rectify this problem puzzled her, since in the rest of her life, she had no qualms about asking for what she wanted. Working as a wedding and event planner in Washington, D.C., Marcy was a master at reeling off detailed instructions to caterers, florists, and hotel personnel. Sex, however, was different. Emotions and egos were at stake. At certain points, Marcy sensed that Jim might suspect that she was faking. Even so, Jim never mentioned it. Maybe he was too scared to know the truth. And even if he had asked, Marcy isn't sure she'd set him straight. "If I'd told him early on I was faking, it would have stung, but I imagine that finding out your girlfriend has been faking for five months would be devastating," she says. Fake orgasms, in her opinion, kept her relationship running smoothly, at least for now. But would there come a day when she couldn't take it? Was faking a sign their relationship would eventually crash and burn?

Marcy's concerns about why she fakes and what it means are amazingly common. According to one online survey of more than 16,000 respondents, 72 percent of women claim they've faked an orgasm at least once in their current or previous relationship. Fifty-five percent of men claimed they could tell when their partners were faking, although clearly, they aren't catching all the counterfeits. In another study of eighty-six couples, Randy Thornhill at the University of Mexico calculated that women faked orgasms 20 percent more often than their partners thought they did. In one particularly sad case, one woman said all her orgasms were shams, while her partner believed she climaxed 100 percent of the time.

Thornhill also found that women who faked were also more likely to neglect their partners and flirt with other men—a sign that eventually, fake climaxes can catch up with us, and that perhaps it's better to speak up sooner rather than later.

Here's something else that women might not realize: One in four men say they've faked orgasms, too. Mark, a lawyer from Raleigh, North Carolina, feels he puts on a fairly convincing performance. "One night I had had too much to drink, and the sex I was having with my girlfriend was going on fifteen, twenty, then thirty minutes," he recalls. He was pretty certain his partner had had an orgasm or two already, but at this point, the odds that he'd get there seemed slim. "I was kind of lacking sensitivity, and was getting tired, and I didn't feel like I was getting any closer to finishing . . . so I pretended. Basically did the full-on push thing then stopped abruptly—my standard M.O. when having an orgasm—while tensing up all over everywhere else. Then I relaxed, lay limp for a minute or two before pulling out and doing the post-coital cuddling thing." Mark doesn't think she had a clue. And he doesn't regret doing it. If it became a regular thing, then he'd worry. But for the right occasion, a fake climax is the perfect solution.

In addition to theorizing why orgasms happen (or not), scientists have developed an array of techniques to make the orgasms we do have even more satisfying. Let's explore their discoveries next.

How to Have Bigger, Better Orgasms

In the 1940s, Arnold Kegel invented an exercise for a muscle in the body that few people even knew they had: the pubococcygeus muscle (or PC for short), which stretches like a hammock from pubic bone to tailbone inside the pelvic cavity.

Kegel, an obstetrician-gynecologist in the suburbs of Los Angeles, had seen scores of women whose PC muscles had been stretched or torn during childbirth, leading to urinary incontinence. At the time, treating this condition often involved surgery, but Kegel decided to try a different Rx. *Go home and contract your PC muscle repetitively.* Kegel's recommendation worked—and not only for better bladder control. His patients returned raving about an unforeseen side benefit—during sex, they were experiencing longer, stronger orgasms.

An orgasm, after all, is like any other physical activity. Muscle tone matters. In the same way that beefy biceps win arm-wrestling matches and regular stints on a treadmill can keep you from getting winded in a 5K race, working out your PC muscles can help you reach even higher peaks during sex. Both women and men can benefit from Kegel's workout, which involves regularly clenching and relaxing your PC muscle (it's the one you use to stop and start urinating). The more reps you do, the better, although experts generally suggest starting out with three rounds of ten reps and building from there. Men and women who want to really whip their PC muscle into shape can use exercise equipment, including the Kegelmaster 2000 for women (as seen on *Oprah*) or the Kegelmale, which incorporate springs and weights for added resistance.

Kegels may provide the pre-sex prep work, but once couples are in bed, there are plenty of other things they can do to improve their orgasmic abilities. For one, adding a little more variety to your repertoire can work wonders. To find out how much variety was ideal, Juliet Richters at the University of New South Wales in Australia asked nearly 20,000 men and women what they did during their last sexual encounter, as well as whether they had an orgasm. Of those who engaged in straight intercourse, only 50 percent of women reached their peak. Couples who threw in two extra activities, such as manual stimulation and oral sex, increased a woman's orgasm odds to 90 percent. Five activities was deemed ideal for sending a woman over the edge (men nearly always orgasmed). In many cases, the combination of intercourse with other activities made all the difference. In one study of three hundred women by Seymour Fisher, 35 percent of women who experienced orgasm during intercourse were having "assisted intercourse," which means one partner was reaching down and stimulating her clitoris manually while they were joined at the hip.

Experimenting with different sexual positions during intercourse can also up the odds of orgasm—and often it's the tiniest tweaks that can tip the scales. During intercourse, raising your legs higher or lower, keeping them together or apart, or positioning your pelvises at a slightly differently angle can be all it takes to get the right parts rubbing up against each other better. Researchers have even forged new sex positions that all

Assisted intercourse (with manual stimulation of the clitoris) can help up a woman's odds of having an orgasm.

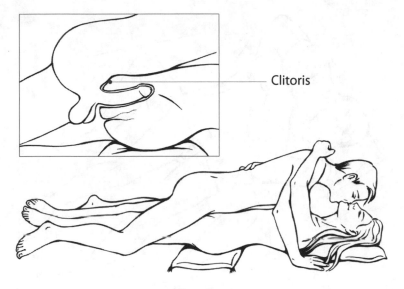

Clitoris

The Coital Alignment Technique (CAT)

but guarantee a fireworks-worthy finale. The Coital Alignment Technique (or "CAT" for short), was coined by New York psychotherapist Edward Eichel, who trained couples how to do it. In 1998, Eichel published his findings, announcing that the CAT allowed a surprising number of women to reach climax during intercourse and many to do so simultaneously with their partners. To try the CAT, the man on top moves his torso up a few inches so that his chin is closer to her forehead. Then he rocks rather than thrusts into his partner, keeping his pubic bone connected to hers at all time. This, in turn, increases stimulation in the clitoral area, turning intercourse into a more pleasurable experience for a woman.

Another position that has proven highly successful is the Lateral Coital Position, which was invented by research team William Masters and Virginia Johnson and became the pre-

The Lateral Coital Position

ferred position of 75 percent of their study subjects once they learned the ropes. To do it, you start out in your typical woman-on-top position, then shift so that the man's legs are parted and the woman's right leg is between his. The woman then leans forward on top of him and the couple rolls slightly to the right so that she can rest her head and shoulders on the bed. The benefit, according to Masters and Johnson in their work *Human Sexual Inadequacy*, is that "there is no pinning of either the male or female partner. There is mutual freedom of pelvic movement in any direction, and there will be no cramping of muscles or necessity for tiring support of body weight." It's a low-impact, highly maneuverable pose that puts both couples equally in control of the action, upping the odds that orgasms will ensue.

How to Improve Your O's

Practice Kegels. Kegel exercises can be performed any-where, while sitting in traffic or watching TV. Regularly clench and relax your PC muscle (it's the one you use to stop and start urinating). Start out with three rounds of ten reps and build from there.

Try new positions. Certain sexual positions can increase the odds that you will both reach some extremely satisfy-ing peaks. Two to try are the Coital Alignment Technique, or CAT (described on page 303 and pictured on page 303) and the Lateral Coital Position (described on pages 303–304 and pictured on page 304).

Lend a helping hand. One third of women who have or-gasms during intercourse do so by having "assisted inter-course" where either the man or woman reaches down and stimulates her clitoris manually. Here's how to pull it off in each position:

> **Missionary:** The woman reaches down between their bodies.

> **Woman on top:** The man places both hands on the front of her hips so that his thumbs are on each side of the clitoris. Then, he paddles his thumbs.

> **Doggy style:** The man can reach around his partner's body to stimulate her clitoris, or the woman can reach between her legs while supporting her torso on one shoulder.

Sideways (with the woman's back to his front): Both the man's and woman's hands are free to roam into clitoris territory.

Speak up. People can be bashful about offering up instructions in bed since they're afraid of hurting their partner's feelings, but their ego will most likely be *more* hurt if you aren't enjoying yourself. So, go ahead and offer up a quick comment like "Could you do that a little softer/harder?" or "Could you move a little to the left/right?" to keep your partner on course.

Don't fake it. Faking an orgasm might seem like an easy way out of a tricky situation, but you're essentially leading your partner further astray by encouraging him to continue techniques that just don't work. This, in turn, puts future orgasms even further out of reach, which can all too easily result in more faking. If an orgasm isn't in the cards, just say so and try some of the above-mentioned techniques to up the odds that it'll happen for real.

Moregasms: How Women *and* Men Can Achieve Multiples

If you've mastered the Big O basics and are looking to expand your horizons, science can point you in plenty of directions. While women struggle more often than men to reach orgasms in general, multiple orgasms are one area where they've got the edge. That's because after men orgasm, they typically enter a refractory period where no stimulus, no matter how pleasurable, will produce a second climax, a period that can last anywhere from a few minutes in young men to a few days in older ones. Women, on the other hand, have much shorter refractory periods, and many women can have multiple orgasms easily. Scientists aren't sure why men need a longer recovery time than women, although they theorize that each gender processes the post-orgasmic rush of neurochemicals differently in a way that affects sensitivity. Studies estimate that between 13 and 40 percent of women have experienced multiple orgasms, and there are actually two different types depending on how quickly orgasm number two, three, and so on arrive on the scene. "Sequential multiples" are orgasms that occur two to ten minutes apart; "serial multiples" are orgasms separated by mere seconds or minutes.

Most Multi-orgasmic Woman . . .

According to the Center for Marital and Sexual Studies, the most multiple orgasms ever achieved, by one anonymous twenty-six-year-old woman, was 134 orgasms in the span of one hour.

A woman's overall attitude toward sex can also increase her odds of having multiple orgasms, according to a study by Carol Darling published in the *Archives of Sexual Behavior*, which polled over eight hundred nurses about what they did in bed and how they felt about it. Darling picked nurses since they, by trade, would likely possess a comfort level with bodily functions that women in other professions—say, floral arrangement or hedge fund management—might lack. True to this finding, a full 43 percent of those nurses said they had experienced multiple orgasms, far higher than the national average. In this group, certain behaviors and attitudes tended to be highly correlative to the ability to achieve multiple orgasms. Most had examined their clitorises up close, had begun masturbating at an early age, and had no qualms about fantasizing, watching porn, receiving cunnilingus, or talking about sex with their partners. Multi-orgasmic women, in other words, didn't just get that way by accident. They had identified what they liked and weren't shy about discussing those needs with their partners.

Most Multi-orgasmic Man . . .

The most multiple orgasms ever achieved, by one anonymous man, was sixteen orgasms in the span of an hour.

For many years, it was thought that men couldn't achieve multiple orgasms at all. Then one day in 1970, a young student walked into the office of researcher William Hartman and claimed he was multi-orgasmic. Skeptical, Hartman asked for a demonstration—and the student dropped trough and delivered, masturbating his way to sixteen orgasms in the span of an hour. Intrigued, Hartman and his co-researcher Marian Fithian set off in search of other multi-orgasmic men and found thirty-two, whom they studied further. In 1984, they published their findings in the book *Any Man Can,* which, true to its title, declared that any man could become multi-orgasmic. But how?

The secret is simply understanding that a man's orgasm is

How to Become Multi-orgasmic

For women: The solution is simple—keep going. Once you've had one orgasm, don't throw in the towel. Instead, continue stimulation however feels best. If you're hypersensitive, ease off on the intensity for a minute or so then try building up again.

For men: Try the Stop-Start Technique, which was developed by a urologist at Duke University named James Semans (no name jokes, please). Semans picked up this trick after a sex surrogate (someone who has sex with patients to achieve therapeutic goals) informed him that it worked wonders helping men who suffered from premature ejaculation last longer in bed. Regular guys, however, can also use this technique to make their already lengthy lovemaking sessions last longer and become multi-orgasmic. To do it, bring yourself to the brink of orgasm, then stop all stimulation to allow the sensation to subside, then build again from there, repeating as many times as you like. Occasionally, you may feel the pleasurable sensation of orgasm, but if you stop stimulation before it gets too intense, you can avoid ejaculating until you decide the time is right.

The second technique, called the Squeeze Technique, was developed by Masters and Johnson. When you feel that you're about to ejaculate, squeeze the tip of your penis with the thumb on top and two fingers underneath. This should help stem the floodtide but allow orgasms to come and go as they please.

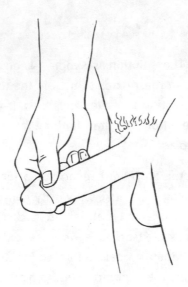

The squeeze technique can help
men become multi-orgasmic.

actually a two-part process: orgasm (those pleasurable muscle contractions) and ejaculation (that splash of seminal fluid). Most times, orgasm and ejaculation arrive on the scene simultaneously. As a result, most people assume that orgasm and ejaculation *have* to arrive at the same time. Not so. Men can ejaculate without orgasm (a medical condition known as ejaculatory anhedonia) and can orgasm without ejaculating (that's called being multi-orgasmic). Clearly, it's the latter group you'll want to join, and given ejaculation is what puts a guy out of commission, the key is to keep those little swimmers from getting loose, but allow orgasms to pass through unhindered. Scientists have developed two techniques for doing just that (described in "How to Become Multi-orgasmic" on page 309).

"I'll Have Mine Blended"

Multiple orgasms may inspire a lot of *oohs* and *ahhs*, but they're not the only type of orgasm scientists have serendipitously stumbled across in their travails. In 1982, a team of researchers including John Perry and Beverly Whipple noted that different parts of the genitals were connected to different nerve pathways, and each produced its own unique sensations. The clitoris is connected to the pudendal nerve, resulting in sensations that feel "sharp" and "superficial." The vagina (including the G spot) is connected to the pelvic nerve, which sends pleasurable sensations rippling throughout the pelvic region that feel "deeper" and "broader" than clitoral stimulation. Last but not least, in the 1990s, Whipple and Komisaruk determined that the cervix is connected to three nerves hypogastric, vagus, and pelvic—and produces the strangest sensation of all. To find out exactly how it felt, Komisaruk and Whipple handed female study subjects in their laboratories a device that's attached to a diaphragm, which stimulates and can create suction on the cervix. Study subjects with the stimulator said it produced pleasurable sensations deep in their abdomen unlike any they'd ever experienced; one woman reported it felt "all encompassing" or like "a shower of stars." This study also included women with complete spinal cord injury, who also experienced orgasm—a shocking and pleasant surprise for many of these study subjects, some of whom had been informed that they'd never experience the sensations of sexual pleasure again.

Simultaneously stimulate all three areas—clitoris, vagina, and cervix—and you'll produce a "blended orgasm," so named because they mix together sensations from different sources.

How to Have a Blended Orgasm

Choose multiple hot spots instead of just one. Blended orgasms mix together sensations from two or more areas of the body. To get started, pick two erogenous zones you'd like to try stimulating. Women might choose their clitoris and G spot. Men might choose their penis and prostate. Other options you might want to consider are the testicles, cervix, anus, A spot, U spot, breast/chest, or any other area where you find stimulation arousing.

Start off stimulating your favorite area. Get warmed up by focusing your initial efforts on the more reliable eroge-

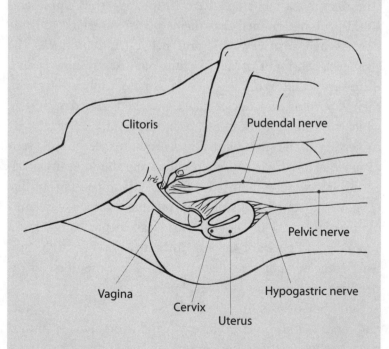

nous zone of the two you picked. Typically, the clitoris (on women) and penis (on men) are the most obvious starting points. This step is important because the sensations you feel from the second erogenous zone might not feel pleasurable unless you're already aroused.

Once you're aroused, switch to stimulating erogenous zone #2. If it's the G spot, insert a finger and crook it in a come-hither motion against the front wall of the vagina around one to three inches in. If it's the prostate, press up on the perineum (the area between the testicles and the anus). (For more detailed instructions on how to turn on these erogenous zones and others, review chapter 5.) This sensation will most likely feel different from the first: the point is to learn to appreciate each in its own right.

Try stimulating both spots at once. Now that you've got the hang of how each hot spot feels when stimulated, try putting them together. On women, try stimulating the G spot manually while treating the clitoris to some oral action. On men, treat the penis to oral sex and reach around with your hand to stimulate the prostate by pressing up on the perineum.

Try turning on three spots. Once you get the hang of stimulating two erogenous zones at once, try for three to triple your pleasure potential. If the man's penis is long enough to come into contact with a woman's cervix, for example, you can try stimulating her clitoris, G spot, and cervix all at once during intercourse. Choose a sex position that's conducive to G spot stimulation (typically, this is doggy style). Deep thrusting should rouse the cervix, while either the man or woman can reach down and manually stimulate the woman's clitoris to round out the sensations she receives. On men, three spots you might want to try stimulating might include the penis, anus, and prostate. While performing oral sex, reach behind and insert a well-lubed finger into the anus. Now that you've got two of his hot spots humming, press along the front wall of the rectum two to three inches to get his prostate in on the fun.

Blended orgasms can also be brought about by stimulating the anus (in men or women), prostate gland (in men), or any other erogenous zone on the body in addition to the genitals. Each area might feel great when rubbed on its own, but put them together, and the combination might be even better than any hot spot by itself. Some people might find that stimulation of certain areas (like the anus) isn't pleasurable *unless* it's combined with stimulation of other spots. That's the beauty of blended orgasms—with a little mixing and matching, a whole new smorgasbord of sensations await. The more parts you play with, the more nerve pathways you stimulate, and the richer the orgasmic results.

Orgasms: All in Our Heads?

"Have you ever come to orgasm without any kind of touch?"

In 1979, Gina Ogden, a doctoral student at the Institute for Human Sexuality in San Francisco, posed this question to fifty women who claimed to be "easily orgasmic" and had volunteered to serve as her study subjects. To Ogden's surprise, more than half said they could orgasm in this manner—through sheer mind power alone. "Oh, you mean thinking off," one woman said off-handedly. "I do it all the time."

Ogden was intrigued. Eight years later, she came across the perfect person who could help her explore this phenomenon in depth: Beverly Whipple. "Beverly was all science. I was all poetry and radical questions," Ogden recalls. Together, they invited ten women into Whipple's laboratory at Rutgers University and attached them to the proper equipment to measure physiological changes during orgasm—both from physical self-stimulation and from imagery alone so they could compare these responses—then asked them to demonstrate their abilities. And they did. Some of the women lay perfectly still during their imagery-induced orgasm, but their thoughts alone triggered the same physiological changes—increases in heart rates, blood pressure, pupil dilation, and pain thresholds—as orgasms achieved through genital self-stimulation. Since then, Barry Komisaruk, who was also involved in these initial studies, has performed fMRI scans of these women's brains. He found that the same areas of the brain light up during thought orgasms as traditional ones, proving beyond a doubt that these climaxes are the real McCoys.

Exactly *how* these women think their way to an orgasm, however, remains a mystery that scientists are still trying to piece together. "One theory is that we have a lot more control over our minds and bodies than we might think," says Komisaruk. While some people in Ogden's study might possess this talent naturally, training through meditation might also help. Tibetan monks, for example, can use meditation to increase circulation to the surface of their skin and raise their body temperature to such an extent that they could steam-dry wet sheets thrown on their shoulders. The same principle could apply to thinking your way to an orgasm, which sounds a whole lot more fun than drying wet sheets. If you're still skeptical, consider the fact that nearly all men and 37 percent of women have orgasms in their sleep. No direct genital stimulation occurs then, either, which suggests they might not be as impossible to achieve during our waking hours as we might think.

So what do these women think about? In Ogden's interviews with these women, many reported fantasizing about scenarios that turned them on, and included everything from Chippendale dancers to Red Riding Hood costumes. Not all women, though, thought about sex. Some women dreamed of pastoral scenes, or emptied their mind entirely. Still others— students of tantra, Taoism, or other Eastern disciplines that work with energy—said they visualized energy in their body, built it up, moved it around, and eventually released it in the form of an orgasm. While it's tempting to think these women are just wired differently, one of Ogden's study subjects, a sexologist named Annie Sprinkle, believes that pretty much anyone—man or women—can think their way to an orgasm if they get a little guidance.

For others, exercise does the trick. Chelsea, a writer in New York who trained as a gymnast during high school, discovered that certain types of stomach crunches weren't only good for her lower abdominals. "There was one exercise where we'd hang from the bar and raise our legs," she recalls. "After maybe two or three, I'd get this incredible rush of sensation in the nether regions. The only way I could maintain my composure was to cross my ankles and squeeze my legs together, as if tightening all my muscles would somehow make it less obvious. I was so young at the time I don't think I even knew it was an orgasm. Still, I knew it was *something*, since I didn't tell

How to Think Your Way to Orgasm

Advice from Annie Sprinkle, who offers classes on how to do it (go to AnnieSprinkle.org for more information):

1. Get comfortable. Lie down on your back with your knees bent and your feet flat on the floor, bed, or other surface. You'll need fifteen to forty-five minutes to get revved up.

2. Breathe deeply. Slowly inhale through your nose, pulling air into your belly so it rises. Then exhale slowly through your mouth as if you're blowing through a straw.

3. Rock your body. Arch your lower back when you inhale then flatten it when you exhale. Start undulating your pelvis as if you're having intercourse. For added oomph, squeeze your PC muscles, since this will increase blood flow and subtly stimulate the right areas.

4. Visualize your energy. While still undulating your body and squeezing your PC muscles, imagine energy building in your pelvic region. Then, slowly, visualize moving it up to your stomach then back down in a circular fashion. Once you feel the energy in your stomach, move it up to your chest in the same circular manner, then to your throat. You should spend at least a few minutes on each stage of the process.

5. Let go. Speed your breathing up to near-panting levels as if you were on the verge of orgasm during traditional sex. Then, start moaning, squealing, or making any noises that seem natural. This should help get the energy flowing up and out the top of your head.

Don't expect instant fireworks. At first, Sprinkle says, these brain orgasms might feel different from your classic climax. The first time you try them, they might produce little more than a few quivers and chills. You might even miss them entirely if you're not tuned in. The more you become aware of these sensations, though, the more you can harness them, and the higher they'll take you. Or, try combining these techniques for brain orgasms with the tactics you use for more traditionally achieved climaxes so you can simultaneously reap the benefits of both physical and psychological input at once.

anyone about it. It was my secret." Later, she discovered that sit-ups could produce the same effects. "Needless to say, I have a very strong stomach!" she says. "But I've always been curious why this happens."

Where on earth are these orgasms coming from? Scientists can't say for sure, although they have some theories. Abdominal exercises, for one, stimulate the diaphragm, which, in turn, activates the vagus nerve running down to the pelvis, which can cause climactic finales. Traumatic or shocking events can trigger a whole cascade of physiological changes—skyrocketing heart rates, blood pressure, and electrical activity in the brain—that could produce an orgasm under the right circumstances. Certain medications can also have some surprisingly sexy side effects. A small percentage of people taking certain antidepressants will experience orgasms out of the blue, often while yawning. In one case documented in the *Journal of Biological Psychiatry,* a thirty-five-year-old woman "experienced a three-hour, sudden-onset spontaneous orgasm while shopping." She stopped taking the medication. In these cases, the drugs alter dopamine levels in the brain—and since dopamine levels surge naturally during orgasm, it's not entirely surprising to scientists that in certain cases, orgasm can ensue.

Still other unexplained cases of orgasms have scientists stumped. In Taiwan, neurologists at Chang Gung Memorial Hospital closely examined a woman who could have orgasms while brushing her teeth. Neither the smell nor the toothpaste nor rubbing her gums alone would produce this effect—just tooth-brushing (the woman soon switched to mouthwash for oral hygiene). In a letter published in the *British Journal of Psychiatry* titled "Spontaneous Orgasms—Any Explanations?" a case was described of a forty-five-year-old Muslim mother of three who "complained bitterly of repeated, uncontrolled orgasms" that "occurred up to 30 times per day without any sort of sexual contact." Not surprisingly, socializing had become a challenge, and the woman had stopped visiting holy shrines. Gynecologists could find no physical cause for this phenomenon; her hormone levels were all within the normal limits.

As yet, there is no explanation or cure for these out-of-the-blue orgasms. Still, while these stories inspire plenty of head scratching and speculation, there remains one aspect of sex that may be even more mystifying and moving than any climax you could encounter. I'm talking about what happens after couples reach their peaks, share some pillow talk, then drift off to sleep. At that moment, millions of sperm could be en route to the egg. What determines whether they meet? In our final chapter, we'll explore the answer to that question by delving into the inner workings of conception.

CHAPTER 12

First Comes Love, Then Comes . . . a Baby? How Conception Really Happens

The pregnancy test was positive. Jane stared at the plus sign in disbelief. She was thrilled, but also baffled. How could this have happened so fast? Jane and John had married last year, and just recently had decided to try having a baby. They'd heard endless complaints from couples who'd struggled for years to conceive. Nonetheless, here Jane was, just weeks off the Pill and poof—a baby was on its way.

In retrospect, Jane realized it all made sense. While she hadn't suffered from morning sickness, she had noticed she'd been feeling a little nauseated lately. Some out-of-character food cravings had cropped up, too—maybe this was why she'd felt compelled to order a bucket of buffalo wings last night. Then there were those throw pillows she'd bought for the couch last week, and her overzealous rearranging of their pantry . . . in essence, Jane had been nesting and hadn't known it.

John was as excited as Jane was when she told him the news; a trip to the doctor made it official. As news of their impending parenthood spread, many marveled at how easily they conceived. What was their secret? Did they have sex in certain positions? Did they eat certain foods? Were John and Jane just blessed with supersonic sperm and eggs, or was something else entirely at work?

PRETTY MUCH EVERYONE past age eight knows more or less where babies come from. And yet, beyond the basics, confusion reigns, even among adults. Any couple who has embarked on a baby-making mission has heard—and maybe even followed—some bizarre advice. Some women stand on their head after sex to get more sperm flowing where it needs to go. Some say missionary-style sex is best, others doggy-style. Still others down yams and potatoes believing bland foods will make them more fertile. So which tips are merely old wives' tales, and what really works?

According to scientists, none of the aforementioned advice will get you very far on the baby-making front. The most crucial factor is something else entirely: timing. In general, sperm remain fertile for two to three days. By day five, pretty much all sperm are spoiled. A woman's wares have an even tighter expiration date. Eggs remain fertile for only 12 to 24 hours after ovulation—the point when the egg is released from the ovary. After that, the egg spoils, foiling whatever efforts sperm might make to mingle until next month. Given there's only a slim window of opportunity when sperm and egg are fresh enough to mix in a meaningful way, when should couples have sex if they want to conceive? In 1995, Allen Wilcox at the National Institute of Environmental Health

Strange Facts About Sperm and Eggs

Smallest cell in the body . . . Sperm.

Largest cell in the body . . . The egg. 1,500 sperm equal the weight of one egg.

Amount of sperm produced per second . . . 1,500 sperm are produced per second per testicle.

Amount of time sperm wait to see the light of day . . . On average, it takes sperm two months from the minute it's made to the moment it's ejaculated.

Number of sperm ejected per orgasm . . . 300 million sperm—that's the population of the United States.

Number of calories in semen . . . 5 calories per teaspoon.

Average speed of sperm as it's ejaculated . . . 28 miles per hour.

Average speed of sperm once it's inside the vagina . . . 8 inches per hour.

First known contraceptive . . . Crocodile dung inside the vagina, a method used by the Egyptians in 2000 BC. This was later replaced with elephant droppings.

Woman with the most children . . . Mrs. Vassilyev, wife of Feodor Vassilyev of Siberia, got pregnant 27 times resulting in 16 pairs of twins, 7 sets of triplets, and 4 sets of quadruplets for a total tally of 69 offspring.

Man with the most children . . . Moulay Ismail, the last emperor of Morocco who died in 1727, had a harem of 500 women who bore him at least 888 children. Throw in the illegitimate ones, and other estimates put that number as high as 1,042.

Sciences pinpointed this window of opportunity by tracking the efforts of 221 couples who were trying to get pregnant. During the trial, women jotted down the days of the month they had sex, and also took daily ovulation detection kits to pinpoint when they were ovulating.

A full 625 menstrual cycles later, 192 pregnancies were recorded. After crunching the numbers, Wilcox found that couples were most likely to conceive during a six-day window leading up to ovulation. Five days prior to ovulation, couples had a one in ten chance of conceiving; on the day of ovulation itself (day six), those odds rose to one in three. As for how often couples should have sex during this six-day period, since men's sperm remain in optimal condition for only two to three days, couples should have sex every other day. Of course, couples could also have sex *every* day if they like, although Wilcox found this didn't significantly increase couples' success rates. Sex every third day, however, is too infrequent. Only 6 percent of conceptions in Wilcox's study could be attributed to sperm that was more than three days old.

While ovulation typically occurs at mid-cycle—which, for a twenty-eight-day cycle, would be day fourteen after the start of a woman's last period—that timing can vary tremendously from month to month. A woman can even ovulate a new egg right when she's menstruating and getting rid of her old one (which is why you can still get pregnant on your period). Couples who want to cut down on the guesswork have two options. One, a woman can keep track of her basal body temperature, which rises by 0.4 to 0.6 degrees Fahrenheit at ovulation to create a prime environment for fertilization. Or, women can use ovulation detection kits, which test their urine for surges in luteinizing hormone, which occurs twenty-four to thirty-six hours before ovulation. Both methods, however, will put you behind the curve. Given basal body temperature only indicates when you're ovulating, you'll only be able to catch the last day of that six-day fertility window. Ovulation detection kits are slightly better, allowing couples to catch the last two or three days of this window. Currently, there's no test that will allow you to detect the onset of this six-day window, so you're best off having sex throughout the month if you want to increase the odds that you'll conceive.

Intercourse may actually *trigger* ovulation. Many mammals including rabbits and cats ovulate in response to sexual intercourse. In another study, Wilcox tracked 171 ovulatory cycles of 68 women, who also jotted down the days of the week they had sex. Not surprisingly, many got it on during the weekend. Far more surprising, though, was that these women tended to ovulate on Sunday, Monday, and Tuesday, which suggests that intercourse got ovulation rolling. But how? The answer, researchers surmised, must be something in the semen. After sifting through its components, researchers found what they think is the culprit. Seminal fluid contains trace amounts of follicle stimulating hormone (FSH), which is also produced naturally in women and causes the egg to ripen and burst out of the ovary. The FSH in semen could be absorbed through the vaginal walls and have the same effect, prompting a timely meeting of sperm and egg.

Timing aside, is there anything else couples can do to increase their chances of getting pregnant? One common-sense tip you've probably heard is to get gravity working in your favor—say, by having sex in the missionary position verses woman on top, or by elevating the woman's hips after intercourse. And yet, while these tactics certainly seem to make sense, the reality is, there's no proof they make a bit of difference. "There hasn't been a study where we track the conception rates of couples who have sex in certain positions," says Wilcox. "But our bodies don't need gravity to get things inside it where they need to go. Our bodies defy gravity all the time." Every day, blood gets pumped to the brain in spite of its tough uphill route. That burrito we ate for lunch gets moved through our small intestines whether we're sitting, lying down, hanging upside down, or astronauts in space with no gravity at all. That's because our digestive tract ripples in waves, nudging particles where they need to go, a process called peristalsis.

Peristalsis doesn't just happen during digestion. Women's reproductive tracts ripple in peristaltic waves as well. While a woman can't feel it happening, her reproductive organs are undulating upward, shuttling sperm toward the egg like moving sidewalks at an airport. In fact, for the majority of their journey, sperm could theoretically kick back and get carried upward at a decent clip; one 1996 study tracing the movement of inactive radioactive particles in a woman's reproductive tract showed that they could get ferried from the vagina to the fallopian tube in one minute flat. Women's bodies even know which fallopian tube to usher sperm into, due to signals sent out by the ovary that released the egg, which cause the closest fallopian tube to widen in diameter, thus allowing more sperm traffic to enter.

Want a Boy? Or a Girl? Why Timing May Matter Here, Too

Typically, after sex, Nick and Gina would lounge around in bed. Once they decided to have a baby, though, Gina adopted a different agenda. "I'll never forget the first time I saw it," says Nick, a telecommunications specialist in Denver, Colorado. The second sex was over, Gina jumped out of bed and started dancing hysterically around the bedroom as if she were in a mosh pit at a Smashing Pumpkins concert. After watching in disbelief for a few seconds, Nick asked Gina what on earth she was doing.

"We want a boy, right?" she said breathlessly between jumps. Gina had heard that male sperm were better swimmers; by jumping around, she'd ensure that the female sperm wouldn't have a chance, and that only male sperm would reach the egg. Nick was dubious. A year later, though, they gave birth to a boy. Two years after that, after more sex and more dancing, they conceived another boy. *I told you it works*, Gina told Nick with a sly smile after the ultrasound specialist announced the sex of their second child. Now, Nick doesn't know what to make of Gina's boy-baby dance. "I'm still not a diehard believer it works," he says. "Still, given we're two for two, I can't say it's complete hogwash, either. Frankly, I don't know what to think."

Call Them Nuts, but . . .

Back in the Middle Ages, it was believed that male sperm originated in the right testicle, female sperm in the left. As a result, men hoping for a boy would often place a rubber band around their left testicle, or have it permanently removed through surgery.

Gina's theory, however odd it might seem to her husband, isn't entirely off base. There is some evidence that couples can take measures to have a say in the sex of the child they conceive. Dancing, however, isn't the answer. Yet again, it's tim-

How to Get Pregnant

Time it right. Ovulation is the prime time to conceive, and in a typical twenty-eight-day menstrual cycle, ovulation occurs on day fourteen after the start of a woman's last period. Given that ovulation rarely occurs on schedule, ovulation detection kits can help you cut down on the guesswork.

Stay fit. Being overweight or underweight can alter hormone levels and render men and women less fertile. The ideal Body Mass Index (BMI) for conception is in the range of 20 to 25. If you're over or under this mark, it may be time to revisit your diet and exercise regimen.

Have a say in the sex of your child. According to the Shettles method, if you want a boy, have sex in the two-and-a-half-to-three-day window leading up to ovulation. If you want a girl, have sex any time before that.

ing. Back in the 1960s, Landrum Shettles theorized that sperm carrying the genetic blueprint for boys (which are contained on the Y chromosome) are faster but more fragile than sperm carrying the blueprint for girls (on the X chromosome). As a result, male sperm will win the race to fertilize the egg if the distance is short—meaning, the egg is perfectly poised for fertilization and waiting when the first wave of contenders arrives. But if, on the other hand, the egg is waylaid farther up the fallopian tube, male sperm will get pooped before they close the deal. This, in turn, leaves the sturdier, slower-moving female sperm clear for landing later. Based on these observations, Shettles argued that having sex right around ovulation will increase the odds you'll have a boy, while sex outside this time frame will up the odds you'll have a girl.

Don't Worry, Sex Won't Harm the Baby

Once couples conceive, many abstain from sex for fear they'll injure the developing fetus or induce early labor. In spite of these widespread concerns, countless studies have shown that, provided there are no complications such as vaginal bleeding or STDs, couples can get busy right up until birth if they're so inspired. In fact, one study found that couples who continue having sex throughout the pregnancy are *less* likely to deliver prematurely. In 2006, Jonathan Schaffir, a gynecologist at Ohio State University, kept tabs on the sex lives of ninety-three pregnant women. Forty-seven reported having sex up until the birth of their child; on average, their delivery occurred at 39.9 weeks—four days *longer* than those who refrained from sex, who gave birth at 39.3 weeks. This doesn't mean sex will actually prolong a pregnancy; more likely, women who are comfortable enough to have sex at this late stage have healthier pregnancies than women who don't have sex due to discomfort.

Another method that might help you select the sex of your child is the Ericsson method, where seminal fluid is deposited in a test tube of viscous liquid and allowed to swim awhile, which separates male from female sperm based on the distance they travel. From there, the appropriate lineup is used for artificial insemination. The founder of this method, Ronald Ericsson, claimed it was successful in predicting the sex of a child up to 70 percent of the time, although not all researchers agree that the accuracy levels are that high. Still, if you really want a boy or a girl, these and other high-tech options may well be worth exploring.

That's how sperm and egg meet. It might not always work perfectly, but you've got to admit, your reproductive organs are much craftier than we usually give them credit for.

Where Will the Science of Sex Take Us Next?

Flash forward five hundred years: What will dating and mating look like then? If they had to guess, most scientists would say it won't look much different than it does for John, Jane, and millions of men and women today. Given all the advances we've made over the years, sex is the one thing that remains largely the same no matter where or when we live. Whether people meet in caves huddled over a fire, in bars over martinis, or thousands of miles up on the moon, they will most likely be asking themselves the very same questions you've asked yourself. Who do you like? Does this person like you back? Can the joys you experience together, in bed and out, keep you together?

No matter how much we know about sex, there's always more to explore. Scientists will be there every step of the way, examining the old in-and-out in an effort to understand what turns us on, and why. So far, they've made incredible progress getting to the bottom of many mysteries we ponder every day. The sexy son hypothesis explains why women go for bad boys. The men-are-pigs hypothesis explains why men sleep around more than women. Lovemaps explain why some of us end up kinky. The poleax hypothesis explains why orgasms feel so good. Whatever quandary in your love life has you stumped, scientists can shed some light on the subject so we can sally forth armed with information that will make sex better than ever.

Sex, however, will always have its secrets. The minute scientists solve one piece of the puzzle, other questions inevitably take its place. Take Stuart Meloy from chapter 11, for instance. Since accidentally stumbling upon his orgasmatron, he's been designing a smaller version (the remote control is the size of a pager) that's also more affordable at $12,000. Meloy estimates that FDA approval of the orgasmatron is still a few years away, although he anticipates the device might cause as many problems as it solves. During trials where he outfitted a handful of female study subjects with the device, one woman asked Meloy, "Would it be considered adultery if I gave the remote control to someone other than my husband?"

Science brings us unimagined powers. But should we use it? Suppose you were dating someone and weren't sure if it was love or lust. If brain scans were made available so that confused couples could gauge how deep their feelings were for each other, would you head to your local MRI clinic for an evaluation? Or consider the cheating screen if it were available for humans—would you request partners get tested to see if they'd remain true? And if that test revealed they were genetically predisposed to cheat, would you ask them to get vaccinated to reduce their odds of straying?

Scientists may not have all the answers, but give them time. They've figured out how to trigger orgasms with the push of a button. They've pinpointed what couples can do to make love last for the long haul. They've even convinced a promiscuous meadow vole named Clinton to happily settle down with one mate. If they can do that, then perhaps anything is possible.

Chapter 1

3 **"I was bored":** Meston, C. M., and D. M. Buss (2007). "Why humans have sex." *Archives of Sexual Behavior* 36 (4): 488–93.

5 **even shopping:** Kahneman, D., A. B. Krueger, D. A. Schkade, N. Schwarz, and A. A. Stone (2004). "A survey method for characterizing daily life experience: The day reconstruction method." *Science* 306 (5702): 1775.

5 **$50,000 per year:** Dash, Eric. "Sex may be happiness, but wealth isn't sexiness." *New York Times*, July 11, 2004, section 4, page 14, column 1.

7 **below-average incomes:** Blanchflower, D. G., and A. J. Oswald (2004). "Money, sex and happiness: An empirical study." *Scandinavian Journal of Economics* 106 (3): 393.

8 **quickly dissipated:** Ney, P. G. (1986). "The intravaginal absorption of male generated hormones and their possible effect on female behavior." *Medical Hypotheses* 20: 226.

8 **depressed at 11.3:** Gallup, G. G. Jr., R. L. Burch, and S. M. Platek (2002). "Does semen have antidepressant properties?" *Archives of Sexual Behavior* 31 (3): 290.

9 **clean, and smooth:** Lai, Hsi. *The Sexual Teachings of the White Tigress*. Rochester, Vermont: Destiny Books, 2001, p. 52.

10 **at some point during this time period:** Brody, S. (2006). "Blood pressure reactivity to stress is better for people who recently had penile-vaginal intercourse than for people who had other or no sexual activity." *Biological Psychology* 71 (2): 214.

10 **day of the trials:** O'Connor, Anahad. *Never Shower in a Thunderstorm*. New York: Macmillan, 2007, p. 32.

11 **physiological performance:** McGlone, S., and I. Shrier (2000). "Does sex the night before competition decrease performance?" *Clinical Journal of Sport Medicine* 10 (4): 233.

12 **had sex more than once per week:** Smith, G. D., S. Frankel, and J. Yarnell (1997). "Sex and death: Are they related? Findings from the Caerphilly cohort study." *BMJ* 315: 1641–44.

12   father's age at death: Palmore, E. B. (1982). "Predictors of the longevity difference: A 25-year follow-up." *Gerontologist* 6: 515.

13   table tennis: Kita, Joe. *Guy Q: The Best Health, Fitness, Stress, Weight-Loss, Sex and Style Tips Ever.* Emmaus, Pennsylvania: Rodale Press, 2003, p. 126.

13   who had sex less frequently: Smith et al, "Sex and death: Are they related?," pp. 1641–44.

13   blood clots: Feldman, H. A., C. B. Johannes, J. B. McKinlay, and C. Longcope (1998). "Low dehydroepiandrosterone sulfate and heart disease in middle-aged men: Cross-sectional results from the Massachusetts male aging study." *Annals of Epidemiology* 8: 217.

13   "with alcohol": Komisaruk, Barry R., Carlos Beyer-Flores, and Beverly Whipple. *The Science of Orgasm.* Baltimore, Maryland: Johns Hopkins University Press, 2006, p. 51.

14   "since we began": Hall, Celia. "Nipple stimulation can protect women against breast cancer, researcher says." *Vancouver Sun*, April 23, 1994, p. B5.

14   men who did so less often: Komisaruk et al, *The Science of Orgasm*, pp. 50–51.

15   moderation is key: Charnetski, Carl J., and Francis X. Brennan. *Feeling Good Is Good for You: How Pleasure Can Boost Your Immune System and Lengthen Your Life.* Emmaus, Pennsylvania: Rodale Press, 2001, p. 114.

16   males or females: Bogaert, A. F., 2004. "Asexuality: Prevalence and associated factors in a national probability sample." *Journal of Sex Research* 41 (3): 279.

16   having sex at all: Roselli, C. E., K. Larkin, J. M. Schrunk, and F. Stormshak (2004). "Sexual partner preference, hypothalamic morphology and aromatase in rams." *Physiology & Behavior* 83 (2): 235.

17   ten times per year: Deveny, Kathleen. "We're not in the mood." *Newsweek*, June 30, 2003, p. 40.

17   vacation per year: Aguiar, M., and E. Hurst (2007). "Measuring trends in leisure: The allocation of time over five decades." *The Quarterly Journal of Economics* 122 (3): 969.

17   job they dislike: Hyde, J. S., J. D. DeLamater, and E. C. Hewitt (1998). "Sexuality and the dual-earner couple: Multiple roles and sexual functioning." *Journal of Family Psychology* 12 (3): 354.

17   positive impact on the frequency of sex: Call, V., S. Sprecher, and P. Schwartz (1995). "The incidence and frequency of marital sex in a national sample." *Journal of Marriage and the Family* 57: 647.

18   confidence in the president: Student, John. "No sex, please . . . we're college graduates." *American Demographics*, February, 1998, pp. 18–23.

19   because they're online: Gaudin, Sharon. "Americans can go without sex longer than the Internet, study finds." *Information Week*, September 21,

2007, unpaginated electronic work or go to: http://www.informationweek.com/news/internet/showArticle.jhtml?articleID=201808208

19 smoking marijuana: CNN.com, "E-mails 'hurt IQ more than pot.'" April 22, 2005, unpaginated electronic work or go to: http://www.cnn.com/2005/WORLD/europe/04/22/text.iq/.

19 biggest libido killers: Reuters, "TV in the bedroom bad for sex life." January 17, 2006.

21 and profanity: Cunningham, M. R., S. R. Shamblen, A. P. Barbee, and L. K. Ault (2005). "Social allergies in romantic relationships: Behavioral repetition, emotional sensitization, and dissatisfaction in dating couples." *Personal Relationships* 12 (2): 280–81.

21 same old stuff: Aron, A. P., C. C. Norman, and E. N. Aron (2000). "Couples' shared participation in novel and arousing activities and experienced relationship quality." *Journal of Personality and Social Psychology* 78 (2): 273.

Chapter 2

25 messing with hair gel: Morgan, Tom. "Men spend almost as long as women preening themselves." *Daily Express*, February 6, 2008, p. 3.

27 (11, 14, and 14): Garwood, S. G., L. Cox, B. Kaplan, N. Wasserman, and J. L. Sulzer (1980). "Beauty is only 'name' deep: The effect of first-name on ratings of physical attraction." *Journal of Applied Social Psychology* 10 (5): 433.

27 (like Anne, Kate, or Mindy): Perfors, A. "What's in a name? The effect of sound symbolism on facial attractiveness." Presented at the 26th Annual Conference for Cognitive Science, Chicago, August 7, 2004. Go to: http://www.mit.edu/~perfors/hotornot.pdf.

29 feel insecure: Jones, J. T., B. W. Pelham, M. Carvallo, and M. C. Mirenberg (2004). "How do I love thee? Let me count the Js: Implicit egotism and interpersonal attraction." *Journal of Personality and Social Psychology* 87 (5): 675.

30 mode of transportation: Gallup, A. C., D. B. White, and G. G. Gallup Jr. (2007). "Handgrip strength predicts sexual behavior, body morphology, and aggression in male college students." *Evolution and Human Behavior* 28 (6): 424.

30 ovulating and most fertile: Petralia, S. M., and G. G. Gallup, Jr. (2002). "Effects of a sexual assault scenario on handgrip strength across the menstrual cycle." *Evolution and Human Behavior* 23 (1): 3.

30 higher fertility levels: Manning, John T. *Digit Ratio: A Pointer to Fertility, Behavior, and Health.* Piscataway, New Jersey: Rutgers University Press, 2002, pp. 52, 61.

31 $50 in between: Miller, G., J. M. Tybur, and B. D. Jordan (2007).

"Ovulatory cycle effects on tip earnings by lap dancers: Economic evidence for human estrus?" *Evolution and Human Behavior* 28 (6): 379.

32 as their favorites: Singh, D. (1991). "Female body odour is a potential cue to ovulation." *Proceedings: Biological Sciences* 268: 797.

32 attract more attention: Haselton, M. G., M. Mortezaie, E. G. Pillsworth, A. Bleske-Rechek, and D. A. Frederick (2007). "Ovulatory shifts in human female ornamentation: Near ovulation, women dress to impress." *Hormones and Behavior* 51 (1): 40.

33 "less well endowed": Hatfield, Elaine, and Susan Sprecher. *Mirror, Mirror: The Importance of Looks in Everyday Life*. Albany, New York: State University of New York Press, 1986, p. 112.

34 sitting across from them was hot: Kurzban, R., and J. Weeden (2005). "HurryDate: Mate preferences in action." *Evolution and Human Behavior* 26 (3): 227.

34 pretty rather than plain: Cunningham, M. (1986). "Measuring the physical in physical attractiveness: Quasi-experiments on the sociobiology of female facial beauty." *Journal of Personality and Social Psychology* 50 (5): 932.

34 paraded before their eyes: Kenrick, D. T., S. E. Gutierres, and L. L. Goldberg (1989). "Influence of popular erotica on judgments of strangers and mates." *Journal of Experimental Social Psychology* 25 (2): 159.

35 white lie to be polite: Pines, Ayala Malach. *Falling in Love* (second edition). New York: Routledge, 2005, p. 28.

35 average-looking folks: Kleinke, Chris. *First Impressions: The Psychology of Encountering Others*. Englewood Cliffs, New Jersey: Prentice-Hall, 1975, pp. 2–3.

35 homelier peers: Moran, J. D., and J. C. McCullers (1984). "A comparison of achievement scores on physically attractive and unattractive students." *Family and Consumer Sciences Research Journal* 13 (1): 39.

35 they were good-looking: Major, B., P. I. Carrington, and P. J. D. Carnevale (1984). "Physical attractiveness and self-esteem: Attributions for praise from other-sex evaluator." *Personality and Social Psychology Bulletin* 10 (1): 43.

36 cute slackers got uglier: Kniffin, K. M., and D. S. Wilson (2004). "The effect of nonphysical traits on the perception of physical attractiveness." *Evolution and Human Behavior* 25 (2): 98.

36 different hue: Elliot, A. J., and D. Niesta (2008). "Romantic red: Red enhances men's attraction to women." *Journal of Personality and Social Psychology* 95 (5): 1160.

37 in American culture, slim wins: Sitton, S., and S. Blanchard (1995). "Men's preferences in romantic partners: Obesity vs. addiction." *Psychological Reports* 77: 1186.

37 within the normal range: Tovée, M. J., S. Reinhardt, J. L. Emery, and P. L. Cornelissen (1998). "Optimum body-mass index and maximum sexual attractiveness." *The Lancet* 352: 548.

37 **little extra padding, either:** Maisey, D. S., E. L. E. Vale, P. L. Cornelissen, and M. J. Tovée (1999). "Characteristics of male attractiveness for women." *The Lancet* 353: 1500.

38 **fat women fatter:** Nelson, L. D., and E. L. Morrison (2005). "The symptoms of resource scarcity: Judgments of food and finances influence preferences for potential partners." *Psychological Science* 16 (2): 172.

38 **size of the hourglass:** Singh, D. (1993). "Adaptive significance of female physical attractiveness: Role of waist-to-hip ratio." *Journal of Personality and Social Psychology* 65 (2): 296.

40 **paired randomly:** Hatfield and Sprecher, *Mirror, Mirror*, pp. 203–4.

41 **same gentleman both times:** Etcoff, Nancy. *Survival of the Prettiest*. New York: Doubleday, 1999, pp. 174–75.

41 **$62,500 per year:** Hitsch, G., A. Hortaçsu, and D. Ariely (2006). "What makes you click? Mate preferences and matching outcomes in online dating." Unpublished, p. 28.

41 **diameter of his shoulders:** Weeden, J., and J. Sabini (2005). "Physical attractiveness and health in western societies: A review." *Psychological Bulletin* 131(5): 640.

41 **(5'9 to 5'11):** Hatfield and Sprecher, *Mirror Mirror . . .* , p. 202.

43 **lower their ratings:** Pellegrini, R. J. (1973). "Impressions of the male personality as a function of beardedness." *Psychology* 10: 30.

43 **which dimensions were deemed ideal:** Leyvand, T., D. Cohen-Or, G. Dror, and D. Lischinski (2008). "Data-driven enhancement of facial attractiveness." *ACM SIGGRAPH*, article 38.

44 **5 to 7 percent:** Gangestad, S. W., R. Thornhill, and R. A. Yeo (1994). "Facial attractiveness, developmental stability, and fluctuating asymmetry." *Ethology and Sociobiology* 15: 73.

44 **rated better dancers:** Brown, W. M., L. Cronk, K. Grochow, A. Jacobson, K. Liu, Z. Popović, and R. Trivers (2005). "Dance reveals symmetry especially in young men." *Nature* 438 (7071): 1148–50.

44 **more orgasms than asymmetrical sorts:** Thornhill, R., S. W. Gangestad, and R. Comer (1995). "Human female orgasm and mate fluctuating asymmetry." *Animal Behavior* 50 (6): 1601.

46 **chosen more than others:** Thornhill, R., and S. W. Gangestad (1999). "The scent of symmetry: A human sex pheromone that signals fitness?" *Evolution and Human Behavior* 20 (3): 175.

46 **symmetrical sorts won the most votes:** Hughes, S. M., M. A. Harrison, and G. G. Gallup, Jr. (2002). "The sound of symmetry: Voice as a marker of developmental instability." *Evolution and Human Behavior* 23: 173.

46 **photographed from the right:** Etcoff, *Survival of the Prettiest*, p. 161.

47   waiting to get on: Meston, C. M., and P. Frohlich (2003). "Love at first fright: Partner salience moderates roller-coaster-inducted excitation transfer." *Archives of Sexual Behavior* 32 (6): 537.

47   intensify our attraction to others: Dutton, D. G., and A. P. Aron (1974). "Some evidence for heightened sexual attraction under conditions of high anxiety." *Journal of Personality and Social Psychology* 30 (4): 512.

48   on a happy note: Pines, *Falling in Love*, p. 17.

48   heading in: Cohen, B., G. Waugh, and K. Place (1989). "At the movies: An unobtrusive study of arousal attraction." *Journal of Social Psychology* 129: 692–93.

49   without any impediments: Fraley, B., and A. P. Aron (2004). "The effect of a shared humorous experience on closeness in initial encounters." *Personal Relationships* 11: 67.

49   almost perfect: Pines, *Falling in Love*, p. 39.

49   more spacious): Hirsch, A. R., and J. J. Gruss, "Odors and perception of room size." Presented at the 148th Annual Meeting of the American Psychiatric Association, Miami, Florida, 1995.

50   14 percent: Hirsch, Alan. *Scentsational Sex: The Secret to Using Aroma for Arousal.* Lanham, Maryland: Element Books, 1998, p. 100.

50   actual weight: Hirsch, A. R., J. R. Hoogeveenb, A. M. Bussec, and E. T. Allend (2007). "The effects of odour on weight perception." *International Journal of Essential Oil Therapeutics* 1: 21.

51   distinct from their own: Wedekind, C., T. Seebeck, F. Bettens, and A. J. Paepke (1995). "MHC-dependent mate preferences in humans." *Proceedings: Biological Sciences* 260 (1359): 245.

53   "sociosexual behaviors": McCoy, N. L., and L. Pitino (2002). "Pheromonal influences on sociosexual behavior in young women. *Physiology and Behavior* 75 (3): 367.

53   concoctions can make a difference: Cutler, W. B., E. Friedmann, and N. L. McCoy (1998). "Pheromonal influences on the sociosexual behavior of men." *Archives of Sexual Behavior* 27(1): 1.

55   one-night stand: Kruger, D. J., M. Fisher, and I. Jobling (2003). "Proper and dark heroes as dads and cads: Alternative mating strategies in British romantic literature." *Human Nature* 14: 313.

56   who took better care of their young: Gustafsson, L., and A. Qvarnstro (2006). "A test of the 'sexy son' hypothesis: Sons of polygynous collared flycatchers do not inherit their fathers' mating status." *The American Naturalist* 167 (2): 297.

58   Eight years younger: Buss, David M. *The Evolution of Desire: Strategies of Human Mating.* New York: Basic Books, 2003, p. 52.

58   six years younger than they are: Fieder, M., S. Huber (2007). "Parental age difference and offspring count in humans." *Biology Letters* 3: 689.

58   **men under age thirty:** Kidd, S. A., B. Eskenazi, and A. J. Wyrobek (2001). "Effects of male age on semen quality and fertility: A review of the literature." *Fertility and Sterility* 75 (2): 237.

59   **unknown causes:** Fisch, Harry. *The Male Biological Clock.* New York: Free Press, 2005, p. 3.

59   **ninety-two in 1992:** Noah, Timothy. "Bellow the fertility king." Slate, January 17, 2000, unpaginated electronic work or go to: http://www.slate .com/id/1004389/.

59   **At thirty-six or forty-five, the woman was attractive:** Marchant, Joanna. "Men choose beauty before age." *New Scientist*, June 27, 2001, unpaginated work or go to: http://www.newscientist.com/article/dn940-men-choose-beauty-before-age.html.

59   **at the age of fifty-nine:** Farmer, Ben. "UK woman, 59, world's oldest natural mother." *The Telegraph*, August 20, 2007, unpaginated electronic resource or go to: http://www.telegraph.co.uk/news/uknews/1560739/UK-woman%2C-59%2C-world%27s oldest natural-mother.html.

59   **age of seventy:** *Daily Mail*, "World's oldest mother gives birth to twins at 70." July 5, 2008, unpaginated electronic resource or go to: http://www.dailymail.co.uk/news/worldnews/article-1031722/Worlds-oldest-mother-gives-birth-twins-70.html.

61   **indifferent onlookers:** Jones, B. C., L. M. De Bruine, A. C. Little, R. P. Burriss, and D. R. Feinberg (2007). "Social transmission of face preferences among humans." *Proceedings: Biological Sciences* 274: 899.

62   **magnetic than the single ones:** Eva, K., and T. Wood (2006). "Are all the taken men good? An indirect examination of mate-choice copying in humans." *CMAJ* 175 (12): 1574.

62   **where the relationship stood fairly accurately:** Aloni, M., and F. J. Bernieri (2004). "Is love blind? The effects of experience and infatuation on the perception of love." *Journal of Nonverbal Behavior* 28: 287.

63   **didn't find attractive:** Pennebaker, J. W., M. A. Dyer, R. S. Caulkins, D. L. Litositz, P. L. Ackreman, D. B. Anderson, and K. M. McGraw (1979). "Don't the girls get prettier at closing time: A country and western application to psychology. *Personality and Social Psychology Bulletin* 5: 124.

64   **beer holder:** Jones, B. T., B. C. Jones, A P. Thomas, and J. Piper (2003). "Alcohol consumption increases attractiveness ratings of opposite-sex faces: A possible third route to risky sex." *Addiction* 98 (8): 1069.

64   **covered in graffiti:** Pennebaker, J. W., and D. Y. Sanders (1976). "American graffiti: Effects of authority and reactance arousal." *Personality and Social Psychology Bulletin* 2 (3): 264–67.

66   **biggest ego boost of all:** Walster, E., G. W. Walster, J. Piliavin, and L. Schmidt (1973). "'Playing hard to get': Understanding an elusive phenomenon." *Journal of Personality and Social Psychology* 26 (1): 113.

67   **668 male suitors:** Strassberg, D. S., and S. Holty (2003). "An exper-

imental study of women's internet personal ads." *Archives of Sexual Behavior* 32 (3): 254.

68   pick up the tab for dinner: Strassberg, "An experimental study of women's internet personal ads," p. 258.

68   earning potential, says Worner: Worner, S. M. "'I just want to get married—I don't care to who!' Marriage, life satisfaction and educational differences in Australian couples." Presented at the HILDA conference, 2007, p. 26.

68   for $1.5 million: Frank, Robert. "Marrying for love . . . of money." *Wall Street Journal*, December 14, 2007, unpaginated electronic resource or go to: http://online.wsj.com/public/article/SB119760031991928727-uxLp-STF5YqrHVllxjIWGE2HxLWM_20091126.html.

69   cold hard cash: Cunningham, M. A., A. F. Barbee, C. R. Graves, D. E. Lundy, S. C. Lister, and W. Rowatt (1996). "Can't buy me love: The effects of male wealth and personal qualities on female attraction." Paper presented at the Convention of the American Psychological Association, Toronto.

69   admiring their own mugs: De Bruine, L. M. (2005) "Trustworthy but not lustworthy: Context-specific effects of facial resemblance." *Proceedings: Biological Sciences* 272 (1566): 919.

71   stable but different: Kleinke, *First Impressions*, p. 101.

71   opposite-sex parent: Little, A. C., I. S. Penton-Voak, D. M. Burt, and D. I. Perrett (2003). "Investigating an imprinting-like phenomenon in humans: Partners and opposite-sex parents have similar hair and eye colour." *Evolution and Human Behavior* 24 (1): 43.

71   romantic partners: Perrett, D. I., I. S. Penton-Voak, A. C. Little, B. P. Tiddeman, D. M. Burt, and N. Schmidt (2002). "Facial attractiveness judgments reflect learning of parental age characteristics." *Proceedings: Biological Sciences* 269 (1494): 873.

72   extremely similar to their own: Penton-Voak, I., D. I. Perrett, and J. Pierce (1999). "Computer graphic studies of facial similarity and judgements of attractiveness." *Current Psychology* 18: 110.

72   faces that looked different: De Bruine, "Trustworthy but not lustworthy," pp. 919.

72   were nearly mirror images of each other: Anderson, C., D. Keltner, and O. P. John (2003). "Emotional convergence between people over time." *Journal of Personality and Social Psychology* 84 (5): 1064.

72   who'd married whom: Zajonc, R. B., P. K. Adelman, S. T. Murphy, and P. M. Niedenthal (1987). "Convergence in physical appearance of spouses." *Motivation and Emotion* 11 (4): 341.

73   who made fewer appearances: Pines, *Falling in Love*, p. 6.

73   gotten more screen time: Ibid., pp. 7–8.

74   Kiesler and Baral concluded: Kiesler, S. B., and R. L. Baral. "The search for a romantic partner: The effects of self-esteem and physical attractiveness on romantic behavior." In K. Gergen and D. Marlow (eds.), *Per-*

sonality and Social Behavior. New York: Addison-Wesley, 1992, pp. 162–63.

78 permanent and positive way: Pines, *Falling in Love*, p. 41.

Chapter 3

81 four people during that time period: Moore, M. M. (1985). "Nonverbal courtship patterns in women: Context and consequences." *Ethology and Sociobiology* 6: 244.

86 dating agency average: Pease, Allan, and Barbara Pease. *The Definitive Book of Body Language.* New York: Bantam Dell, 2004, p. 185.

86 "passionate love" for one another: Kellerman, J., J. Lewis, J. D. Laird (1989). "Looking and loving: The effects of mutual gaze on feelings of romantic love." *Journal of Research in Personality* 23: 145.

86 these study subjects got married: Pincott, Jennifer. *Do Gentlemen Really Prefer Blondes?* New York: Delacorte Press, 2008, p. 4.

87 "small talk": Fukada, Shiho. "Eyes only for each other, at least for the next three minutes." *New York Times*, December 11, 2005, Section 14; p. 6; Column 1.

89 never once looked like they were: Pease and Pease, *The Definitive Book of Body Language*, p. 176.

90 prone to indulge their cravings: Larsson, M., N. L. Pedersen, and H. Stattin (2007). "Associations between iris characteristics and personality in adulthood." *Biological Psychology* 75: 165.

91 no matter what opening line they used: Cunningham, M. R. (1989). "Reactions to heterosexual opening gambits." *Personality and Social Psychology Bulletin* 15 (1): 31.

91 "Saint-Rémy": Bale, C., R. Morrison, and P. G. Caryl (2006). "Chat-up lines as male sexual displays." *Personality and Individual Differences* 40: 655.

91 yielded to the other person's opinion: Kleinke, Chris. *First Impressions: The Psychology of Encountering Others.* Englewood Cliffs, New Jersey: Prentice-Hall, 1975, pp. 123–24.

93 gushed constant accolades: Kleinke, *First Impressions*, p. 120.

94 a good listener: Madan, A., R. Caneel, and A. S. Pentland (2004). "Voices of attraction." Cambridge, Massachusetts: MIT Media Laboratory, unpaginated electronic resource or go to: http://web.media.mit.edu/~anmol/TR-584.pdf.

94 having sex on their very first date: Padgett, P. M. (2007). "Personal safety and sexual safety for women using online personal ads." *Sexual Research & Social Policy* 4 (2): 27.

94 they've known for only a day or two: Laumann, Edward O., John H. Gagnon, Robert T. Michael, and Stuart Michaels. *The Social Organiza-*

tion of Sexuality. Chicago: The University of Chicago Press, 1994, pp. 398–99.

95   provided we smile when we say it: Clark, A.P. (2007). "Attracting interest: Displays of proceptivity increase the attractiveness of men and women." Unpublished.

96   genuinely happy: Pease and Pease, *The Definitive Book of Body Language*, pp. 66-67.

97   someone to smile back: Dimberg, U. M. Thunberg, and K. Elmehed (2000). "Unconscious facial reactions to emotional facial expressions." *Psychological Science* 11 (1): 86–89.

98   screaming or retching): Warren, J. E., D. A. Sauter, F. Eisner, J. Wiland, J. A. Dresner, R. J. S. Wise, S. Rosen, and S. K. Scott (2006). "Positive emotions preferentially engage an auditory-motor 'mirror' system." *The Journal of Neuroscience* 26 (50): 13067.

98   factor when picking women to date: Bressler, E., R. Martin, and S. Balshine (2006). "Production and appreciation of humor as sexually selected traits." *Evolution and Human Behavior* 27 (2): 121.

99   "Lost your wheel?": Shuster, S. (2007). "Sex, aggression, and humour: Responses to unicycling." *BMJ* 335: 1321.

100   hit on someone else: Givens, David. *Love Signals: A Practical Field Guide to the Body Language of Courtship*. New York: St. Martin's Press, 2005, pp. 6–7.

100   zero chance of sharing a bed later: Pease and Pease, *The Definitive Book of Body Language*, p. 103.

100   Let's cuddle: Givens, *Love Signals*, p. 47.

102   redeem yourself: Pease and Pease, *The Definitive Book of Body Language*, p. 222.

103   usually on a more subtle level: Ibid., p. 312.

103   resulted in a date: MSN/Carpoint.com (2002). "MSN Carpoint.com Valentine's Day fast facts reveals 30 percent of respondents judge their date by the type of car they drive." Unpaginated electronic work or go to: http://www.microsoft.com/presspass/press/2002/feb02/02-12fastfactspr.mspx.

104   mirror their actions: Chartrand, T. L., and J. A. Bargh (1999). "The chameleon effect: The perfection-behavior link and social interaction." *Journal of Personality and Social Psychology* 76 (6): 893.

106   waltzing around the room: Pease and Pease, *The Definitive Book of Body Language*, p. 203.

109   returned the dime: Brockner, J., B. Pressman, J. Cabitt, and P. Moran (1982). "Nonverbal intimacy, sex, and compliance: A field study." *Journal of Nonverbal Behavior* 6 (4): 256.

109   handing over the menu: Guéguen, N., C. Jacob, and G. Boulbry (2007). "The effect of touch on compliance with a restaurant's employee suggestion." *Hospitality Management* 26: 1019.

Chapter 4

113   only 50 percent of the men did: Clark, R., and E. Hatfield (1989). "Gender differences in receptivity to sexual offers." *Journal of Psychology and Human Sexuality* 2 (1): 50.

113   women four: Mosher, W. E., A. Chandra, and J. Jones. "Sexual behavior and selected health measures: Men and women 15–44 years of age, United States, 2002." *Advance Data from Vital and Health Statistics #362*, September 15, 2005, p. 3.

114   four or five: Buss, David M. *The Evolution of Desire: Strategies of Human Mating.* New York: Basic Books, 2003, p. 77.

115   downplay their experience levels: Alexander, M. G., and T. D. Fisher (2003). "Truth and consequences: Using the bogus pipeline to examine sex differences in self-reported sexuality." *Journal of Sex Research* 40 (1): 32.

116   men 11.9: Brown, N. R., and R. C. Sinclair (1999). "Estimating number of lifetime sexual partners: Men and women do it differently." *The Journal of Sex Research* 36 (3): 292–97.

116   to be going at it: Kohut, John, and Roland Sweet. *Real Sex: Titillating but True Tales of Bizarre Fetishes, Strange Compulsions, and Just Plain Weird Stuff.* New York: Plume, 2000, p. 68.

118   high self-esteem 16 partners: Walsh, A. (1991). "Self-esteem and sexual behavior: Exploring gender differences." *Sex Roles* 25 (7/8): 446.

119   as many people as possible: Markey, P. M., and C. N. Markey (2007). "The interpersonal meaning of sexual promiscuity." *Journal of Research in Personality* 41 (6): 1199.

119   three to four partners: Nettle, D., and H. Clegg (2006). "Schizotypy, creativity and mating success in humans." *Proceedings: Biological Sciences* 273: 613.

119   5.9 percent had an STD: Michael, Robert T., John H. Gagnon, and Edward O. Laumann. *Sex in America: A Definitive Survey.* Boston: Little, Brown, & Company, 1994, p. 194.

120   full thirty-seven steps apart: Bearman, P. S., J. Moody, and K. Stovel (2004). "Chains of affection: The structure of adolescent romantic and sexual networks." *AJS* 110 (1): 59.

121   trichomoniasis and chlamydia: Weinstock, S. B., and W. Cates, Jr. (2004). "Sexually transmitted diseases among American youth: Incidence and prevalence estimates, 2000." *Perspectives on Sexual and Reproductive Health* 36 (1): 6.

122   admitted to it): Bechtel, Stefan, Laurence Roy Stains, and the editors of Men's Health books. *Sex: A Man's Guide.* Emmaus, Pennsylvania: Rodale Press, 1996, p. 516.

125   sleep with twelve people, then pick the best after that: Todd, P. M. "Coevolved cognitive mechanisms in mate search: Making decisions in a decision-shaped world." In J. P. Forgas, M. G. Haselton, and W. V. Hippel (eds.), *Evolution and the Social Mind: Evolutionary Psychology and Social Cognition*. New York: Psychology Press, 2007, pp. 145–59.

Chapter 5

130 **sex was not one of them:** Schultz, W. W., P. V. Andel, I. Sabelis, and E. Mooyaart (1999). "Magnetic resonance imaging of male and female genitals during coitus and female sexual arousal." *BMJ* 319: 1596–1600.

131 **than to the left:** Güntürkün, O. (2003). "Adult persistence of head-turning asymmetry." *Nature* 421: 711.

132 **lost interest in the person:** Hughes, S. M., M. A. Harrison, and G. G. Gallup Jr. (2007). "Sex differences in romantic kissing among college students: An evolutionary perspective." *Evolutionary Psychology* 5 (3): 626.

132 **45 percent wished they were bigger:** Lever, J., D. Frederick, and L. A. Peplau (2006). "Does size matter? Men's and women's views on penis size across the lifespan." *Psychology of Men & Masculinity* 7 (3): 129.

133 **while smoking marijuana:** Earleywine, M. (2001). "Cannabis-induced Koro in Americans." *Addiction* 96 (11): 1663.

134 **5.5 inches and 6.3 inches:** Ansell Limited (manufacturer of LifeStyles condoms). "The LifeStyles Condoms average penis size survey." March 2001. Unpaginated electronic work or go to: http://www.free-con dom-stuff.com/education/research.htm.

134 **no correlation to their shoe size:** Shah, J., and N. Christopher (2002). "Can shoe size predict penile length?" *BJU International* 90: 586.

134 **happy with the size of their partner's package:** Lever et al., "Does size matter?," p. 129.

135 **11-centimeter-long specimen:** Masters, William H., and Virginia E. Johnson. *Human Sexual Response*. Boston: Little, Brown & Company, 1966, pp. 192–93.

135 **mimic the view men missed:** Morris, Desmond. *The Naked Woman*. New York: Macmillan, 2007, p. 146.

136 **(34.8 inches):** Kleinke, C. L., and R. A. Staneski (1980). "First impressions of female bust size." *Journal of Social Psychology* 110 (1): 123–34.

136 **overall weight distribution:** Lerner, R. M., S. A. Karabenick, and J. L. Stuart (1973). "Relations among physical attractiveness, body attitudes, and self-concept in male and female college students." *Journal of Psychology* 85: 123.

136 **indicator of his arousal level:** Rupp, H. A., and K. Wallen (2007). "Sex differences in viewing sexual stimuli: An eye-tracking study in men and women." *Hormones and Behavior* 51 (4): 524.

139 **"exhibit comparable activity":** Komisaruk, B. R., and B. Whipple (1998). "Love as sensory stimulation: Physiological consequences of its deprivation and expression." *Psychoneuroendocrinology* 23 (8): 937.

140 "Applied on the teeth alone": Kinsey, Alfred, Wardell B. Pomeroy, Clyde E. Martin, and Paul H. Gebhard. *Sexual Behavior of the Human Female*. Bloomington, Indiana: Indiana University Press, 1953, p. 589.

140 "palm-of-the-hand orgasms": Petersen, James. "Playboy Interview: Masters and Johnson." *Playboy*, November, 1979, p. 110.

142 Kinsey noted: Kinsey et al. *Sexual Behavior of the Human Female*, p. 589.

142 women find it highly arousing: Komisaruk, Barry R., Carlos Beyer-Flores, and Beverly Whipple. *The Science of Orgasm*. Baltimore, Maryland: Johns Hopkins University Press, 2006, pp. 8–9.

143 about the same amount as their partners: Miller, S. A., and E. S. Byers (2004). "Actual and desired duration of foreplay and intercourse: Discordance and misperceptions within heterosexual couples." *Journal of Sex Research* 41 (3): 304.

144 raring to go: Masters, William H., and Virginia E. Johnson. *Human Sexual Inadequacy*. Boston: Little, Brown & Company, 1970, pp. 67–84.

145 found breast and nipple stimulation arousing: Levin, R. J., and C. Meston (2006). "Nipple/breast stimulation and sexual arousal in young men and women." *The Journal of Sexual Medicine* 3 (3): 450.

146 "anatomical echoes' of other organs": Morris, *The Naked Woman*, p. 254.

146 women's breasts get 25 percent bigger: Masters and Johnson, *Human Sexual Response*, p. 28.

146 testicles 50 percent bigger: Ibid., p. 208.

149 "mouth," Kinsey noted: Kinsey et al, *Sexual Behavior of the Human Female*, p. 613.

149 surprisingly similar rates: Kukkonen, T. M., Y. M. Binik, R. Amsel, and S. Carrier (2007). "Thermography as a physiological measure of sexual arousal in both men and women." *The Journal of Sexual Medicine* 4 (1): 93.

150 corona at six o'clock: Halata, Z., and B. L. Munger (1986). "The neuroanatomical basis for the protopathic sensibility of the human glans penis." *Brain Research* 371 (2): 205.

152 risk of erectile dysfunction: Marceau, L., K. Kleinman, I. Goldstein, and J. McKinlay (2001). "Does bicycling contribute to the risk of erectile dysfunction? Results from the Massachusetts Male Aging Study (MMAS)." *International Journal of Impotence Research* 13 (5): 298–302.

155 "defective morally.": Maimónides, Moses (translated by Shlomo Pines). *The Guide of the Perplexed*. Chicago: University of Chicago Press, 1963, p. 609.

155 ten days to a man's life: Lawler, F. H., R. S. Bisonni, and D. R. Holtgrave (1991). "Circumcision: A decision analysis of its medical value." *Family Medicine* 23 (8): 587.

156 **Six percent noted improvements:** Kim, D., and M. G. Pang (2007). "The effect of male circumcision on sexuality." *BJU International* 99 (3): 619.

157 **491 percent by abstaining:** Shefi, S., P. E. Tarapore, T. J. Walsh, M. Croughan, and P. J. Turek (2007). "Wet heat exposure: A potentially reversible cause of low semen quality in infertile men." *International Braz J Urol* 33 (1): 50.

157 **laps on a regular basis:** Sheynkin, Y., M. Jung, P. Yoo, D. Schulsinger, and E. Komaroff (2004). "Increase in scrotal temperature in laptop computer users." *Human Reproduction* 20 (2): 453.

157 **sperm count or motility significantly:** Munkelwitz, R., and B. Gilbert (1998). "Are boxer shorts really better? Critical analysis of the role of underwear type in male subfertility." *Journal of Urology* 160 (4): 1329.

158 **below-the-belt protective gear:** Bechtel, Stefan, Laurence Roy Stains, and the editors of Men's Health books. *Sex: A Man's Guide*. Emmaus, Pennsylvania: Rodale Press, 1996, p. 90.

159 **ancient practice:** Paley, Maggie. *The Book of the Penis*. New York: Grove Press, 2000, p. 47.

164 **"sweetness of Venus.":** Laqueur, Thomas. *Making Sex: Body and Gender from the Greeks to Freud*. Cambridge, Massachusetts: Harvard University Press, 1992, p. 64.

164 **witchcraft, and Satanism:** Margolis, Jonathan. *O: the Intimate History of the Orgasm*. New York: Grove Press, 2004, pp. 242–43.

164 **delete this label in 1948:** Moore, L. J., and A. E. Clarke (1995). "Clitoral conventions and transgressions: Graphic representations in anatomy texts." *Feminist Studies* 21 (2): 255–301.

165 **An Illustrated Guide:** Chalker, Rebecca. *The Clitoral Truth: The Secret World at Your Fingertips*. New York: Seven Stories Press, 2002, pp. 34–35.

165 **easier time reaching multiple orgasms:** Ibid., p. 50.

166 **equipment in a sleep lab):** Karacan, I., A. L. Rosenbloom, and R. L. Williams (1970). "The clitoral erection cycle during sleep." *Psychophysiology* 7: 338.

167 **stomping ground of men: ejaculate:** Whipple, Beverly, Alice Kahn Ladas, and John D. Perry. *The G Spot: And Other Discoveries about Human Sexuality*. New York: Macmillan, 2004, p. 21.

168 **"on several occasions," they wrote:** Addiego, F., E. G. Belzer Jr., J. Comolli, W. Moger, J. D. Perry, and B. Whipple (1981). "Female ejaculation: A case study." *The Journal of Sex Research* 17 (1): 16.

168 **11 and 1 o'clock:** Whipple et al., *The G Spot*, p. 33.

169 **blue as could be:** Chalker, *The Clitoral Truth*, p. 97.

169 **found in semen:** Addiego et al, "Female ejaculation: A case study," p. 18.

169 **Certain women have G spots, while others don't:** Gravina, G. L., F. Brandetti, P. Martini, E. Carosa, S. M. Di Stasi, S. Morano, A. Lenzi, and

E. A. Jannini (2008). "Measurement of the thickness of the urethrovaginal space in women with or without vaginal orgasm. *Journal of Sexual Medicine* 5 (3): 610.

173   orgasmic in one to two minutes: Ann, C. C. (1997). "A proposal for a radical new sex therapy technique for the management of vasocongestive and orgasmic dysfunction in women: The AFE zone stimulation technique." *Sexual and Relationship Therapy* 12 (4): 357–70.

174   U spots are getting stimulated: Roach, Mary. *Bonk: The Curious Coupling of Science and Sex.* New York: W. W. Norton & Company, 2008, pp. 71–72.

178   eventually get kicked out: Baker, Robin. *Sperm Wars: The Science of Sex.* New York: Basic Books, 1996, pp. 20–21.

Chapter 6

182   limbic lobes of the brain ablaze: Faro, Scott. "Brain imaging could spot liars." News@nature.com. Presented at the annual meeting of the Radiological Society of North America in Chicago, November 29, 2004. Go to: http://www.nature.com/news/2004/041129/full/news041129-1.html.

186   face in those interesting shapes: Komisaruk, Barry R., Carlos Beyer-Flores, and Beverly Whipple. *The Science of Orgasm.* Baltimore, Maryland: Johns Hopkins University Press, 2006, p. 265.

186   rattles of the real deal: Ross, Emma. "Brain areas shut off during female orgasm." Reuters, June 20, 2005, unpaginated electronic work or go to: http://www.livescience.com/health/050620_ap_female_orgasm.html.

187   seat of sexual urges: Aron, A., H. E. Fisher, D. J. Mashek, G. Strong, H. Li, and L. L. Brown (2005). "Reward, motivation, and emotion systems associated with early-stage intense romantic love." *Journal of Neurophysiology* 94: 332.

188   his former employer: Timesonline.co.uk, "Man whose sex drive rose after injury claims £3.5m." December 13, 2006, unpaginated electronic work or go to: http://business.timesonline.co.uk/tol/business/law/article752461.ece.

188   £1.2 million in damages: *Telegraph,* "Injured biker now obsessed by sex." March 2, 2007, unpaginated electronic work or go to: http://www.telegraph.co.uk/news/uknews/1544273/Injured-biker-now-obsessed-by-sex.html.

189   couple's relationship quickly improved: Amen, Daniel. *Sex on the Brain: 12 Lessons to Enhance Your Love Life.* New York: Harmony Books, 2007, pp. 92–94.

191   Nothing more: Brizendine, Louann. *The Female Brain.* New York: Broadway Books, 2006, p. 5.

191   button-pushing and tons of frustration: Komisaruk et al, *The Science of Orgasm,* pp. 209–10.

195 brake (inhibition): Janssen, E., H. Vorst, P. Finn, and J. Bancroft (2002). "The Sexual Inhibition (SIS) and Sexual Excitation (SES) Scales: I. Measuring sexual inhibition and excitation proneness in men." *The Journal of Sex Research* 39 (2): 125–26.

195 distasteful, or otherwise: Janssen, E., H. Vorst, P. Finn, and J. Bancroft, J. (2002). "The Sexual Inhibition (SIS) and Sexual Excitation (SES) Scales: II. Predicting psychophysiological response patterns." *The Journal of Sex Research* 39 (2): 127.

197 seemed kind of hot: Ariely, D., and G. Lowenstine (2006). "The heat of the moment: The effect of sexual arousal on sexual decision making. *Journal of Behavioral Decision Making* 19: 93.

200 definitely not arousing: Chivers, Meredith L., and J. M. Bailey (2005). "A sex difference in features that elicit genital response." *Biological Psychology* 70 (2): 119.

203 one stage leading to another: Basson, R. (2001). "Female sexual response: The role of drugs in the management of sexual dysfunction." *Obstetrics & Gynecology* 98 (2): 350.

Chapter 7

207 7.2 sexual fantasies per day, women 4.5: Leitenberg, H., and K. Henning (1995). "Sexual fantasy." *Psychological Bulletin* 117 (3): 472.

208 indulge to his heart's content: Buss, David M. *The Evolution of Desire: Strategies of Human Mating.* New York: Basic Books, 2003, p. 82.

209 sex with a close relative: Hsu, B., A. Kling, C. Kessler, K. Knapke, P. Diefenbach, and J. E. Elias (1994). "Gender differences in sexual fantasy and behavior in a college population: A ten-year replication." *Journal of Sex & Marital Therapy* 20 (2): 113–14.

210 something wrong with his marriage?: Kahr, Brett. *Who's Been Sleeping in Your Head? The Secret World of Sexual Fantasies.* New York: Basic Books, 2007, pp. 9–10.

210 who don't daydream that often: Leitenberg and Henning, "Sexual fantasy," p. 490.

211 regardless of what they do in real life: Hicks, T., and H. Leitenberg (2001). "Sexual fantasies about one's partner verses someone else: Gender differences in incidence and frequency." *The Journal of Sex Research* 38 (1): 48.

212 think about nothing in particular: Hekmat, H., P. Staats, A. Staats, and J. Diek (2007). "Do romantic fantasies facilitate coping with acute pain?" *Journal of Pain* 8 (4, supplement 1): S55.

212 more easily aroused and orgasmic than in real life: Becker, M. A., and F. E. Wolf. "Gender differences in sexual fantasy content." Paper presented at the meeting of the American Psychological Association, Boston, 1990.

213 **bring them back later in spades:** Wegner, D. M., D. J. Schneider, S. R. Carter III, and T. L. White (1987). "Paradoxical effects of thought suppression." *Journal of Personality and Social Psychology* 53 (1): 5.

213 **abstain from this form of entertainment:** Coles, C. D., and M. J. Shamp (1984). "Some sexual, personality, and demographic characteristics of women readers of erotic romances." *Archives of Sexual Behavior* 13 (3): 187.

214 **who tried it and were disappointed.":** Bechtel, Stefan, Laurence Roy Stains, and the editors of Men's Health books. *Sex: A Man's Guide.* Emmaus, Pennsylvania: Rodale Press, 1996, p. 209.

215 **Envisioning "real" rape was repugnant:** Bond, S. B., and S. D. Mosher (1986). "Guided imagery of rape: Fantasy, reality, and the willing victim myth." *The Journal of Sex Research* 22 (2): 162.

217 **no relation to women's actual experiences:** Strassberg, D. S., and L. K. Locker (1998). "Force in women's sexual fantasies." *Archives of Sexual Behavior* 27 (4): 403.

217 **"sexual blame avoidance.":** Critelli, J. W., and J. M. Bivona (2008). "Women's erotic rape fantasies: An evaluation of theory and research. *The Journal of Sex Research* 45 (1): 63.

217 **imprinted on her mind since childhood.":** Friday, Nancy. *Women on Top: How Real Life Has Changed Women's Sexual Fantasies.* New York: Simon and Schuster, 1993, pp. 4–5.

Chapter 8

221 **He took them to bed with him.:** Krafft-Ebing, Richard von (translated by Francis Joseph Rebman). *Psychopathia Sexualis, with Especial Reference to the Antipathic Sexual Instinct: A Medico-forensic Study.* New York: Medical Art Agency, 1922, pp. 129, 258, 280.

225 **regular control group:** Cross, P. A., and K. Matheson. "Understanding sadomasochism: An empirical examination of four perspectives." From *Sado-masochism: Powerful Pleasures*, P. J. Kleinplatz and C. Moser (eds.). Philadelphia, Pennsylvania: Harrington Park Press, 2006, pp. 145–46.

227 **analgesic rather than distracting:** Whipple, B., and B. R. Komisaruk (1985). "Elevation of pain thresholds by vaginal stimulation in women." *Pain* 21: 357.

229 **and other risky professions:** Sprott, Richard (2005). "Kink sexuality and personality: Pilot study." Unpublished.

231 **feet as a turn-on quadrupled:** Giannini, A. J., G. Colapietro, A. E. Slaby, S. M. Melemis, and R. K. Bowman (1998). "Sexualization of the female foot as a response to sexually transmitted epidemics." *Psychological Reports* 83: 496.

232 **Ellis loved watching women pee:** Brome, Vincent. *Havelock Ellis, Philosopher of Sex: A Biography.* New York: Routledge, 1979, p. 9.

233 damper on his sexuality and have fun: Weiss, J. (1998). "Bondage fantasies and beating fantasies." *Psychoanalytic Quarterly* 67 (4): 631–36.

234 they feel guilty for it: Bader, Michael. *Arousal: The Secret Logic Behind Sexual Fantasies.* New York: St. Martin's Press, 2002, pp.115–40.

237 their affinity for boots faded: Rachman, S. (1966). "Sexual fetishism: An experimental analogue." *The Psychological Record* 16: 293–96.

238 triple-X movies when they became available: Zillmann, D., and J. Bryant (1986). "Shifting preferences in pornography consumption." *Communication Research* 13 (4): 560.

Chapter 9

240 cheat on their spouse at some point: Smith, T. W. "American sexual behavior: Trends, socio-demographic differences, and risk behavior." Chicago: National Opinion Research Center, 2006, p. 54.

241 watching porn as cheating: MSNBC.com, "Your unadulterated thoughts on adultery: The lowdown on the MSNBC.com/iVillage lust, love & loyalty survey." April 16, 2007, unpaginated electronic work or go to: http://www.msnbc.msn.com/id/18055526/.

241 total count up to 60 percent: Buss, David M. *The Evolution of Desire: Strategies of Human Mating.* New York: Basic Books, 2003, p. 133.

243 dildos with no glans removed only 35 percent: Gallup, G. G. Jr., R. L. Burch, M. L. Zappieri, R. A. Parvez, M. L. Stockwell, and J. A. Davis (2003). "The human penis as a semen displacement device." *Evolution and Human Behavior* 24: 280.

244 biologically designed to stray occasionally: Buss, *The Evolution of Desire*, pp. 74–75.

244 Other men's sperm: Baker, Robin. *Sperm Wars: The Science of Sex.* New York: Basic Books, 1996, pp. 42–43.

246 712 million sperm per ejaculate: Baker, R. R., and M. A. Bellis (1989). "Number of sperm in human ejaculate varies in accordance with sperm competition theory." *Animal Behavior* 37 (5): 867–69.

247 spiked right around ovulation: Haselton, M. G., and S. W. Gangestad (2006). "Conditional expression of women's desires and men's mate guarding across the ovulatory cycle." *Hormones and Behavior* 49: 509.

247 affairs right when they're ovulating: Bellis, M. A., and R. R. Baker (1990). "Do females promote sperm competition? Data for humans." *Animal Behaviour* 40: 997–98.

247 who is not his own: Bellis, M. A., K. Hughes, S. Hughes, and J. R. Ashton (2005). "Measuring paternal discrepancy and its public health consequences." *Journal of Epidemiology and Community Health* 59: 752.

248 "very happy.": Glass, Shirley, and Jean Coppock Staeheli. *Not Just Friends: Rebuilding Trust and Recovering Your Sanity After Infidelity.* New York: Simon and Schuster, 2004, p. 221.

249 triumvirate of personality traits spells trouble: Buss, *The Evolution of Desire*, pp. 148–51.

249 likelihood to cheat by 1 percent: Treas, J., and D. Giesen (2000). "Sexual infidelity among married and cohabiting Americans." *Journal of Marriage and the Family* 62 (1): 56.

250 actually glad they cheated: MSNBC.com, "Your unadulterated thoughts on adultery."

250 more likely to fool around: Walster, E., J. Traupmann, and G. W. Walster (1978). "Equity and extramarital sexuality." *Archives of Sexual Behavior* 7 (2): 127.

252 if you pay for it: Druckerman, Pamela. *Lust in Translation: Infidelity from Tokyo to Tennessee.* New York: Penguin, 2007, p. 180.

252 adultery during your marriage by 39 percent: Treas, J., and D. Giesen (2000). "Sexual infidelity among married and cohabiting Americans," p. 54.

252 my hand down your smooth back . . .": Maheu, Marlene. *Infidelity on the Internet.* Naperville, Illinois: Sourcebooks, 2001, p. 3.

252 engaged in an online affair: MSNBC.com, "Your unadulterated thoughts on adultery."

253 touchy-feely stuff occurred: Gergen, Kenneth, Mary Gergen, and William Barton. "Deviance in the dark." *Psychology Today*, October 1973, pp. 129–30.

254 thirteen real-life affairs: Mileham, B. L. A. (2007). "Online infidelity in Internet chat rooms: An ethnographic exploration." *Computers in Human Behavior* 23: 13.

257 hiring a private investigator: MSNBC.com, "Your unadulterated thoughts on adultery."

258 got it right 58 percent of the time: Anderson (unpublished).

258 the ones who'd cheated: Ali, Lorraine, and Lisa Miller. "The secret lives of wives." *Newsweek*, July 12, 2004, p. 46.

258 women's infidelity rates rival men's: Schmitt, D. P. (2004). "Patterns and universals of mate poaching across 53 nations: The effects of sex, culture, and personality on romantically attracting another person's partner." *Journal of Personality and Social Psychology* 86 (4): 577.

258 number had risen to 82 percent: Druckerman, *Lust in Translation*, p. 15.

258 polygamy or human cloning: Gallup poll, "Moral Issues." Conducted May 8–11, 2006.

260 only 24 percent end up packing their bags: Glass and Staehali, *Not Just Friends*, p. 127

260 never sign on the dotted line: Ibid., p. 116.

261 even in this extreme circumstance: Buss, David. M. *The Dangerous Passion: Why Jealousy Is as Necessary as Love and Sex.* New York: Free Press, 2000, p. 156.

261 invested in the relationship already: Ibid., p. 202.
261 without bringing sex into the picture: Ibid., pp. 57–59.
262 outshine the interloper: Ibid., pp. 190–91.
262 verify info like that?): Ibid., p. 201.
263 displaying greater affection: Ibid., p. 192.
263 rig you with blinders: Gonzaga, G. C., M. G. Haselton, J. Smurda, M. S. Davies, and J. C. Poore (2008). "Love, desire, and the suppression of thoughts of romantic alternatives." *Evolution and Human Behavior* 29 (2): 119.

266 followed in Clinton's footsteps and settled down: Young, L. J. (1999). "Oxytocin and vasopressin receptors and species-typical social behaviors." *Hormones and Behavior* 36 (3): 212–21.

267 34 percent reported marital discord: Walum, H., L. Westerberg, S. Henningsson, J. M. Neiderhiser, D. Reiss, W. Igl, J. M. Ganiban, E. L. Spotts, N. L. Pedersen, E. Eriksson, and P. Lichtenstein (2008). "Genetic variation in the vasopressin receptor 1a gene (*AVPR1A*) associates with pair-bonding behavior in humans." *Proceedings of the National Academy of Sciences in the United States of America* 105 (37): 14153–56.

267 harbor these cheating genes: Cherkas, L. F., E. C. Oelsner, Y. T. Mak, A. Valdex, and T. D. Spector (2004). "Genetic influences on female infidelity and number of sexual partners in humans: A linkage and association study of the role of the vasopressin receptor gene (*AVPR1A*)." *Twin Research* 7 (6): 649.

Chapter 10

270 crocodile hearts right on the penis: Conis, Elena. "Historic, and nutty, treatments for male impotence." *Los Angeles Times*, March 17, 2008, unpaginated electronic work or go to: http://www.latimes.com/features/health/la-he-esoterica17mar17,1,4065807.column?track=rss.

270 guinea pigs and dogs into his body: Nuland, Sherwin. "How to grow old." *Best American Science Writing*, edited by Dava Sobel. New York: HarperCollins, 2004, pp. 69–70.

271 ring around the base of his penis: Lewis, R. W., and R. Witherington (1997). "External vacuum therapy for erectile dysfunction: Use and results." *World Journal of Urology* 15 (1): 78.

272 Papaverine injections were one possibility: Klotz, L. (2005). "How (not) to communicate new scientific information: A memoir of the famous Brindley lecture." *BJU International* 96 (7): 956–57.

272 give it away to men in need: Fisher, Ian. "$1 million gift for new charity case: The Viagra-needy." *New York Times*, June 10, 1998, Section B; page 3; column 1.

274 experiments simulated eastbound flights: Agostino, P. V., Plano, S. A., and D. A. Golombek (2007). "Sildenafil accelerates reentrainment of

circadian rhythms after advancing light schedules." *Proceedings of the National Academy of Sciences in the United States of America* 104 (23): 9834.

274 color vision is often crucial for flights, particularly at night: Borrillo, D. J. (1998). "Dangers of Viagra use in pilots." *Federal Air Surgeon's Medical Bulletin* 98 (3): 9–10.

274 40 percent fewer embryos than other mice: Glenn, D. R. J., N. McClure, S. L. Cosby, M. Stevenson, and S. E. M. Lewis (2008). "Sildenafil citrate (Viagra) impairs fertilization and early embryo development in mice." *Fertility and Sterility*, pp. 1–6, not yet published in print, doi:10.1016/j.fertnstert.2007.12.014.

275 rendering sperm infertile: Glenn, D. R. J., C. M. McVicar, N. M. McClure, and S. E. M. Lewis (2005). "Sildenafil citrate improves sperm motility but causes a premature acrosome reaction in vitro." *Fertility and Sterility* 87 (5): 1067.

275 approved the drug for this purpose: Roach, Mary. *Bonk: The Curious Coupling of Science and Sex.* New York: W. W. Norton & Company, 2008, p. 250.

275 brain such as serotonin: Carey, John. "Viagra for women?" BusinessWeek, December 28, 2006, unpaginated electronic resource or go to: http://www.businessweek.com/bwdaily/dnflash/content/dec2006/db2006 1228_315249.htm.

276 shipped to the Playboy mansion: Moore, Jenny. "Falling for Niagara." *The Independent*, May 6, 2001, p. 19.

276 Adam Sandler discussed making a movie about it: Bowen, Kit. "A little sex drink for Roberts and Sandler." Hollywood.com, April 26, 2001, unpaginated electronic work or go to: http://www.hollywood.com/news/A_little_sex_drink_for_Roberts_and_Sandler/386442.

276 Sabucedo's team sounded the alarm: Sabucedo, A., M. A. Gutierrez, and K. C. Mueller (2004). "Sex, lies, and Niagra." *JAMA* 291 (5): 560–62.

277 died of heart failure: Centers for Disease Control and Prevention (1995). "Deaths associated with a purported aphrodisiac—New York City, February 1993–May 1995." *Morbidity and Mortality Weekly Report* 44 (46): 853–55, 861.

278 those who took a placebo: Hong, B., Y. H. Ji, J. H. Hong, K. Y. Nam, and T. Y. Ahn (2002). "A double-blind crossover study evaluating the efficacy of Korean red ginseng in patients with erectile dysfunction: A preliminary report." *The Journal of Urology* 168: 270–73.

279 and a cute name: Ferguson, D., C. Steidle, G. Singh, S. Alexander, Mary K. Weihmiller, and M. Crosby (2003). "Randomized, placebo-controlled, double-blind, crossover design trial on the efficacy and safety of Zestra for women in women with and without female sexual arousal disorder." *Journal of Sex & Marital Therapy* 29 (supplement 1): 38.

279 could inhibit PDE-5 as well as sildenafil, he says: Dell'Agli, M., G. V. Valli, E. D. Cero, F. Belluti, R. Matera, E. Zironi, G. Pagliuca, and E.

Bosisio (2008). "Potent inhibition of human phosphodiesterase-5 by Icariin derivatives." *Journal of Natural Products* 71 (9): 1513.

280 produced more mounting activity: Gauthaman K., P. G. Adaikan, and R. N. Prasad (2002). "Aphrodisiac properties of Tribulus Terrestris extract (Protodioscin) in normal and castrated rats." *Life Sciences* 71 (12): 1385.

280 whether they were taking *Tribulus* or not: Neychev, V. K., and V. I. Mitev (2005). "The aphrodisiac herb *Tribulus terrestris* does not influence the androgen production in young men." *Journal of Ethnopharmacology* 101 (1–3): 319.

280 Women in all three groups scored similarly: Salonia, A., F. Fabbi, G. Zanni, M. Scavini, G. V. Fantini, A. Briganti, R. Naspro, F. Parazzii, E. Gori, P. Rigatti, and F. Montorsi (2006). "Chocolate and women's sexual health: An intriguing correlation." *The Journal of Sexual Medicine* 3 (3): 476.

281 more frequent sex will ensue: Antoniou, L. D., T. Sudhaker, R. J. Shathoub, and J. C. Smith (1977). "Reversal of uraemic impotence by zinc." *Lancet* 2 (8044): 895.

281 returned for another romp: Guarraci, F. A., and A. Benson (2005). "'Coffee, Tea and Me': Moderate doses of caffeine affect sexual behavior in female rats." *Pharmacology, Biochemistry and Behavior* 82 (3): 522.

282 significantly more often than those popping a placebo: Brody, S. (2002). "High-dose ascorbic acid increases intercourse frequency and improves mood: A randomized controlled clinical trial." *Biological Psychiatry* 52 (4): 371.

Chapter 11

288 contracting at 0.8-second intervals: Masters, William H., and Virginia E. Johnson. *Human Sexual Response.* Boston: Little, Brown & Company, 1966, p. 78.

288 twenty-five contractions over forty-three seconds: Giustina, Anthony. *Sex World Records.* Morrisville, North Carolina: Lulu Publishing, 2005, p. 5.

290 unable to reach orgasm at all: Mourik, Orli Van. "Sex, love and SSRIs." *Psychology Today*, April 3, 2007. Unpaginated electronic work or go to: http://www.psychologytoday.com/articles/index.php?term=pto-20070403-000003&page=1.

291 dubious investments: Kosfeld, M., M. Heinrichs, P. J. Zak, U. Fischbacher, and E. Fehr (2005). "Oxytocin increases trust in humans." *Nature* 435: 674.

291 based on their eye movements: Domes G., M. Heinrichs, A. Michel, C. Berger, and S. C. Herpertz (2007). "Oxytocin improves 'mind-reading' in humans." *Biological Psychiatry* 61 (6): 731.

291 might have more luck smoothing things over: Ditzen, B., G. Bodenmann, U. Ehlert, and M. Heinrichs (2006). "Effects of social support and oxytocin on psychological and physiological stress responses during marital conflict." *Frontiers in Neuroendocrinology* 27 (1): 134.

292 **"subjectively the same.":** Vance, E. B., and N. N. Wagner (1976). "Written descriptions of orgasm: A study of sex differences." *Archives of Sexual Behavior* 5 (1): 93.

293 *téléclitoridiennes* (*télé* meaning **"far"**): Roach, Mary. *Bonk: The Curious Coupling of Science and Sex.* New York: W. W. Norton & Company, 2008, pp. 66–67.

294 **your thumb, you are likely to come:** Ibid., p. 68.

294 **34 percent of a woman's abilities to reach orgasm are genetic:** Dunn, K. M., L. F. Cherkas, and Tim D. Spector (2005). "Genetic influences on variation in female orgasmic function: a twin study." *Biology Letters* 1 (3): 260.

295 **All they needed was an attitude adjustment:** Margolis, Jonathan. *O: The Intimate History of the Orgasm.* New York: Grove Press, 2004, p. 66.

295 **in strength, duration, and rhythm):** Bohlen, J. G. (1982). "The female orgasm: Pelvic contractions." *Archives of Sexual Behavior* 11 (5): 367–68.

296 **climax outside this time frame:** Komisaruk, Barry R., Carlos Beyer-Flores, and Beverly Whipple. *The Science of Orgasm.* Baltimore, Maryland: Johns Hopkins University Press, 2006, pp. 38–39.

298 **vulva and right hip.":** Margolis, *O: The Intimate History of the Orgasm,* p. 66.

298 **pat their heads with the other.":** Maines, Rachel. *The Technology of Orgasm: "Hysteria," the Vibrator, and Women's Sexual Satisfaction.* Baltimore, Maryland: Johns Hopkins University Press, 1999, p. 4.

299 **current or previous relationship:** Mialon, H. M. (2008). "The economics of ecstasy." Unpublished. Go to: http://userwww.service.emory.edu/~hmialon/Ecstasy.pdf.

300 **flirt with other men:** Thornhill, R., S. W. Gangestad, and R. Comer (1995). "Human female orgasm and mate fluctuating asymmetry." *Animal Behaviour* 50 (6): 1610.

300 **One in four men say they've faked orgasms, too:** Mialon, "The economics of ecstasy."

302 **(men nearly always orgasmed):** Richters, J. R. de Visser, C. Rissel, and A. Smith (2006). "Sexual practices at last heterosexual encounter and occurrence of orgasm in a national survey." *The Journal of Sex Research* 43 (3): 221.

303 **simultaneously with their partners:** Eichel, E. W. (1988). "The technique of coital alignment and its relation to female orgasmic response and simultaneous orgasm." *Journal of Sex & Marital Therapy* 14 (2): 129.

304 **tiring support of body weight.":** Masters, William H., and Virginia E. Johnson. *Human Sexual Inadequacy.* Boston: Little, Brown & Company, 1970, pp. 310–11.

307 **40 percent of women have experienced multiple orgasms:**

O'Connor, Anahad. *Never Shower in a Thunderstorm*. New York: Macmillan, 2007, p. 27.

307   134 orgasms in the span of one hour: Giustina, *Sex World Records*, p. 5.

308   talking about sex with their partners: Darling, C. A. (1991). "The female sexual response revisited: Understanding the multiorgasmic experience in women." *Archives of Sexual Behavior* 20 (6): 532–35.

308   sixteen orgasms in the span of an hour: Ibid., p. 6.

308   any man could become multi-orgasmic: Bechtel, Stefan, Laurence Roy Stains, and the editors of Men's Health books. *Sex: A Man's Guide*. Emmaus, Pennsylvania: Rodale Press, 1996, pp. 300–305.

311   "shower of stars.": Komisaruk et al., *The Science of Orgasm*, p. 10.

315   orgasms achieved through genital self-stimulation: Whipple, B., G. Ogden, and B. R. Komisaruk (1992). "Physiological correlates of imagery-induced orgasm in women." *Archives of Sexual Behavior* 21 (2): 121.

316   37 percent of women have orgasms in their sleep: Kinsey, Alfred, Wardell B. Pomeroy, Clyde E. Martin, and Paul H. Gebhard. *Sexual Behavior of the Human Female*. Bloomington, Indiana: Indiana University Press, 1953, p. 196.

316   eventually released it in the form of an orgasm: Ogden, Gina. *Women Who Love Sex: An Inquiry into the Expanding Spirit of Women's Erotic Experience*. Cambridge, Massachusetts: Womanspirit Press, 1999, pp. 97–98.

318   the higher they'll take you: Sprinkle, Annie. *Dr. Sprinkle's Spectacular Sex: Make Over Your Love Life with One of the World's Great Sex Experts*. New York: Penguin, 2005, pp. 259–60.

319   She stopped taking the medication: Grimes, J., and L. Labbate (1996). "Spontaneous orgasm with the combined use of Bupropion and Sertraline." *Journal of Biological Psychiatry* 40: 1184.

319   *mouthwash for oral hygiene):* Chuang, Y. C. (2004). "Tooth-brushing epilepsy with ictal orgasms." *Seizure* 13: 181.

319   hormone levels were all within the normal limits: Al-Sheikhli, A. K. (1989). "Spontaneous orgasms—an explanation?" *The British Journal of Psychiatry* 155: 269–70.

Chapter 12

323   it's ejaculated: Baker, Robin. *Sperm Wars: The Science of Sex*. New York: Basic Books, 1996, pp. 20–21.

323   United States: Roizen, Michael F., Mehmet Oz, Lisa Oz, and Ted Spiker. *You: The Owner's Manual*. New York: HarperCollins, 2005, p. 222.

323   5 calories per teaspoon: Foley, Salli, Sally A Kope, and Dennis P. Sugrue. *Sex Matters for Women*. New York: Guilford Press, 2001, p. 241.

323 **28 miles per hour:** Scardino, Peter T., and Judith Kelman. *Dr. Peter Scardino's Prostate Book*. New York: Avery, 2006, p. 30.

323 **8 inches per hour:** Ibid., p. 30.

323 **69 offspring:** Giustina, Anthony. *Sex World Records*. Morrisville, North Carolina: Lulu Publishing, 2005, p. 16.

323 **high as 1,042:** Ibid., p. 7.

324 **more than three days old:** Wilcox, A. J., C. R. Weinberg, and D. D. Baird (1995). "Timing of sexual intercourse in relation to ovulation—effects on the probability of conception, survival of the pregnancy, and sex of the baby." *The New England Journal of Medicine* 333 (23): 1517.

325 **a timely meeting of sperm and egg:** Wilcox, A. J., D. D. Baird, D. B. Dunson, D. R. McConnaughey, J. S. Kesner, and C. R. Weinberg (2004). "On the frequency of intercourse around ovulation: Evidence for biological influences." *Human Reproduction* 19 (7): 1541.

326 **fallopian tube in one minute flat:** Komisaruk, Barry R., Carlos Beyer-Flores, and Beverly Whipple. *The Science of Orgasm*. Baltimore, Maryland: Johns Hopkins University Press, 2006, p. 38.

326 **thus allowing more sperm traffic to enter:** Ibid., p. 40.

329 **women who don't have sex due to discomfort:** Schaffir, J. (2006). "Sexual intercourse at term and onset of labor." *Obstetrics & Gynecology* 107 (6): 1310.

329 **up the odds you'll have a girl:** Shettles, Landrum Brewer, and David M. Rorvik. *How to Choose the Sex of Your Baby*. New York: Random House, 1996, p. 142.

Addiego, F., E. G. Belzer Jr., J. Comolli, W. Moger, J. D. Perry, and B. Whipple (1981). "Female ejaculation: A case study." *The Journal of Sex Research* 17 (1): 13–21.

Agostino, P. V., S. A. Plano, and D. A. Golombek (2007). "Sildenafil accelerates reentrainment of circadian rhythms after advancing light schedules." *Proceedings of the National Academy of Sciences in the United States of America* 104 (23): 9834–39.

Aguiar, M., and E. Hurst (2007). "Measuring trends in leisure: The allocation of time over Five Decades." *The Quarterly Journal of Economics* 122 (3): 969–1006.

Al-Sheikhli, A. K. (1989). "Spontaneous orgasms—an explanation?" *The British Journal of Psychiatry* 155: 269–70.

Alexander, M. G., and T. D. Fisher (2003). "Truth and consequences: Using the bogus pipeline to examine sex differences in self-reported sexuality." *The Journal of Sex Research* 40 (1): 27–35.

Ali, Lorraine, and Lisa Miller. "The secret lives of wives." *Newsweek*, July 12, 2004, p. 46.

Aloni, M., and F. J. Bernieri (2004). "Is love blind? The effects of experience and infatuation on the perception of love." *Journal of Nonverbal Behavior* 28: 287–95.

Amen, Daniel. *Sex on the Brain: 12 Lessons to Enhance Your Love Life.* New York: Harmony Books, 2007.

Anderson, C., D. Keltner, and O. P. John (2003). "Emotional convergence between people over time." *Journal of Personality and Social Psychology* 84 (5): 1054–68.

Anderson, Eric. Unpublished.

Ann, C. C. (1997). "A proposal for a radical new sex therapy technique for the management of vasocongestive and orgasmic dysfunction in women: The AFE zone stimulation technique." *Sexual and Relationship Therapy* 12 (4): 357–70.

Ansell Limited (manufacturer of LifeStyles Condoms). "The LifeStyles Condoms average penis size survey." March, 2001. Unpaginated electronic work or go to: http://www.free-condom-stuff.com/education/research.htm.

Antoniou, L. D., T. Sudhaker, R. J. Shathoub, and J. C. Smith (1977). "Reversal of uraemic impotence by zinc." *Lancet* 2 (8044): 895–98.

Ariely D., and G. Lowenstine (2006). "The heat of the moment: The effect of sexual arousal on sexual decision making. *Journal of Behavioral Decision Making* 19: 87–98.

Aron, A. P., C. C. Norman, and E. N. Aron (2000). "Couples' shared participation in novel and arousing activities and experienced relationship quality." *Journal of Personality and Social Psychology* 78 (2): 273–84.

Aron, A., H. E. Fisher, D. J. Mashek, G. Strong, H. Li, and L. L. Brown (2005). "Reward, motivation, and emotion systems associated with early-stage intense romantic love. *Journal of Neurophysioly* 94: 327–37.

Aronson, E., and D. Linder (1965). "Gain and loss of esteem as determinants of interpersonal attractiveness," *Journal of Experimental Social Psychology* 1: 156–72.

Bader, Michael. *Arousal: The Secret Logic Behind Sexual Fantasies.* New York: St. Martin's Press, 2002.

Baker, R. R., and M. A Bellis (1989). "Number of sperm in human ejaculate varies in accordance with sperm competition theory." *Animal Behavior* 37 (5): 867–69.

Baker, Robin. *Sperm Wars: The Science of Sex.* New York: Basic Books, 1996.

Bale, C., R. Morrison, P. G. Caryl (2006). "Chat-up lines as male sexual displays." *Personality and Individual Differences* 40: 655–64.

Basson, R. (2001). "Female sexual response: The role of drugs in the management of sexual dysfunction." *Obstetrics & Gynecology* 98 (2): 350–53.

Bearman, P. S., J. Moody, and K. Stovel (2004). "Chains of affection: The structure of adolescent romantic and sexual networks." *AJS* 110 (1): 44–91.

Bechtel, Stefan, Laurence Roy Stains, and the editors of Men's Health books. *Sex: A Man's Guide.* Emmaus, Pennsylvania: Rodale Press, 1996.

Becker, M.A., and F. E. Wolf. "Gender differences in sexual fantasy content." Paper presented at the meeting of the American Psychological Association, Boston, 1990.

Bellis, M. A., and R. R. Baker (1990). "Do females promote sperm competition? Data for humans." *Animal Behaviour*, 40: 997–99.

Bellis, M. A., K. Hughes, S. Hughes, and J. R. Ashton (2005). "Measuring paternal discrepancy and its public health consequences." *Journal of Epidemiology and Community Health* 59: 749–54.

Belzer, E. G. Jr. (1981). "Orgasmic Expulsions of Women: A Review and Heuristic Inquiry." *The Journal of Sex Research* 17 (1): 1–12.

Blanchflower, D. G., and A. J. Oswald (2004). "Money, sex and happiness: An empirical study." *Scandinavian Journal of Economics* 106 (3): 393–415.

Bogaert, A. F. (2004). "Asexuality: Prevalence and associated factors in a national probability sample." *The Journal of Sex Research* 41 (3): 279–87.

Bohlen, J. G. (1982). "The female orgasm: Pelvic contractions." *Archives of Sexual Behavior* 11 (5): 367–86.

Bond, S., and D. Mosher (1986). "Guided imagery of rape: Fantasy, reality, and the willing victim myth." *The Journal of Sex Research* 22 (2): 162–83.

Borrillo, D. J. (1998). "Dangers of Viagra use in pilots." *Federal Air Surgeon's Medical Bulletin* 98 (3): 9–10.

Bowen, Kit. "A little sex drink for Roberts and Sandler." Hollywood.com, April 26, 2001, unpaginated electronic work or go to: http://www .hollywood.com/news/A_little_sex_drink_for_Roberts_and_Sandler/ 386442.

Bressler, E., R. Martin, and S. Balshine (2006). "Production and appreciation of humor as sexually selected traits." *Evolution and Human Behavior* 27 (2): 121–30.

Brizendine, Louann. *The Female Brain*. New York: Broadway Books, 2006.

Brockner, J., B. Pressman, J. Cabitt, and P. Moran (1982). "Nonverbal intimacy, sex, and compliance: A field study." *Journal of Nonverbal Behavior* 6 (4): 253–58.

Brody, S. (2002). "High-dose ascorbic acid increases intercourse frequency and improves mood: A randomized controlled clinical trial." *Biological Psychiatry* 52 (4): 371–74.

——— (2006). "Blood pressure reactivity to stress is better for people who recently had penile–vaginal intercourse than for people who had other or no sexual activity." *Biological Psychology* 71 (2): 214–22.

Brome, Vincent. *Havelock Ellis, Philosopher of Sex: A Biography*. New York: Routledge, 1979.

Brown, N. R., and R. C. Sinclair (1999). "Estimating number of lifetime sexual partners: Men and women do it differently." *The Journal of Sex Research* 36 (3): 292–97.

Brown, W. M., L. Cronk, K. Grochow, A. Jacobson, K. Liu, Z. Popović, and R. Trivers (2005). "Dance reveals symmetry especially in young men." *Nature* 438 (7071): 1148–50.

Buss, D. M., and D. P. Schmitt (1993). "Sexual strategies theory: An evolutionary perspective on human mating." *Psychological Review* 100: 204–32.

Buss, David. *The Dangerous Passion: Why Jealousy Is as Necessary as Love and Sex*. New York: Free Press, 2000.

Buss, David M. *The Evolution of Desire: Strategies of Human Mating*. New York: Basic Books, 2003.

Call, V., S. Sprecher, and P. Schwartz (1995). "The incidence and frequency of marital sex in a national sample." *Journal of Marriage and the Family* 57: 639–52.

Carey, John. "Viagra for women?" *BusinessWeek*, December 28, 2006,

unpaginated electronic resource or go to: http://www.businessweek
.com/bwdaily/dnflash/content/dec2006/db20061228_315249.htm.

Centers for Disease Control and Prevention (1995). "Deaths associated with
a purported aphrodisiac—New York City, February 1993–May 1995."
Morbidity and Mortality Weekly Report 44 (46): 853–55, 861.

Chalker, Rebecca. *The Clitoral Truth: The Secret World at Your Fingertips.*
New York: Seven Stories Press, 2002.

Charnetski, Carl J., Francis X. Brennan. *Feeling Good Is Good for You: How
Pleasure Can Boost Your Immune System and Lengthen Your Life.* Emmaus, Pennsylvania: Rodale Press, 2001.

Chartrand, T. L., J. A. Bargh (1999). "The chameleon effect: The perfection-
behavior link and social interaction." *Journal of Personality and Social
Psychology* 76 (6): 893–910.

Cherkas, L. F., E. C. Oelsner, Y. T. Mak, A. Valdex, and T. D. Spector (2004).
"Genetic influences on female infidelity and number of sexual partners in
humans: A linkage and association study of the role of the vasopressin receptor gene (*AVPR1A*)." *Twin Research* 7 (6): 649–58.

Chivers, Meredith L., J. M. Bailey (2005). "A sex difference in features that
elicit genital response." *Biological Psychology* 70 (2): 115–20.

Chuang, Y. C. (2004). "Tooth-brushing epilepsy with ictal orgasms." *Seizure*
13: 179–82.

Clark, A.P. (2007). "Attracting interest: Displays of proceptivity increase the
attractiveness of men and women." Unpublished.

Clark, R., and E. Hatfield (1989). "Gender differences in receptivity to sexual
offers." *Journal of Psychology and Human Sexuality* 2 (1): 39–55.

CNN.com, "E-mails 'hurt IQ more than pot.'" April 22, 2005, unpaginated
electronic work or go to: http://www.cnn.com/2005/WORLD/europe/
04/22/text.iq/.

Cohen, B., G. Waugh, and K. Place (1989). "At the movies: An unobtrusive
study of arousal attraction." *Journal of Social Psychology* 129: 691–93.

Coles, C. D., M. J. Shamp (1984). "Some sexual, personality, and demographic characteristics of women readers of erotic romances." *Archives of
Sexual Behavior* 13 (3): 187–209.

Conis, Elena. "Historic, and nutty, treatments for male impotence." *Los Angeles Times,* March 17, 2008, unpaginated electronic work or go to: http://
www.latimes.com/features/health/la-he-esoterica17mar17,1,4065807
.column?track=rss.

Conway, C. A., B. C. Jones, L. M. De Bruine, and A. C. Little (2008). "Evidence for adaptive design in human gaze preference." *Proceedings: Biological Sciences* 275 (1630): 63–69.

Critelli, J. W., and J. M. Bivona (2008). "Women's erotic rape fantasies:
An evaluation of theory and research. *The Journal of Sex Research* 45
(1): 57–70.

Cross, P. A., and K. Matheson. "Understanding sadomasochism: An empirical examination of four perspectives." From *Sado-masochism: Powerful Pleasures*, P. J. Kleinplatz and C. Moser (eds.). Philadelphia, Pennsylvania: Harrington Park Press, 2006, pp. 133–66.

Cunningham, M. (1986). "Measuring the physical in physical attractiveness: Quasi-experiments on the sociobiology of female facial beauty." *Journal of Personality and Social Psychology* 50 (5): 925–35.

Cunningham, M. A., A. F. Barbee, C. R. Graves, D. E. Lundy, S. C. Lister, and W. Rowatt (1996). "Can't buy me love: The effects of male wealth and personal qualities on female attraction." Paper presented at the Convention of the American Psychological Association, Toronto.

Cunningham, M. R. (1989). "Reactions to heterosexual opening gambits." *Personality and Social Psychology Bulletin* 15 (1): 27–41.

Cunningham, M. R., S. R. Shamblen, A. P. Barbee, and L. K. Ault (2005). "Social allergies in romantic relationships: Behavioral repetition, emotional sensitization, and dissatisfaction in dating couples." *Personal Relationships* 12 (2): 273–95.

Cutler, W. B., E. Friedmann, and N. L. McCoy (1998). "Pheromonal influences on the sociosexual behavior of men." *Archives of Sexual Behavior* 27(1): 1–13.

Daily Mail, "World's oldest mother gives birth to twins at 70." July 5, 2008. Unpaginated electronic resource or go to: http://www.dailymail.co.uk/news/worldnews/article-1031722/Worlds-oldest-mother-gives-birth-twins-70.html.

Darling, C. A. (1991). "The female sexual response revisited: Understanding the multiorgasmic experience in women." *Archives of Sexual Behavior* 20 (6): 527–40.

Dash, Eric. "Sex may be happiness, but wealth isn't sexiness." *New York Times*, July 11, 2004, Section 4; Column 1; Week in Review Desk; Ideas & Trends; p. 14.

De Bruine, L. M. (2005) "Trustworthy but not lustworthy: Context-specific effects of facial resemblance." *Proceedings: Biological Sciences* 272 (1566): 919–22.

Dell'Agli, M., G. V. Valli, E. D. Cero, F. Belluti, R. Matera, E. Zironi, G. Pagliuca, and E. Bosisio (2008). "Potent inhibition of human phosphodiesterase-5 by Icariin derivatives." *Journal of Natural Products* 71 (9): 1513–17.

Deveny, Kathleen. "We're not in the mood." *Newsweek*, June 30, 2003, p. 40.

Dimberg, U., M. Thunberg, and K. Elmehed (2000). "Unconscious facial reactions to emotional facial expressions." *Psychological Science* 11 (1): 86–89.

Ditzen, B., G. Bodenmann, U. Ehlert, and M. Heinrichs (2006). "Effects of social support and oxytocin on psychological and physiological stress responses during marital conflict." *Frontiers in Neuroendocrinology* 27 (1): 134.

Domes G., M. Heinrichs, A. Michel, C. Berger, and S. C. Herpertz (2007). "Oxytocin improves 'mind-reading' in humans." *Biological Psychiatry* 61 (6): 731–33.

Druckerman, Pamela. *Lust in Translation: Infidelity from Tokyo to Tennessee.* New York: Penguin. 2007.

Dunn, K. M., L. F. Cherkas, and Tim D. Spector (2005). "Genetic influences on variation in female orgasmic function: a twin study." *Biology Letters* 1 (3): 260–63.

Dutton, D. G., and A. P. Aron (1974). "Some evidence for heightened sexual attraction under conditions of high anxiety." *Journal of Personality and Social Psychology* 30 (4): 510–17.

Earleywine, M. (2001). "Cannabis-induced Koro in Americans." *Addiction* 96 (11): 1663–66.

Eichel, E. W. (1988). "The technique of coital alignment and its relation to female orgasmic response and simultaneous orgasm." *Journal of Sex & Marital Therapy* 14 (2): 129–41.

Elliot, A. J., and D. Niesta (2008). "Romantic red: Red enhances men's attraction to women." *Journal of Personality and Social Psychology* 95 (5): 1150–64.

Etcoff, Nancy. *Survival of the Prettiest.* New York: Doubleday, 1999.

Eva, K., and T. Wood (2006). "Are all the taken men good? An indirect examination of mate–choice copying in humans." *CMAJ* 175 (12): 1573–74.

Farmer, Ben. "UK woman, 59, world's oldest natural mother." *The Telegraph,* August 20, 2007. Unpaginated electronic resource or go to: http://www.telegraph.co.uk/news/uknews/1560739/UK-woman%2C-59%2C-world%27s-oldest-natural-mother.html.

Faro, Scott. "Brain imaging could spot liars." News@nature.com. Presented at the annual meeting of the Radiological Society of North America in Chicago, November 29, 2004. Go to: http://www.nature.com/news/2004/041129/full/news041129-1.html.

Feldman, H. A., C. B. Johannes, J. B. McKinlay, and C. Longcope (1998). "Low dehydroepiandrosterone sulfate and heart disease in middle-aged men: Cross-sectional results from the Massachusetts male aging study." *Annals of Epidemiology* 8: 217–28.

Ferguson, D., C. Steidle, G. Singh, S. Alexander, Mary K. Weihmiller, and M. Crosby (2003). "Randomized, placebo-controlled, double-blind, crossover design trial on the efficacy and safety of Zestra for women in women with and without female sexual arousal disorder." *Journal of Sex & Marital Therapy* 29 (supplement 1): 33–44.

Fieder, M., and S. Huber (2007). "Parental age difference and offspring count in humans." *Biology Letters* 3: 689–91.

Fisch, Harry. *The Male Biological Clock.* New York: Free Press, 2005.

Fisher, Helen. *Why We Love: The Nature and Chemistry of Romantic Love.* New York: Macmillan, 2004.

Fisher, Ian. "$1 million gift for new charity case: the Viagra-needy." *New York Times*, June 10, 1998, Section B; page 3; Column 1.

Fraley, B., and A. P. Aron (2004). "The effect of a shared humorous experience on closeness in initial encounters." *Personal Relationships* 11: 61–78.

Frank, Robert. "Marrying for love . . . of money." *Wall Street Journal*, December 14, 2007. Unpaginated electronic resource or go to: http://online .wsj.com/public/article/SB119760031991928727-uxLpSTF5YqrHVllxj IWGE2HxLWM_20091126.html.

Friday, Nancy. *Women on Top: How Real Life Has Changed Women's Sexual Fantasies*. New York: Simon and Schuster, 1993.

Fukada, Shiho. "Eyes only for each other, at least for the next three minutes." *New York Times*, December 11, 2005, Section 14; p. 6; Column 1.

Gallup, G. G. Jr., R. L. Burch, M. L. Zappieri, R. A. Parvez, M. L. Stockwell, and J. A. Davis (2003). "The human penis as a semen displacement device." *Evolution and Human Behavior* 24: 277–89.

Gallup, A. C., D. B. White, and G. G. Gallup Jr. (2007). "Handgrip strength predicts sexual behavior, body morphology, and aggression in male college students." *Evolution and Human Behavior* 28 (6): 423–29.

Gallup, G. G. Jr., R. L. Burch, and S. M. Platek (2002). "Does semen have antidepressant properties?" *Archives of Sexual Behavior* 31 (3): 289–93.

Gallup poll, "Moral Issues." Conducted May 8–11, 2006.

Gangestad, S. W., R. Thornhill, and R. A. Yeo (1994). "Facial attractiveness, developmental stability, and fluctuating asymmetry." *Ethology and Sociobiology* 15: 73–85.

Garwood, S. G., L. Cox, B. Kaplan, N. Wasserman, and J. L. Sulzer (1980). "Beauty is only 'name' deep: The effect of first-name on ratings of physical attraction." *Journal of Applied Social Psychology* 10 (5): 431–35.

Gaudin, Sharon. "Americans can go without sex longer than the Internet, study finds." *Information Week*, September 21, 2007, [unpaginated electronic work], or go to: http://www.informationweek.com/news/ internet/showArticle.jhtml?articleID=201808208.

Gauthaman K., P. G. Adaikan, and R. N. Prasad (2002). "Aphrodisiac properties of Tribulus Terrestris extract (Protodioscin) in normal and castrated rats." *Life Sciences* 71 (12): 1385–96.

Gergen, Kenneth, Mary Gergen, and William Barton. "Deviance in the dark." *Psychology Today*, October 1973, pp. 129–30.

Giannini, A. J., G. Colapietro, A. E. Slaby, S. M. Melemis, and R. K. Bowman (1998). "Sexualization of the female foot as a response to sexually transmitted epidemics." *Psychological Reports* 83: 491–98.

Giustina, Anthony. *Sex World Records*. Morrisville, North Carolina: Lulu Publishing, 2005.

Givens, David. *Love Signals: A Practical Field Guide to the Body Language of Courtship*. New York: St. Martin's Press, 2005.

Glass, Shirley, and Jean Coppock Staeheli. *Not Just Friends: Rebuilding*

Trust and Recovering Your Sanity After Infidelity. New York: Simon and Schuster, 2004.

Glenn, D. R. J., C. M. McVicar, N. M. McClure, and S. E. M. Lewis (2005). "Sildenafil citrate improves sperm motility but causes a premature acrosome reaction in vitro." *Fertility and Sterility* 87 (5): 1064–70.

Glenn, D. R. J., N. McClure, S. L. Cosby, M. Stevenson, and S. E. M. Lewis (2009). "Sildenafil citrate (Viagra) impairs fertilization and early embryo development in mice." *Fertility and Sterility* 91 (3): 893–99.

Gonzaga, G. C., M. G. Haselton, J. Smurda, M. S. Davies, and J. C. Poore (2008). "Love, desire, and the suppression of thoughts of romantic alternatives." *Evolution and Human Behavior* 29 (2): 119–26.

Foley, Salli, Sally A. Kope, and Dennis P. Sugrue. *Sex Matters for Women.* New York: Guilford Press, 2001.

Gravina, G. L., F. Brandetti, P. Martini, E. Carosa, S. M Di Stasi, S. Morano, A. Lenzi, and E. A. Jannini (2008). "Measurement of the thickness of the urethrovaginal space in women with or without vaginal orgasm. *Journal of Sexual Medicine* 5 (3): 610–18.

Graziano, W., T. Brothen, and E. Berscheid (1978). "Height and attraction: Do men and women see eye-to-eye?" *Journal of Personality* 46: 128–45.

Grimes, J., and L. Labbate (1996). "Spontaneous orgasm with the combined use of Bupropion and Sertraline." *Journal of Biological Psychiatry* 40: 1184.

Guarraci, F. A., and A. Benson (2005). "'Coffee, Tea and Me': Moderate doses of caffeine affect sexual behavior in female rats." *Pharmacology, Biochemistry and Behavior* 82 (3): 522–30.

Guéguen, N., C. Jacob, and G. Boulbry (2007). "The effect of touch on compliance with a restaurant's employee suggestion." *Hospitality Management* 26: 1019–23.

Güntürkün, O. (2003). "Adult persistence of head-turning asymmetry." *Nature* 421: 711–12.

Gustafsson, L., and A. Qvarnstro (2006). "A test of the 'sexy son' hypothesis: Sons of polygynous collared flycatchers do not inherit their fathers' mating status." *The American Naturalist* 167 (2): 297–302.

Halata, Z., and B. L. Munger (1986). "The neuroanatomical basis for the protopathic sensibility of the human glans penis." *Brain Research* 371 (2): 205–30.

Hall, Celia. "Nipple stimulation can protect women against breast cancer, researcher says." *The Vancouver Sun*, April 23, 1994, p. B5.

Haselton, M. G., M. Mortezaie, E. G. Pillsworth, A. Bleske-Rechek, and D. A. Frederick (2007). "Ovulatory shifts in human female ornamentation: Near ovulation, women dress to impress." *Hormones and Behavior* 51 (1): 40–45.

Haselton, M. G., and S. W. Gangestad (2006). "Conditional expression of women's desires and men's mate guarding across the ovulatory cycle." *Hormones and Behavior* 49: 509–18.

Hatfield, Elaine, and Susan Sprecher. *Mirror, Mirror: The Importance of Looks in Everyday Life*. Albany, New York: State University of New York Press, 1986.

Hekmat, H., P. Staats, A. Staats, and J. Diek (2007). "Do romantic fantasies facilitate coping with acute pain?" *The Journal of Pain* 8 (4, supplement 1): S55.

Hicks T., and H. Leitenberg (2001). "Sexual fantasies about one's partner verses someone else: Gender differences in incidence and frequency." *The Journal of Sex Research* 38 (1): 43–50.

Hirsch, A. R., and J. J. Gruss, "Odors and perception of room size." Presented at the 148th Annual Meeting of the American Psychiatric Association, Miami, Florida, 1995.

Hirsch, A. R., J. R. Hoogeveenb, A. M. Bussec, and E. T. Allend (2007). "The effects of odour on weight perception." *International Journal of Essential Oil Therapeutics* 1: 21–28.

Hirsch, Alan. *Scentsational Sex: The Secret to Using Aroma for Arousal*. Lanham, Maryland: Element Books, 1998.

Hitsch, G., A. Hortaçsu, and D. Ariely (2006). "What makes you click? Mate preferences and matching outcomes in online dating." Unpublished, pp. 1–38.

Hong, B., Y. H. Ji, J. H. Hong, K. Y. Nam, and T. Y. Ahn (2002). "A double-blind crossver study evaluating the efficacy of Korean red ginseng in patients with erectile dysfunction: A preliminary report." *The Journal of Urology* 168: 270–73.

Hsu, B., A. Kling, C. Kessler, K. Knapke, P. Diefenbach, and J. E. Elias (1994). "Gender differences in sexual fantasy and behavior in a college population: A ten-year replication." *Journal of Sex & Marital Therapy* 20 (2): 103–18.

Hughes, S. M., M. A. Harrison, and G. G. Gallup, Jr. (2002). "The sound of symmetry: Voice as a marker of developmental instability." *Evolution and Human Behavior* 23: 173–80.

Hughes, S. M., M. A. Harrison, and G. G. Gallup Jr. (2007). "Sex differences in romantic kissing among college students: An evolutionary perspective." *Evolutionary Psychology* 5 (3): 612–31.

Hyde, J. S., J. D. DeLamater, and E. C. Hewitt (1998). "Sexuality and the dual-earner couple: Multiple roles and sexual functioning." *Journal of Family Psychology* 12 (3): 354–68.

Janssen, E., H. Vorst, P. Finn, and J. Bancroft (2002). "The Sexual Inhibition (SIS) and Sexual Excitation (SES) Scales: I. Measuring sexual inhibition and excitation proneness in men." *The Journal of Sex Research* 39 (2): 114–26.

Janssen, E., H. Vorst, P. Finn, and J. Bancroft (2002). "The Sexual Inhibition (SIS) and Sexual Excitation (SES) Scales: II. Predicting psychophysiological response patterns." *The Journal of Sex Research* 39 (2):
127–32.

Jones, B. C., L. M. De Bruine, A. C. Little, R. P. Burriss, and D. R. Feinberg
(2007). "Social transmission of face preferences among humans." *Proceedings: Biological Sciences* 274: 899–903.

Jones, B. T., B. C. Jones, A P. Thomas, and J. Piper (2003). "Alcohol consumption increases attractiveness ratings of opposite-sex faces: A possible third route to risky sex." *Addiction* 98 (8): 1069–75.

Jones, J. C., and D. H. Barlow (1990). "Self-reported frequency of sexual
urges, fantasies, and masturbatory fantasies in heterosexual males and
females." *Archives of Sexual Behavior* 19 (3): 269–79.

Jones, J. T., B. W. Pelham, M. Carvallo, and M. C. Mirenberg (2004). "How
do I love thee? Let me count the Js: Implicit egotism and interpersonal
attraction." *Journal of Personality and Social Psychology* 87 (5): 665–83.

Kahneman, D., A. B. Krueger, D. A. Schkade, N. Schwarz, and A. A. Stone
(2004). "A survey method for characterizing daily life experience: The
day reconstruction method." *Science* 306 (5702): 1776 –80.

Kahr, Brett. *Who's Been Sleeping in Your Head? The Secret World of Sexual
Fantasies*. New York: Basic Books, 2007.

Kampe, K. K. W., C. D. Frith, R. J. Dolan, and U. Frith (2001). "Reward value
of attractiveness and gaze." *Nature* 413 (6856): 589.

Karacan, I., A. L. Rosenbloom, and R. L. Williams (1970). "The clitoral erection cycle during sleep." *Psychophysiology* 7: 338.

Kellerman, J., J. Lewis, and J. D. Laird (1989). "Looking and loving: The effects of mutual gaze on feelings of romantic love." *Journal of Research in
Personality* 23: 145–61.

Kenrick, D. T., S. E. Gutierres, and L. L. Goldberg (1989). "Influence of popular erotica on judgments of strangers and mates." *Journal of Experimental Social Psychology* 25 (2): 159–67.

Kidd, S. A., B. Eskenazi, and A. J. Wyrobek (2001). "Effects of male age on
semen quality and fertility: A review of the literature." *Fertility and
Sterility* 75 (2): 237–48.

Kiesler, S. B., and R. L. Baral. "The search for a romantic partner: The effects
of self-esteem and physical attractiveness on romantic behavior." In K.
Gergen and D. Marlow (eds.), *Personality and Social Behavior*. New
York: Addison-Wesley, 1992.

Kim, D., and M. G. Pang (2007). "The effect of male circumcision on sexuality." *BJU International* 99 (3): 619–22.

Kinsey, Alfred, Wardell B. Pomeroy, Clyde E. Martin, and Paul H. Gebhard.
Sexual Behavior of the Human Female. Bloomington, Indiana: Indiana
University Press, 1953.

Kita, Joe. *Guy Q: The Best Health, Fitness, Stress, Weight-Loss, Sex and Style Tips Ever.* Emmaus, Pennsylvania: Rodale Press, 2003.

Kleinke, Chris. *First Impressions: The Psychology of Encountering Others.* Englewood Cliffs, New Jersey: Prentice-Hall, 1975.

Kleinke, C. L., and R. A. Staneski (1980). "First impressions of female bust size." *Journal of Social Psychology* 110 (1): 123–34.

Klotz, L. (2005). "How (not) to communicate new scientific information: A memoir of the famous Brindley lecture." *BJU International* 96 (7): 956–57.

Kniffin, K. M., and D. S. Wilson (2004). "The effect of nonphysical traits on the perception of physical attractiveness." *Evolution and Human Behavior* 25 (2): 88–101.

Kohut, John, and Roland Sweet. *Real Sex: Titillating but True Tales of Bizarre Fetishes, Strange Compulsions, and Just Plain Weird Stuff.* New York: Plume, 2000, p. 68.

Kolata, Gina. "Pfizer gives up testing Viagra on women." *New York Times,* February 28, 2004, Section C; p. 1; Column 5.

Komisaruk, Barry R., Carlos Beyer-Flores, and Beverly Whipple. *The Science of Orgasm.* Baltimore, Maryland: Johns Hopkins University Press, 2006.

Komisaruk, B. R., and B. Whipple (1998). "Love as sensory stimulation: physiological consequences of its deprivation and expression." *Psychoneuroendocrinology* 23 (8): 927–44.

Kosfeld, M., M. Heinrichs, P. J. Zak, U. Fischbacher, and E. Fehr (2005). "Oxytocin increases trust in humans." *Nature* 435: 673–76.

Krafft-Ebing, Richard von (translated by Francis Joseph Rebman). *Psychopathia Sexualis, with Especial Reference to the Antipathic Sexual Instinct: A Medico-forensic Study.* New York: Medical Art Agency, 1922.

Kruger, D. J., M. Fisher, and I. Jobling (2003). "Proper and dark heroes as dads and cads: Alternative mating strategies in British romantic literature." *Human Nature* 14: 305–17.

Kukkonen, T. M., Y. M. Binik, R. Amsel, and S. Carrier (2007). "Thermography as a physiological measure of sexual arousal in both men and women." *The Journal of Sexual Medicine* 4 (1): 93–105.

Kurzban, R., and J. Weeden (2005). "HurryDate: Mate preferences in action." *Evolution and Human Behavior* 26 (3): 227–44.

Lai, Hsi. *The Sexual Teachings of the White Tigress.* Rochester, Vermont: Destiny Books, 2001.

Laqueur, Thomas. *Making Sex: Body and Gender from the Greeks to Freud.* Harvard University Press, 1992.

Larsson, M., N. L. Pedersen, and H. Stattin (2007). "Associations between iris characteristics and personality in adulthood." *Biological Psychology* 75: 165–75.

Laumann, Edward O., John H. Gagnon, Robert T. Michael, and Stuart

Michaels. *The Social Organization of Sexuality*. Chicago: The University of Chicago Press, 1994.

Lawler, F. H., R. S. Bisonni, and D. R. Holtgrave (1991). "Circumcision: A decision analysis of its medical value." *Family Medicine* 23 (8): 587–93.

Leitenberg, H., and K. Henning (1995). "Sexual fantasy." *Psychological Bulletin* 117 (3): 469–96.

Lerner, R. M., S. A. Karabenick, and J. L. Stuart (1973). "Relations among physical attractiveness, body attitudes, and self-concept in male and female college students." *Journal of Psychology* 85: 119–29.

Lever, J., D. Frederick, and L. A. Peplau (2006). "Does size matter? Men's and women's views on penis size across the lifespan." *Psychology of Men & Masculinity* 7 (3): 129–43.

Levin, R. J., and C. Meston (2006). "Nipple/breast stimulation and sexual arousal in young men and women." *The Journal of Sexual Medicine* 3 (3): 450–54.

Lewis, R. W., and R. Witherington (1997). "External vacuum therapy for erectile dysfunction: Use and results." *World Journal of Urology* 15 (1): 78–82.

Leyvand, T., D. Cohen-Or, G. Dror, and D. Lischinski (2008). "Data-driven enhancement of facial attractiveness." *ACM SIGGRAPH*, article 38.

Little, A. C., I. S. Penton-Voak, D. M. Burt, and D. I. Perrett (2003). "Investigating an imprinting-like phenomenon in humans: Partners and opposite-sex parents have similar hair and eye colour." *Evolution and Human Behavior* 24 (1): 43–51.

Lloyd, Elisabeth Anne. *The Case of the Female Orgasm: Bias in the Science of Evolution*. Cambridge, Massachusetts: Harvard University Press, 2005.

Madan, A., R. Caneel, and A. S. Pentland (2004). "Voices of attraction." Cambridge, Massachusetts: MIT Media Laboratory. Go to: http://web.media.mit.edu/~anmol/TR-584.pdf.

Maheu, Marlene. *Infidelity on the Internet*. Naperville, Illinois: Sourcebooks, 2001.

Maimónides, Moses (translated by Shlomo Pines). *The Guide of the Perplexed*. Chicago: University of Chicago Press, 1963.

Maines, Rachel. *The Technology of Orgasm: "Hysteria," the Vibrator, and Women's Sexual Satisfaction*. Baltimore, Maryland: Johns Hopkins University Press, 1999.

Maisey, D. S., E. L. E. Vale, P. L. Cornelissen, and M. J. Tovée (1999). "Characteristics of male attractiveness for women." *The Lancet* 353: 1500.

Major, B., P. I. Carrington, and P. J. D. Carnevale (1984). "Physical attractiveness and self-esteem: Attributions for praise from other-sex evaluator." *Personality and Social Psychology Bulletin* 10 (1): 43–50.

Manning, John T. *Digit Ratio: A Pointer to Fertility, Behavior, and Health*. Piscataway, New Jersey: Rutgers University Press, 2002.

Maravilla, K. A., J. R. Heiman, P. A. Garland, Y. Cao, B. T. Peterson, and R. H. Weisskoff (2003). "Dynamic MR imaging of the sexual arousal response in women." *Journal of Sex & Marital Therapy* 29 (supplement 1): 71–76.

Marceau, L., K. Kleinman, I. Goldstein, and J. McKinlay (2001). "Does bicycling contribute to the risk of erectile dysfunction? Results from the Massachusetts Male Aging Study (MMAS)." *International Journal of Impotence Research* 13 (5): 298–302.

Marchant, Joanna. "Men choose beauty before age." *New Scientist*, June 27, 2001, unpaginated work or go to: http://www.newscientist.com/article/dn940-men-choose-beauty-before-age.html.

Margolis, Jonathan. *O: The Intimate History of the Orgasm*. New York: Grove Press, 2004.

Markey, P. M., C. N. Markey (2007). "The interpersonal meaning of sexual promiscuity." *Journal of Research in Personality* 41 (6): 1199–1212.

Masters, William H., and Virginia E. Johnson. *Human Sexual Inadequacy*. Boston: Little, Brown & Company, 1970.

Masters, William H., and Virginia E. Johnson. *Human Sexual Response*. Boston: Little, Brown & Company, 1966.

McCoy, N. L., and L. Pitino (2002). "Pheromonal influences on sociosexual behavior in young women. *Physiology and Behavior* 75 (3): 367–75.

McGlone, S., and I. Shrier (2000). "Does sex the night before competition decrease performance?" *Clinical Journal of Sport Medicine* 10 (4): 233–34.

Meston, C. M., and D. M. Buss (2007). "Why humans have sex." *Archives of Sexual Behavior* 36 (4): 477–507.

Meston, C. M., and P. Frohlich (2003). "Love at first fright: Partner salience moderates roller–coaster–inducted excitation transfer." *Archives of Sexual Behavior* 32 (6): 537–44.

Mialon, H. M. (2008). "The economics of ecstasy." Unpublished. Go to: http://userwww.service.emory.edu/~hmialon/Ecstasy.pdf

Michael, Robert T., John H. Gagnon, and Edward O. Laumann. *Sex in America: A Definitive Survey*. Boston: Little, Brown, & Company, 1994.

Mileham, B. L. A. (2007). "Online infidelity in Internet chat rooms: An ethnographic exploration." *Computers in Human Behavior* 23: 11–31.

Miller, G., J. M. Tybur, and B. D. Jordan (2007). "Ovulatory cycle effects on tip earnings by lap dancers: Economic evidence for human estrus?" *Evolution and Human Behavior* 28 (6): 375–81.

Miller, S. A., and E. S. Byers (2004). "Actual and desired duration of foreplay and intercourse: Discordance and misperceptions within heterosexual couples." *The Journal of Sex Research* 41 (3): 301–09.

Moore, Jenny. "Falling for Niagara." *The Independent*, May 6, 2001, p. 19.

Moore, L. J., and A. E. Clarke (1995). "Clitoral conventions and transgressions: Graphic representations in anatomy texts." *Feminist Studies* 21 (2): 255–301.

Moore, M. M. (1985). "Nonverbal courtship patterns in women: Context and consequences." *Ethology and Sociobiology* 6: 237–47.

Moran, J. D., and J. C. McCullers (1984). "A comparison of achievement scores on physically attractive and unattractive students." *Family and Consumer Sciences Research Journal* 13 (1): 36–40.

Morgan, Tom. "Men spend almost as long as women preening themselves." *Daily Express*, February 6, 2008, p. 3.

Morris, Desmond. *The Naked Woman.* New York: Macmillan, 2007.

———. *The Naked Ape.* New York: McGraw Hill, 1967.

Mosher, W. E., A. Chandra, and J. Jones. "Sexual behavior and selected health measures: Men and women 15–44 years of age, United States, 2002." *Advance Data from Vital and Health Statistics #362*, September 15, 2005, pp. 1–56.

Mourik, Orli Van. "Sex, love and SSRIs." *Psychology Today*, April 3, 2007. Unpaginated electronic work or go to: http://www.psychologytoday.com/articles/index.php?term=pto-20070403-000003&page=1.

MSNBC.com, "Your unadulterated thoughts on adultery: The lowdown on the MSNBC.com/iVillage lust, love & loyalty survey." April 16, 2007, unpaginated electronic work or go to: http://www.msnbc.msn.com/id/18055526/.

MSN/Carpoint.com (2002). "MSN Carpoint.com Valentine's Day fast facts reveals 30 percent of respondents judge their date by the type of car they drive." Unpaginated electronic work or go to: http://www.microsoft.com/presspass/press/2002/feb02/02-12fastfactspr.mspx.

Muller, J. E., M. A. Mittleman, M. Maclure, J. B. Sherwood, and G. H. Tofler (1996). "Triggering of myocardial infarction by sexual activity: Low absolute risk and prevention by regular physical exertion." *JAMA* 275:1405–09.

Munkelwitz, R., and B. Gilbert (1998). "Are boxer shorts really better? Critical analysis of the role of underwear type in male subfertility." *Journal of Urology* 160 (4): 1329–33.

Nelson, L. D., and E. L. Morrison (2005). "The symptoms of resource scarcity: Judgments of food and finances influence preferences for potential partners." *Psychological Science* 16 (2): 167–73.

Nettle, D., and H. Clegg (2006). "Schizotypy, creativity and mating success in humans." *Proceedings: Biological Sciences* 273, 611–15.

Ney, P. G. (1986). "The intravaginal absorption of male generated hormones and their possible effect on female behavior." *Medical Hypotheses* 20: 221–51.

Neychev, V. K., and V.I. Mitev (2005). "The aphrodisiac herb *Tribulus ter-*

restris does not influence the androgen production in young men." *Journal of Ethnopharmacology* 101 (1–3): 319–23.

Noah, Timothy. "Bellow the fertility king." Slate, January 17, 2000. Unpaginated electronic work or go to: http://www.slate.com/id/1004389/.

Nuland, Sherwin. "How to grow old." *Best American Science Writing*, edited by Dava Sobel. New York: HarperCollins, 2004.

O'Connor, Anahad. *Never Shower in a Thunderstorm*. New York: Macmillan, 2007.

Ogden, Gina. *Women Who Love Sex: An Inquiry into the Expanding Spirit of Women's Erotic Experience*. Cambridge, Massachusetts: Womanspirit Press, 1999.

Padgett, P. M. (2007). "Personal safety and sexual safety for women using online personal ads." *Sexual Research & Social Policy* 4 (2): 27–37.

Paley, Maggie. *The Book of the Penis*. New York: Grove Press, 2000.

Palmore, E. B. (1982). "Predictors of the longevity difference: A 25-year follow-up." *Gerontologist* 6: 513–18.

Pease, Allan, and Barbara Pease. *The Definitive Book of Body Language*. New York: Bantam Dell, 2004.

Pellegrini, R. J. (1973). "Impressions of the male personality as a function of beardedness." *Psychology* 10: 29–33.

Pennebaker, J. W., and D. Y. Sanders (1976). "American graffiti: Effects of authority and reactance arousal." *Personality and Social Psychology Bulletin* 2 (3): 264–67.

Pennebaker, J. W., M. A. Dyer, R. S. Caulkins, D. L. Litositz, P. L. Ackreman, D. B. Anderson, and K. M. McGraw (1979). "Don't the girls get prettier at closing time: A country and western application to psychology. *Personality and Social Psychology Bulletin* 5: 122–25.

Penton-Voak, I., D. I. Perrett, and J. Pierce (1999). "Computer graphic studies of facial similarity and judgements of attractiveness." *Current Psychology* 18: 104–18.

Perfors, A. "What's in a name? The effect of sound symbolism on facial attractiveness." Presented at the 26th Annual Conference for Cognitive Science, Chicago, August 7, 2004. Go to: http://www.mit.edu/~perfors/hotornot.pdf.

Perrett, D. I., I. S. Penton-Voak, A. C. Little, B. P. Tiddeman, D. M. Burt, and N. Schmidt (2002). "Facial attractiveness judgments reflect learning of parental age characteristics." *Proceedings: Biological Sciences* 269 (1494): 873–80.

Petersen, James. "Playboy Interview: Masters and Johnson." *Playboy*, November, 1979, pp. 87–122.

Petralia, S. M., and G. G. Gallup, Jr. (2002). "Effects of a sexual assault scenario on handgrip strength across the menstrual cycle." *Evolution and Human Behavior* 23 (1): 3–10.

Pincott, Jennifer. *Do Gentlemen Really Prefer Blondes?* New York: Delacorte Press, 2008.

Pines, Ayala Malach. *Falling in Love* (second edition). New York: Routledge, 2005.

Provine, Robert. *Laughter: A Scientific Investigation.* New York: Penguin, 2000.

Rachman, S. (1966). "Sexual fetishism: An experimental analogue." *The Psychological Record* 16: 293–96.

Reuters, "TV in the bedroom bad for sex life." January 17, 2006.

Richters, J. R. de Visser, C. Rissel, and A. Smith (2006). "Sexual practices at last heterosexual encounter and occurrence of orgasm in a national survey." *The Journal of Sex Research* 43 (3): 217–26.

Roach, Mary. *Bonk: The Curious Coupling of Science and Sex.* New York: W. W. Norton & Company, 2008.

Roselli, C. E., K. Larkin, J. M. Schrunk, and F. Stormshak (2004). "Sexual partner preference, hypothalamic morphology and aromatase in rams." *Physiology & Behavior* 83 (2): 233–45.

Ross, Emma. "Brain areas shut off during female orgasm." Reuters, June 20, 2005, unpaginated electronic work or go to: http://www.livescience.com/health/050620_ap_female_orgasm.html.

Roizen, Michael F., Mehmet Oz, Lisa Oz, and Ted Spiker. *You: The Owner's Manual.* New York: HarperCollins, 2005.

Rozin, P., and A. Fallon (1988). "Body image, attitudes to weight, and misperceptions of figure preferences of the opposite sex: A comparison of men and women in two generations." *Journal of Abnormal Psychology* 97 (3): 342–45.

Rupp, H. A., and K. Wallen (2007). "Sex differences in viewing sexual stimuli: An eye-tracking study in men and women." *Hormones and Behavior* 51 (4): 524–33.

Sabucedo, A., M. A. Gutierrez, and K. C. Mueller (2004). "Sex, lies, and Niagra." *JAMA* 291 (5): 560–62.

Salonia, A., F. Fabbi, G. Zanni, M. Scavini, G. V. Fantini, A. Briganti, R. Naspro, F. Parazzii, E. Gori, P. Rigatti, and F. Montorsi (2006). "Chocolate and women's sexual health: An intriguing correlation." *The Journal of Sexual Medicine* 3 (3): 476–82.

Scardino, Peter T., and Judith Kelman. *Dr. Peter Scardino's Prostate Book.* New York: Avery, 2006.

Schaffir, J. (2006). "Sexual intercourse at term and onset of labor." *Obstetrics & Gynecology* 107 (6): 1310.

Schmitt, D. P. (2004). "Patterns and universals of mate poaching across 53 nations: The effects of sex, culture, and personality on romantically attracting another person's partner." *Journal of Personality and Social Psychology* 86 (4): 560–84.

Schneider, J. P., M. D. Corley, and R. K. Irons (1998). "Surviving disclosure of infidelity: Results of an international survey of 164 recovering sex addicts and partners." *Sexual Addiction and Compulsivity* 5: 189–217.

Schultz, W. W., P. V. Andel, I. Sabelis, and E. Mooyaart (1999). "Magnetic resonance imaging of male and female genitals during coitus and female sexual arousal." *BMJ* 319: 1596–1600.

Shah, J., and N. Christopher (2002). "Can shoe size predict penile length?" *BJU International* 90: 586–87.

Shefi, S., P. E. Tarapore, T. J. Walsh, M. Croughan, and P. J. Turek (2007). "Wet heat exposure: A potentially reversible cause of low semen quality in infertile men." *International Braz J Urol* 33 (1): 50–57.

Shettles, Landrum Brewer, and David M. Rorvik. *How to Choose the Sex of Your Baby.* New York: Random House, 1996.

Sheynkin, Y., M. Jung, P. Yoo, D. Schulsinger, and E. Komaroff (2004). "Increase in scrotal temperature in laptop computer users." *Human Reproduction* 20 (2): 452–45.

Shuster, S. (2007). "Sex, aggression, and humour: responses to unicycling." *BMJ* 335: 1320–22.

Singh, D. (1993). "Adaptive significance of female physical attractiveness: Role of waist-to-hip ratio." *Journal of Personality and Social Psychology* 65 (2): 293–307.

Singh, D., and P. M. Bronstad (2001). "Female body odour is a potential cue to ovulation." *Proceedings: Biological Sciences* 268 (1469): 797–801.

Sitton, S., and S. Blanchard (1995). "Men's preferences in romantic partners: Obesity vs. addiction." *Psychological Reports* 77: 1185–86.

Smith, G. D., S. Frankel, and J. Yarnell (1997). "Sex and death: Are they related? Findings from the Caerphilly cohort study." *BMJ* 315: 1641–44.

Smith, T. W. "American sexual behavior: Trends, socio-demographic differences, and risk behavior." Chicago: National Opinion Research Center, 2006.

Sprinkle, Annie. *Dr. Sprinkle's Spectacular Sex: Make Over Your Love Life with One of the World's Great Sex Experts.* New York: Penguin, 2005.

Sprott, Richard (2005). "Kink sexuality and personality: Pilot study." Unpublished.

Strassberg, D. S., and L. K. Locker (1998). "Force in women's sexual fantasies." *Archives of Sexual Behavior* 27 (4): 403–14.

Strassberg, D. S., and S. Holty (2003). "An experimental study of women's internet personal ads." *Archives of Sexual Behavior* 32 (3): 253–60.

Student, John. "No sex, please . . . we're college graduates." *American Demographics*, February, 1998, pp. 18–23.

Telegraph, "Injured biker now obsessed by sex." March 2, 2007, unpaginated electronic work or go to: http://www.telegraph.co.uk/news/uknews/1544273/Injured-biker-now-obsessed-by-sex.html.

Thornhill, R., and S. W. Gangestad (1999). "The scent of symmetry: A human sex pheromone that signals fitness?" *Evolution and Human Behavior* 20 (3): 175–201.

Thornhill, R., S. W. Gangestad, and R. Comer (1995). "Human female orgasm and mate fluctuating asymmetry." *Animal Behaviour* 50 (6): 1601–15.

Timesonline.co.uk, "Man whose sex drive rose after injury claims £3.5m." December 13, 2006, unpaginated eletronic work or go to: http://business.timesonline.co.uk/tol/business/law/article752461.ece.

Todd, P. M. "Coevolved cognitive mechanisms in mate search: Making decisions in a decision-shaped world." In J. P. Forgas, M. G. Haselton, and W. V. Hippel (eds.), *Evolution and the Social Mind: Evolutionary Psychology and Social Cognition*. New York: Psychology Press, 2007, pp. 145–59.

Tovée, M. J., S. Reinhardt, J.L. Emery, and P.L. Cornelissen (1998). "Optimum body-mass index and maximum sexual attractiveness." *The Lancet* 352: 548.

Treas, J., and D. Giesen (2000). "Sexual infidelity among married and cohabiting Americans." *Journal of Marriage and the Family* 62 (1): 48–60.

Valenstein, Elliot S. *Brain Control: A Critical Examination of Brain Stimulation and Psychosurgery*. Hoboken, New Jersey: John Wiley & Sons, 1973.

Vance, E. B., and N. N. Wagner (1976). "Written descriptions of orgasm: A study of sex differences." *Archives of Sexual Behavior* 5 (1): 87–98.

Walsh, A. (1991). "Self-esteem and sexual behavior: Exploring gender differences." *Sex Roles* 25 (7/8): 441–50.

Walster, E., G. W. Walster, J. Piliavin, and L. Schmidt (1973). "'Playing hard to get': Understanding an elusive phenomenon." *Journal of Personality and Social Psychology* 26 (1): 113–21.

Walster, E., J. Traupmann, and G. W. Walster (1978). "Equity and extramarital sexuality." *Archives of Sexual Behavior* 7 (2): 127–42.

Walum, H., L. Westerberg, S. Henningsson, J. M. Neiderhiser, D. Reiss, W. Igl, J. M. Ganiban, E. L. Spotts, N. L. Pedersen, E. Eriksson, and P. Lichtenstein (2008). "Genetic variation in the vasopressin receptor 1a gene (*AVPR1A*) associates with pair-bonding behavior in humans." *Proceedings of the National Academy of Sciences in the United States of America* 105 (37): 14153–56.

Warren, J. E., D. A. Sauter, F. Eisner, J. Wiland, J. A. Dresner, R. J. S. Wise, S. Rosen, and S. K. Scott (2006). "Positive emotions preferentially engage an auditory-motor 'mirror' system." *The Journal of Neuroscience* 26 (50): 13067–75.

Wedekind, C., T. Seebeck, F. Bettens, and A. J. Paepke (1995). "MHC-dependent mate preferences in humans." *Proceedings: Biological Sciences* 260 (1359): 245–49.

Weeden, J., and J. Sabini (2005). "Physical attractiveness and health in western societies: A review." *Psychological Bulletin* 131(5): 635–53.

Wegner, D. M., D. J. Schneider, S. R. Carter III, and T. L. White (1987). "Paradoxical effects of thought suppression." *Journal of Personality and Social Psychology* 53 (1): 5–13.

Weinstock, S. B., and W. Cates, Jr. (2004). "Sexually transmitted diseases among American youth: Incidence and prevalence estimates, 2000." *Perspectives on Sexual and Reproductive Health* 36 (1): 6–10.

Weiss, J. (1998). "Bondage fantasies and beating fantasies." *Psychoanalytic Quarterly* 67 (4): 626–44.

Whipple, B., and B. R. Komisaruk (1985). "Elevation of pain thresholds by vaginal stimulation in women." *Pain* 21: 357–67.

Whipple, B., G. Ogden, and B. R. Komisaruk (1992). "Physiological correlates of imagery-induced orgasm in women." *Archives of Sexual Behavior* 21 (2): 121–33.

Whipple, Beverly, Alice Kahn Ladas, and John D. Perry. *The G Spot: And Other Discoveries about Human Sexuality.* New York: Macmillan, 2004.

Wilcox, A. J., C. R. Weinberg, and D. D. Baird (1995). "Timing of sexual intercourse in relation to ovulation—effects on the probability of conception, survival of the pregnancy, and sex of the baby." *The New England Journal of Medicine* 333 (23): 1517–21.

Wilcox, A. J., D. D. Baird, D. B. Dunson, D. R. McConnaughey, J. S. Kesner, and C. R. Weinberg (2004). "On the frequency of intercourse around ovulation: evidence for biological influences." *Human Reproduction* 19 (7): 1539–43.

Worner, S. M. "'I just want to get married—I don't care to who!' Marriage, life satisfaction and educational differences in Australian couples." Presented at the HILDA conference, 2007, pp. 1–36. Go to: http://www .melbourneinstitute.com/hilda/conf/conf2007/HILDA%20Conf%20Pa pers%202007/All%20Papers/Worner,%20Shane_final%20paper.pdf.

Young, L. J., (1999). "Oxytocin and vasopressin receptors and species-typical social behaviors." *Hormones and Behavior* 36 (3): 212–21.

Zajonc, R. B., P. K. Adelman, S. T. Murphy, and P. M. Niedenthal (1987). "Convergence in physical appearance of spouses." *Motivation and Emotion* 11 (4): 333–35.

Zillmann, D., and J. Bryant (1986). "Shifting preferences in pornography consumption." *Communication Research* 13 (4): 560–78.